Stealing with Pride — Volume 1

Advanced OSD Customizations for MDT 2013 and ConfigMgr 2012 R2

Maik Koster
Johan Arwidmark

PUBLISHED BY
Deployment Artist
http://www.deploymentartist.com

ISBN: 978-91-87445-03-3

Warning and Disclaimer

Feedback Information

We'd like to hear from you! If you have any comments about how we could improve the quality
of this book, please don't hesitate to contact us by visiting http://deploymentartist.com, sending an
email to feedback@deploymentartist.com, or visiting our Facebook site
facebook.com/DeploymentArtist.

Acknowledgements

This book would not exist without the support from our families. Our biggest thanks go to Angelika, Louise, and all the kids. Thank you for your patience and understanding. We love you all.

Thank you, Chris Nelson. Without your tireless edits, this book would never have been completed.

Thank you, Keith Garner, Ben Hunter, and Mikael Nystrom for your support.

Special thanks to Michael Niehaus for putting up with all of our questions over the years. Your knowledge is overwhelming.

About the Authors

Maik Koster

Maik Koster works as an infrastructure specialist at an international company with a focus on Enterprise Management and Deployment Solutions. He is an active blogger on maikkoster.com and hosting several deployment related projects on Codeplex. Maik has been awarded Microsoft Most Valuable Professional (MVP) for more than three years.

Johan Arwidmark

Johan Arwidmark is a consultant and all-around geek specializing in Systems Management and Enterprise Windows Deployment Solutions. Johan also speaks at several conferences each year, including Microsoft events around the world. He is actively involved in deployment communities like deploymentresearch.com and myitforum.com. Johan and has been awarded Microsoft Most Valuable Professional (MVP) for more than ten years.

Contents

Introduction

Stealing with Pride: Advanced OSD Customizations for MDT 2013 and ConfigMgr 2012 R2 is the ultimate source for the working IT Pro who wants to customize deployment solutions based on MDT 2013 or ConfigMgr 2012 R2. Most of the examples and scenarios described in this book are targeted to both deployment solutions, but there are solution-specific parts, as well. Please note that even though we used MDT 2013 and ConfigMgr 2012 R2 and tested all examples against that only platform, many of the examples and guides also work on MDT 2012 Update 1 and ConfigMgr 2012 SP1. Some even work on ConfigMgr 2007 (which you should not be using anymore ☺).

Anyway, this is a HOW TO GET IT DONE book, solely focusing on customizing deployment solutions with roots in the real world.

> **Note:** As far as the title goes, we don't mean you should steal things, literally. In this book, *stealing* is just a metaphor for not reinventing the wheel. We don't want you to waste time developing solutions that are already available for free.

Say Hello (Possibly Again) to ViaMonstra Inc.

In this book, you customize deployment solutions for the fictive ViaMonstra Inc. organization. ViaMonstra is a midsized company with a single location and 3000 employees. Their site is located in New York.

ViaMonstra has decided to use ConfigMgr 2012 R2 for its main departments, but it also has a development department using the standalone MDT 2013 solution. BTW, the name ViaMonstra comes from *Viam Monstra*, Latin, meaning "Show me the way."

Structure of the Book

The first chapter is a development essentials school, which explains the terminology and scenarios we use in the book. The second chapter describes the various deployment and development tools that are being used.

Chapter 3 explains the environment used in ViaMonstra organization, including what servers and software are used.

Chapter 4 is a quick introduction to MDT 2013 and why ViaMonstra decided to integrate it with ConfigMgr 2012 R2 as well as running it as a standalone solution. The following two chapters (5 and 6) go into more technical details on MDT and ConfigMgr operating system deployment (OSD) and provide you with guides to set them up for the various solutions used in this book.

Chapter 7 contains general customization guidelines, and then Chapters 8–13 provide technical explanations and guides for commonly used customizations, including frontends, custom scripts, databases, web services, and monitoring. Chapter 14 is about integrating with Orchestrator 2012 R2.

Finally, we have the appendix, which include extra material on how to set up the entire proof-of-concept environment, servers and clients, including their roles and configurations. You also find debugging tips and reference information of MDT functions and properties.

How to Use This Book

We have packed this book with step-by-step guides, which mean you will be able to build your solution as you read along.

In numbered steps, we have set all names and paths in bold typeface. We also have used a standard naming convention throughout the book when explaining what to do in each step. The steps normally are something like this:

1. On the **Advanced Properties** page, select the **Confirm** check box, and then click **Next**.

Sample scripts are formatted like the following example, on a grey background.

```
DoNotCreateExtraPartition=YES
MachineObjectOU=ou=Workstations,dc=corp,dc=viamonstra,dc=com
```

Code and commands that you type in the guides are displayed like this:

1. Install **MDT 2013** by running the following command in an elevated **PowerShell** prompt:

```
& msiexec.exe /i 'C:\Setup\MDT 2013\
MicrosoftDeploymentToolkit2013_x64.msi' /quiet
```

The step-by-step guides in this book assume that you have configured the environment according to the information in Chapter 3, "ViaMonstra Inc. and the Proof-of-Concept Environment," and in Appendix A.

This book is not intended as a reference volume, covering every deployment or development technology, acronym, or command-line switch known to man, but rather is designed to make sure you learn what you need to know to customize your deployment solution.

Sample Files

All sample files used in this book can be downloaded from http://stealingwithpride.com.

Additional Resources

In addition to all tips and tricks provided in this book, you will find extra resources like articles and video recordings on our blogs, www.deploymentresearch.com and http://maikkoster.com.

Topics Not Covered

This book does not cover creating reference images or working with drivers. If you want to learn more about those topics, we recommend reading the book *Deployment Fundamentals* – Volume 4 by Johan Arwidmark and Mikael Nystrom.

Chapter 1

Development Essentials

In this chapter, you get a crash course in the various development technologies that are used in this book. If you are an experienced developer or IT professional already doing some development work, you may want to skip this and continue directly with Chapter 2.

VBScript

VBScript (Visual Basic Scripting Edition) is a scripting language that has been installed by default in every release of Microsoft Windows since Windows 98. VBScript is still heavily used in deployment solutions because it's always available on the target operating system and also in the Windows Preinstallation Environment (WinPE). Here is a short VBScript snippet that gets hardware info (model name) from a machine:

```
strComputer = "."
strConn = "winmgmts:{impersonationLevel=impersonate}!\\" & _
    strComputer & "\root\cimv2"
strQuery = "Select * from Win32_Computersystem"

Set objWMI = GetObject(strConn)
Set colItems = objWMI.ExecQuery(strQuery)
For Each Item In colItems
    Wscript.Echo "Model: " & Item.Model
Next
Set objWMI = Nothing
```

JavaScript

JavaScript (JS) is often used to run client-side scripts inside a web browser. JavaScript does copy many name and naming convention from Java, but is otherwise not the same language as Java. In deployment solutions, JavaScript is primarily used for frontends (HTA). Here is a short JavaScript snippet that sets the window size and position of an HTA page:

```
function Set(){
    var l=(screen.width/2 - 500);
    var t=(screen.height-200);
      self.moveTo(l,t);

      self.resizeTo('900','300');
    }
```

PowerShell

This has to be the coolest technology ever created by Microsoft. PowerShell, or Windows PowerShell, is Microsoft's framework for task automation. It consists of a command-line shell, with an associated scripting language built on top of it, and integrates with .NET Framework, having access to all COM objects and direct access to WMI. PowerShell allows you to perform administrative tasks on both local and remote Windows systems. Since the release of WinPE 4.0, PowerShell also can be added to the boot images used in OSD.

It's a bit unfair to list samples of what you can do in PowerShell, because there are no real limits. Every type of automation task you can imagine can be done in PowerShell, but here are a couple samples:

- Get hardware info (model name) from the machine using PowerShell

```
Get-WmiObject -Class:Win32_ComputerSystem | Select Model
```

- Create a device collection in ConfigMgr 2012 R2

```
New-CMDeviceCollection -Name "Install Windows 8.1"
-LimitingCollectionName "All Systems"
```

Windows Management Instrumentation (WMI)

WMI is a set of extensions to the Windows Driver Model. Windows deployment solutions like MDT 2013 and ConfigMgr 2012 R2 use WMI to get information about the hardware being deployed. ConfigMgr 2012 R2 also uses WMI heavily to store configurations and, for example, to get inventory data. When scripting against ConfigMgr 2012 R2, you can use WMI to read/write configurations, as well. The PowerShell example in the previous section uses WMI to read the hardware info.

HTML Application (HTA)

HTAs give you the features of HTML together with the advantages of scripting languages. The HTA pages are executed fully trusted so they have access to local computer information (unlike normal webpages). HTA is commonly used for frontends and other deployment wizards.

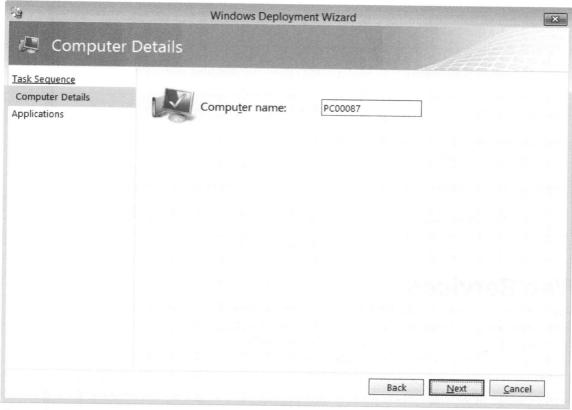

A sample HTA wizard pane (from MDT 2013).

VB.NET and C#

Visual Basic .NET (VB.NET) and C Sharp (C#) are both programming languages used when doing advanced customization for MDT 2013 and ConfigMgr 2012 R2.

VB.NET can be viewed as an evolution of the classic Visual Basic (VB) language, and C# is intended to be a general-purpose, object-oriented programming language.

The two programming languages are not that different to work with, for example converting VB.NET code into C# is often quite straightforward. Compare how to get hardware information using the two languages:

- Get hardware information (model name) from the machine using VB.NET

```
Dim strSearch = "SELECT * FROM Win32_ComputerSystem"
Dim searcher As New ManagementObjectSearcher(strSearch)

For Each mgtObject As ManagementObject In searcher.[Get]()
    Console.WriteLine(mgtObject("Model").ToString())
Next
```

- Get hardware information (model name) from the machine using C#

```
string strSearch = "SELECT * FROM Win32_ComputerSystem";

ManagementObjectSearcher searcher =
    new ManagementObjectSearcher(strSearch);

foreach (ManagementObject mgtObject in searcher.Get())
{
    Console.WriteLine(mgtObject["Model"].ToString());
}
```

Web Services

Web services are used to make it easy for machines to communicate with each other independent of what operating systems they are using. When customizing OSD solutions, web services are mainly used for calling server-side actions. A commonly used scenario is calling a web service that moves a computer from one organizational unit (OU) to another during the deployment process.

Another aspect of web services is reading information, like monitoring information, from the deployment process.

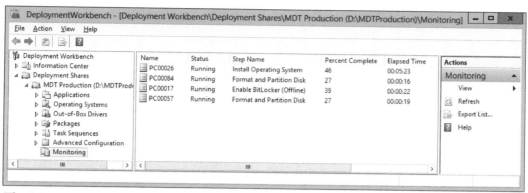

The Monitoring node showing a few Windows 8.1 clients being deployed (data from web service).

Hydration

Hydration is the concept of using a deployment solution, like MDT 2013, to do a fully automated build of an entire lab, proof-of-concept, or production environment. We provide a hydration kit (see Appendix A) that builds the environment used in this book.

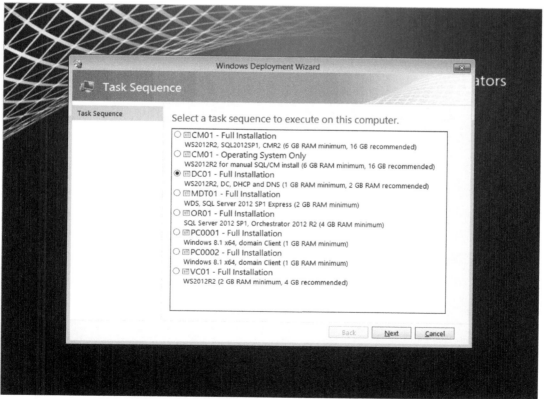

Creating the virtual machines used in this book. See Appendix A for details.

Chapter 2

Development Tools of the Trade

Depending on what you are customizing, and what type of solutions you are developing when it comes to operating system deployment, you use different tools. In this book, you learn about the tools we recommend and use on a daily basis.

Notepad++

This is a great freeware script editor, perfect for editing VBScripts.

Notepad++ displaying one of the book sample scripts.

PowerShell Integrated Scripting Environment (ISE)

For editing PowerShell scripts, we recommend using the built-in ISE editor available in Windows 7, Windows 8.1, Windows Sever 2012, and Windows Server 2012 R2. It provides you with cmdlets help and Intellisense when writing PowerShell scripts.

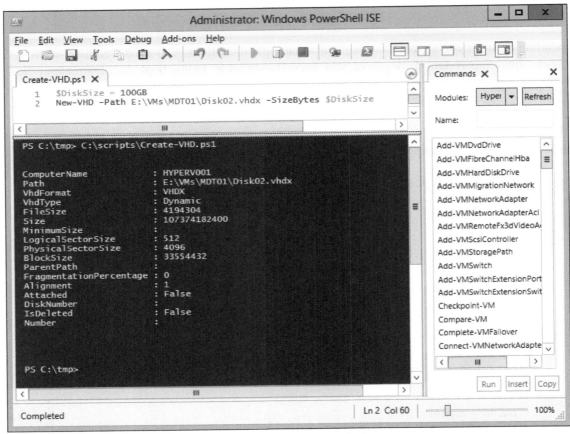

PowerShell ISE running a script to create a virtual hard disk.

Visual Studio 2013

You also can use Visual Studio for editing scripts, and it is very good on that, as well. Editing scripts in this suite of tools also allows for advanced debugging, something that is missing in Notepad++.

However, Visual Studio is mainly used for "real" programming, meaning using non-scripting languages like VB.NET and C#. In this book, you learn to use Visual Studio to write web services, but also to edit scripts, HTA pages, and more.

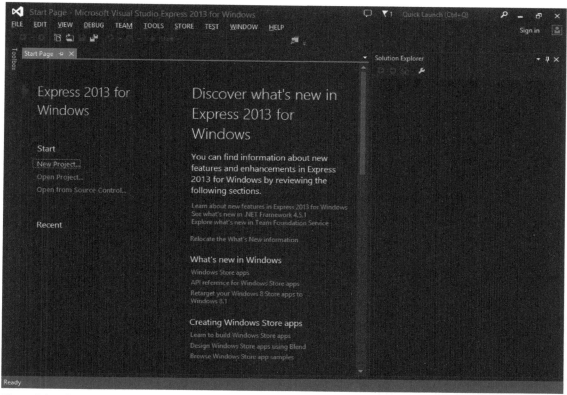

Visual Studio Express 2013 for Windows.

Understand the Different Editions

There are quite a few editions of Visual Studio available, each with its own feature set. The following is a summary of the various editions. In this book, we use the free Visual Studio Express 2013 for Windows edition.

The Visual Studio Express 2013 for Windows edition is good enough for all the solutions presented in this book, but as you start to develop further, beyond this book, the other editions may be of interest to you.

- **Visual Studio 2013 Ultimate with MSDN.** This is the biggest (and most expensive) version of Visual Studio, used primarily when working in large development teams and when you do lots of automated testing. This edition helps you through the complete application lifecycle management.

- **Visual Studio 2013 Premium with MSDN.** The younger brother of the Ultimate edition, Premium contains almost the same feature set but is missing a few features with regard to application lifecycle management.

- **Visual Studio 2013 Test Professional with MSDN.** This is a special version of Visual Studio 2013 Professional that also includes features for automatic testing.

- **Visual Studio 2013 Professional with MSDN.** This edition contains all the core functions for Windows and Web development. Via the MSDN subscription you get access to some testing tools, as well.

- **Visual Studio Online.** Formerly Team Foundation Service, Visual Studio Online is used to store your project data in the cloud, providing you with a central place without the need to set up a local server. This is a monthly subscription and comes in three flavors: Visual Studio Online Basic, Visual Studio Online Professional, and Visual Studio Online Advanced. As Visual Studio Online Basic comes as a free offer for up to five users, it's a very interesting option for managing even smaller projects in a professional manner.

- **Visual Studio Express 2013.** This is the free version, which is nice. Visual Studio Express is not really a single suite; it's rather four products: Express for Web product is used for web development (like web services); Express for Windows is for developing Windows 8-style applications; Express for Windows Desktop is used for standard Windows application development; and Team Foundation Server Express is a source version control solution. The main thing we miss in the Visual Studio Express 2013 product is third-party extensibility support (plugins). In this book, you use Visual Studio Express 2013 for web.

> **Update:** About a week prior to this book release (November 2014), Microsoft announced the free Visual Studio 2013 Community edition. This edition is basically a full version of Visual Studio 2013 for, with no restrictions, except it's only for teams with no more than five people. We have not tested the book code samples and guides with this new edition, but they are likely to work just fine if you want to try the new edition.

Visual Studio Team Foundation Server 2013

Visual Studio Team Foundation Server (TFS) 2013 is the Microsoft version control system. The Team Foundation Server 2013 Express version is free and can be used for up to five developers. The full version is only included in Visual Studio 2013 Professional with MSDN and above editions (Premium and Ultimate).

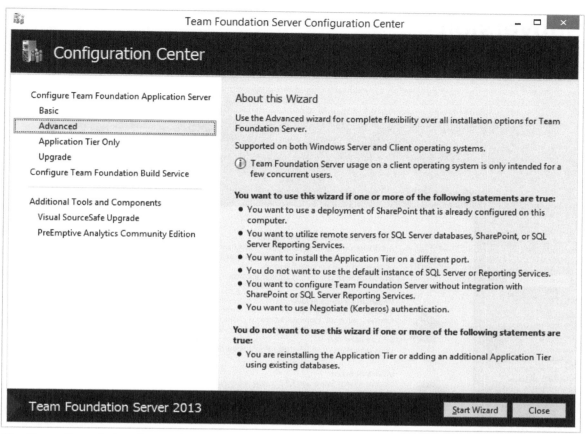

The Team Foundation Server 2013 configuration options.

Subversion

This is a free open-source version control system. One of the many (well, five) Windows binaries of Subversion is the VisualSVN package that includes both the client and server components.

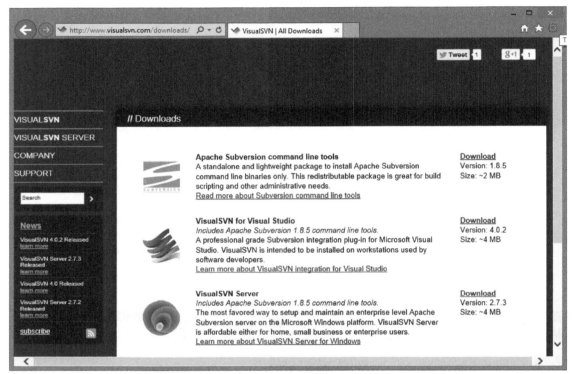

The VisualSVN download page.

Git

Git is a free open-source distributed version control system. As opposed to Subversion, every Git working directory is a full-fledged repository with complete history and full version tracking capabilities, and is not dependent on network access or a central server. Git is most known as the version control system for the Linux kernel development.

One of most well-known adoptions of Git is GitHub (https://github.com/), which provides hosting for Git repositories. Visual Studio Online also supports Git.

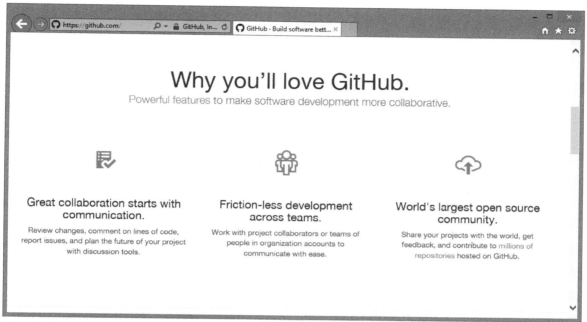

The GitHub web site.

WBEMTest and WMI Tools

These are tools for exploring WMI information on a machine. Used to enumerate WMI classes and methods, but also for other things, such as testing WQL queries, WBEMTest is built into Windows and Windows PE. WMI Tools (or WMI Administrative Tools) is a free download from Microsoft that contains the following tools:

- **WMI CIM Studio.** A tool for viewing and editing WMI classes and properties. It can also generate and compile MOF files.

- **WMI Object Browser.** A tool for viewing WMI objects and editing property values.

- **WMI Event Registration Tool.** A tool for creating and configuring permanent event consumers.

- **WMI Event Viewer.** A tool for displaying events for registered consumers.

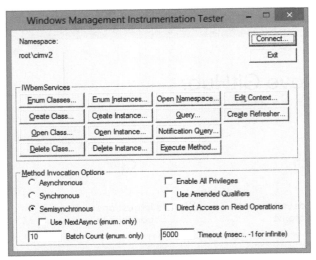

The WBEMTest tool.

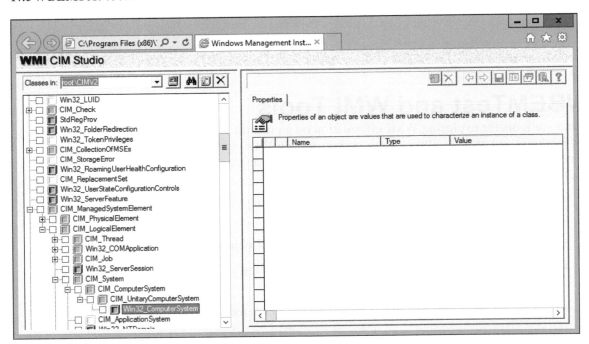

The WMI CIM Studio tool.

SQL Server 2012 SP1

Perhaps not a developer tool per se, this database is in the grey area between development tool and database. There are four main editions of SQL Server 2012 SP1 available: Enterprise, Business Intelligence, Standard, and Express. There also is a special Web edition that we don't cover here.

- **SQL Server 2012 SP1 Enterprise.** This is the full-featured edition of SQL Server for mission-critical applications and data warehousing. It offers advanced high availability and data warehousing capabilities.

- **SQL Server 2012 SP1 Business Intelligence.** This edition adds functionality such as browser-based data exploration and visualization, powerful data mash-up capabilities, and enhanced integration management to the standard edition.

- **SQL Server 2012 SP1 Standard.** This edition delivers basic data management and business intelligence database for departments and small organizations to run their applications and supports common development.

- **SQL Server 2012 SP1 Express.** This is a scaled down, free edition of SQL Server, which includes the core database engine. It's limited to using one socket or four cores, 1 GB of memory, and a 10 GB maximum database size. It is, however, not limited to a specific number of databases and suits almost every operating system (OS) deployment-related scenario.

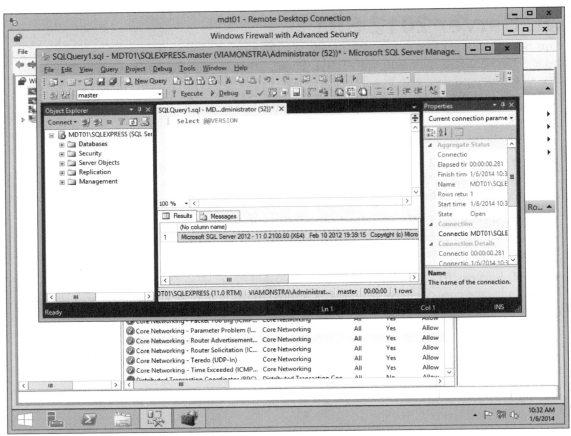

SQL Server 2012 SP1 Express with a simple version query.

MDT Wizard Studio

The Microsoft Deployment Toolkit (MDT) Wizard Studio is an updated and extended version of the MDT Wizard Editor, originally written by Michael Niehaus. The name implies what the tool does; it's a graphical editor for the MDT 2013 Lite Touch Wizard. MDT Wizard Studio is available for download (free) on CodePlex (http://mdtwizardstudio.codeplex.com). You also can find a copy in the book sample files.

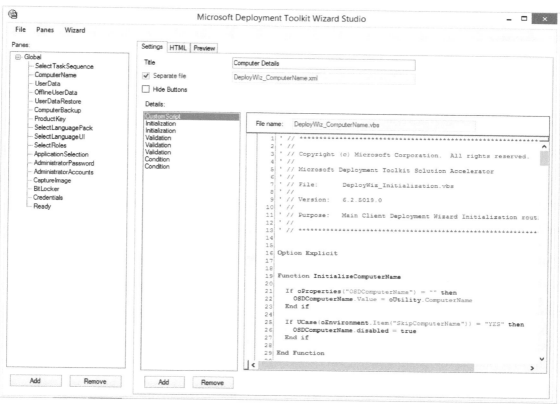

The MDT Wizard Studio showing one of the default scripts in MDT 2013.

NLog 2.0

NLog is a free logging platform for .NET that makes it easy to produce and manage logs for your application. Configuration can happen either programmatically or through configuration files, which allows adjusting the logging on-the-fly. NLog integrates nicely with Visual Studio.

NLog comes with great online documentation, and it has IntelliSense in the code itself and also in the configuration files.

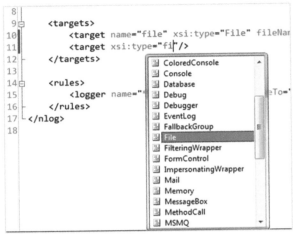

Part of an NLog 2.0 configuration file, showing the code IntelliSense.

ReSharper

This is an extension (a plugin created by JetBrains) that extends IntelliSense, code quality analysis, and documentation in Visual Studio. Please note that ReSharper works only with the full versions of Visual Studio 2013 and not the Express version.

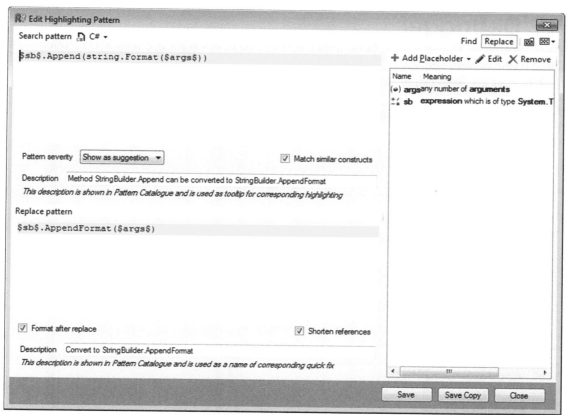

Structural search and replace in ReSharper, one of many useful features.

MDT Debugger

This tool, written by Daniel Oxley, helps debug scripts you develop for use with MDT. Since version 2.0 (the current version is 2.1), this tool also works in WinPE. You can download the MDT Debugger 2.1 from http://tinyurl.com/mdtdebugger21.

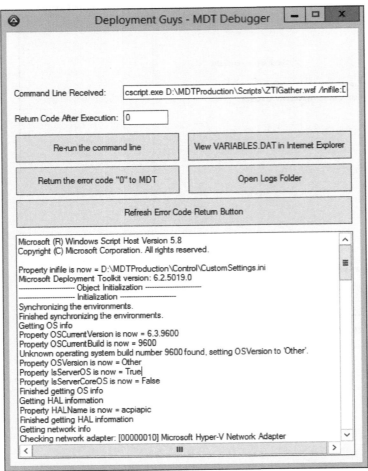

Debugging the MDT 2013 ZTIGather.wsf script in the MDT Debugger.

Chapter 3

ViaMonstra Inc. and the Proof-of-Concept Environment

As you remember from the introduction, ViaMonstra Inc. is the fictive company we use throughout this book. In this chapter, we describe the company in more detail, as well as the proof-of-concept environment we use in our step-by-step guides. Detailed installation instructions on how to set up the environment can be found in Appendix A.

ViaMonstra Inc.

ViaMonstra Inc. was invented for the very purpose of having a "real" company for which to build a deployment solution. These deployment solutions come from multiple real-world consulting engagements we have done, consolidating them into a single generic scenario.

ViaMonstra has 3000 employees and a single location in New York.

Servers

The New York site has the following servers related to software distribution and other supporting infrastructure. All servers are running Windows Server 2012 R2. Detailed configuration of each server is found in the "Servers (Detailed Info)" section in this chapter.

> **Friendly Reminder:** Detailed step-by-step guidance on how to deploy the servers used in the book can be found in Appendix A.

- **DC01.** Domain Controller, DNS, and DHCP
- **MDT01.** File Server, WSUS, WDS, and SQL Server 2012 SP1 Express
- **CM01.** SQL Server 2012 SP1 and ConfigMgr 2012 R2
- **VC01.** File Server and SQL Server 2012 SP1 Express
- **OR01.** Optional Server. SQL Server 2012 SP1 and Orchestrator 2012 R2

> **Note:** The OR01 server is required only if you want to learn or use the advanced integration (automation scenarios) with Orchestrator 2012 R2 that is supported in standalone (Lite Touch) MDT 2013 and ConfigMgr 2012 R2 integrated with MDT 2013.

Clients

In addition to the servers, you have two Windows 8.1 clients that you use when developing or customizing the deployment solutions, as well as for testing. As with the servers, Appendix A helps you deploy these machines.

- **PC0001.** Windows 8.1 Enterprise x64 client

- **PC0002.** Windows 8.1 Enterprise x64 client

Internet Access

Some of the guides in this book require you to have Internet access on the virtual machines. We commonly use a virtual router (running in a VM) to provide Internet access to our lab and test VMs. Our favorite router are the Vyatta and VyOS (Vyatta community fork) routers, but you can use a Windows Server 2012 R2 virtual machine with routing configured, as well.

> **Note:** For detailed guidance on setting up a virtual router for your lab environment, see this article: http://tinyurl.com/usingvirtualrouter.

Software

The following list describe the various applications used by ViaMonstra. To be able to follow all the step-by-step guides and configurations in the book, the following software must be downloaded. They can be either trial or full versions.

- 7-Zip 9.20

- Adobe Reader XI

- Windows Assessment and Deployment Toolkit (ADK) 8.1

- ConfigMgr 2012 R2

- ConfigMgr 2012 R2 Toolkit

- Microsoft Deployment Toolkit (MDT) 2013

- Microsoft Visual Studio Express 2013 for Web

- TortoiseSVN 1.8 (http://tortoisesvn.net/downloads.html)

- VisualSVN Server 2.7.3 (http://www.visualsvn.com)

- Notepad++ (http://notepad-plus-plus.org/download/v6.2.3.html)

- SQL Server 2012 SP1 Express

- SQL Server 2012 SP1

- Windows 8.1

- Windows Server 2012 R2

Servers (Detailed Info)

As mentioned earlier in this chapter, we are using a set of servers in our environment. We use a concept called *hydration* (automated build of entire labs and production environments) when creating the servers.

As mentioned earlier in this chapter, for detailed step-by-step guidance on how to deploy the servers, please review Appendix A, "Using the Hydration Kit to Build the PoC Environment."

To set up a virtual environment with all the servers and clients, you need a host with at least 16 GB of RAM, even though 32 GB RAM is recommended. Either way, make sure you are using SSD drives for your storage. A single 480 GB SSD is enough to run all the scenarios in this book.

Real World Note: If using a laptop or desktop when doing the step-by-step guides in this book, please do use a SSD drive for your virtual machines. Using normal spindle-based disks are just too slow for decent lab and test environments. Also please note that most laptops support at least 16 GB of RAM these days, even if many vendors do not update their specifications with this information.

A detailed description of the servers follows:

- **DC01.** A **Windows Server 2012 R2** machine, fully patched with the latest security updates and configured as Active Directory Domain Controller, DNS Server, and DHCP Server in the **corp.viamonstra.com** domain.
  - Server name: **DC01**
  - IP Address: **192.168.1.200**
  - Roles: **DNS**, **DHCP**, and **Domain Controller**

- **MDT01.** A **Windows Server 2012 R2** machine, fully patched with the latest security updates and configured as a member server in the **corp.viamonstra.com** domain. The server has been configured with the WDS role. The server also has MDT, ADK, and SQL Server 2012 SP1 Express installed.
  - Server name: **MDT01**
  - IP Address: **192.168.1.210**
  - Roles: **WDS**
  - Software: **SQL Server 2012 SP1 Express**

- **CM01.** A **Windows Server 2012 R2** machine, fully patched with the latest security updates and configured as a member server in the **corp.viamonstra.com** domain. The server has SQL Server 2012 SP1 and ConfigMgr 2012 R2 installed.
  - Server name: **CM01**
  - IP Address: **192.168.1.214**
  - Roles: **WDS** and **IIS**
  - Software: **SQL Server 2012 SP1** and **ConfigMgr 2012 R2**

- **OR01.** A **Windows Server 2012 R2** machine, fully patched with the latest security updates and configured as a member server in the **corp.viamonstra.com** domain. This is the file server used for the optional System Center 2012 R2 Orchestrator server.

  o   Server name: **OR01**

  o   IP Address: **192.168.1.218**

  o   Software: **SQL Server 2012 SP1** and **System Center 2012 R2 Orchestrator**

- **VC01.** A **Windows Server 2012 R2** machine, fully patched with the latest security updates and configured as a member server in the **corp.viamonstra.com** domain. This is the file server used for the version control.

  o   Server name: **VC01**

  o   IP Address: **192.168.1.228**

  o   Software: **VisualSVN Server**

Clients (Detailed Info)

In addition to the servers, you also use two clients in the step-by-step guides. The required client virtual machines are the following:

- **PC0001**. A **Windows 8.1 Enterprise x64** machine, fully patched with the latest security updates and configured as a member in the **corp.viamonstra.com** domain.

  o   Client name: **PC0001**

  o   IP Address: **192.168.1.11**

  o   Software: **MDT 2013, Microsoft Visual Studio Express 2013 for Web, TortoiseSVN plugin, CMTrace, Notepad++,** and **MDT Wizard Studio**

- **PC0002**. A **Windows 8.1 Enterprise x64** machine, fully patched with the latest security updates and configured as a member in the **corp.viamonstra.com** domain.

  o   Client name: **PC0002**

  o   IP Address: **192.168.1.12**

  o   Software: **Notepad++** and **CMTrace**

Chapter 4

Why Use MDT?

In later chapters (5 and 6), you get a technical drilldown in the two deployment solutions used in this book, but we thought that an early overview at this point was in order, an overview in which we answer the big "Why use MDT?" question.

If you have been working with previous versions of MDT and ConfigMgr, this will not come a surprise to you; but if you are new into the MDT 2013 and ConfigMgr 2012 R2 world, these two solutions may appear to be totally separate. However, behind the scenes, they really are not separate. They belong together. Let us explain:

Introduction

If you don't have ConfigMgr 2012 R2 in your environment, you can download MDT 2013 and use it as a standalone deployment solution. This solution is called Lite Touch, but has nothing to do with the level of automation. The Lite Touch deployment solution can be as automated as you like it to be. From manual to fully automated, or somewhere in between.

If you are using ConfigMgr 2012 R2 in your environment, you can use MDT 2013 together with ConfigMgr. This configuration, that uses features from MDT 2013, is called Zero Touch, and it extends the OSD capabilities in ConfigMgr with hundreds (well 280) of OSD enhancements.

Not Reinventing the Wheel

When talking to customers around the globe, we often hear them reasoning something like this: No, we don't want to integrate ConfigMgr with MDT, because it adds additional complexity to the solution. But it's actually the exact opposite: by providing ready-made, supported, OSD enhancements to ConfigMgr, you actually reduce the complexity.

> **Put it this way:** If you are using ConfigMgr 2012 R2 today and are missing a function or feature related to OSD, please don't starting developing that feature yourself. Download the MDT 2013 deployment solution and see whether what you are looking for is not already in that download. Most likely it is.

Even if the feature you are searching for is not in MDT, MDT will help you develop that feature quickly. MDT not only adds features to OSD, it in fact also adds a whole framework for development, allowing you to get results within hours, rather than days (or weeks).

Enterprise-Ready

No matter whether you are using the standalone version of MDT 2013 (Lite Touch), or you are integrating MDT with ConfigMgr 2012 R2, the solution was made for the enterprise network. MDT 2013 has been download several hundred thousand times from Microsoft and has become a de facto standard for how to do Windows deployment.

MDT 2013 also is supported by Microsoft, meaning that if you run into any issues, you can use your normal support channels to get support for it.

Sample Features – from the Real World

This section contains a few commonly used deployment features from MDT 2013. We start by listing a few from the standalone version and then a few for the integration with ConfigMgr 2012 R2.

MDT 2013 Lite Touch

As you learn in the next chapter, MDT 2013 Lite Touch doesn't require any management infrastructure but is still a complete deployment solution. Some of its core features are:

- **Fully automated deployments.** You can deploy all supported Windows clients and servers, fully automated.

- **Wizard-based deployment.** If you want a more manual deployment process, you can configure MDT for prompting the user or technician for information during deployment.

- **Create references images.** MDT can be used to create reference images for all the deployment solutions Microsoft has, including MDT, ConfigMgr, SCVMM, VDI, and more.

- **Install software updates.** MDT can install software updates (preferably from your WSUS server) as part of the deployment process.

- **Install applications.** MDT can install applications, run scripts and executables, and so forth, as part of the deployment process.

- **Deployment monitoring.** MDT supports end-to-end monitoring of your deployment.

- **Development framework.** MDT provides ready-made functions for many commonly used configurations.

MDT 2013 Zero Touch (with ConfigMgr 2012 R2)

As you learn in Chapter 6, MDT 2013 Zero Touch adds features to the ConfigMgr 2012 R2 OSD platform (and also supports previous versions of ConfigMgr). Some of its core enhancements are:

- **Orchestrator 2012 R2 integration.** You have the ability to call Orchestrator runbooks from task sequences.

- **Real time monitoring**. MDT monitoring also works with ConfigMgr.

- **User-driven installations.** MDT adds an optional deployment wizard.

- **Full WIM backup.** You can enable an optional full WIM backup during deployment.

- **Enhanced logging.** MDT integration adds additional server-side logging.

- **Roles and features.** Zero Touch allows you to easily install roles and features as part of the operating system deployment.

- **Gather process.** You have access to some 150 extremely useful properties, functions, and settings that can be used in the deployment process.

- **Deployment database.** This version includes an extensible database to facilitate dynamic deployments.

- **Regional settings support.** MDT integration adds support to easily configure language settings.

- **Development framework.** MDT provides ready-made functions for many commonly used configurations.

Supported OSD Scenarios

Both MDT 2013 Lite Touch and ConfigMgr 2012 R2 support the same basic OSD scenarios, and as you learned earlier in this chapter, you can control the level of automation in each scenario.

New Computer Scenario

The new computer scenario is for bare metal deployments and is also called *new machine*. The key signature for this scenario is that you don't have any user data to deal with; it's simply a fresh install of a new operating system.

The deployment process for the new machine scenario is as follows:

1. The setup is started from boot media (CD/USB or PXE).
2. The operating system image is installed.
3. Other applications are installed (as part of the task sequence).
4. The machine is ready to be used.

When using PXE-based deployments, Windows Deployment Services (WDS) is used to allow for network-booting the boot images.

Real World Note: ConfigMgr 2012 R2 by default has slightly better built-in control for pre-staging machines than MDT 2013 Lite Touch has. For MDT 2013, you can solve that by prestaging computers in Active Directory and configuring them to use a specific boot image. In Windows Server 2012 R2, you even find PowerShell cmdlets for WDS that let you prestage the computers.

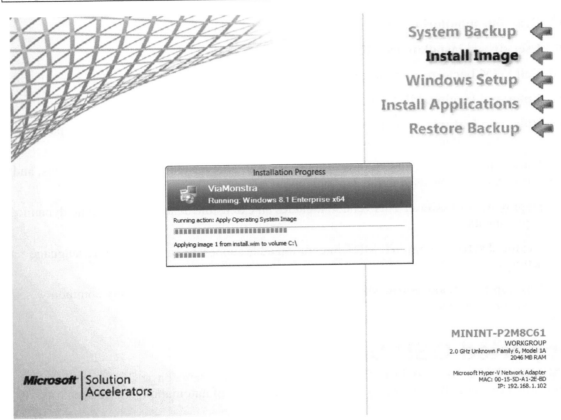

Deploying a bare metal machine using ConfigMgr 2012 R2.

Computer Refresh

Refresh, or *wipe-and-load*, is the new upgrade. This is a scenario you might use, for example, to upgrade from Windows 7 to Windows 8.1. The User State Migration Tool (USMT) is used for backup, and you have an optional full WIM backup you can use, as well.

Please note that the optional WIM backup is only a data .wim file, intended for restoring individual files and folders, and not meant for restoring to a working operating system again.

The deployment process for the wipe and load scenario is as follows:

1. The setup is started through a deployment to a running operating system.

2. User state is saved locally (normally).

3. The operating system image is installed.

4. Other applications are installed.

5. User state is restored.

6. The machine is ready to be used.

Computer Replace Scenario

Simply put, the replace scenario, also called *side-by-side*, is a computer replacement, which is something most organizations do with 20–25 percent of their machines every year. This scenario is similar to the refresh scenario, but because the machine is being replaced, you need to store the backup where the new computer can pick it up.

By default, the USMT backup is stored on a network share. (In ConfigMgr 2012 R2, the network share is controlled by the state migration point by default, but that can be changed.)

The deployment process for the replace scenario is as follows:

1. The user state is saved on the state migration point through an advertisement to a running operating system.

2. Then the new computer is deployed as a normal bare metal deployment.

Offline Media Scenario

Both MDT 2013 Lite Touch and ConfigMgr 2012 R2 also support offline media, or offline deployments. You can generate an ISO file or a bootable USB stick that will hold your task sequence and all the necessary packages.

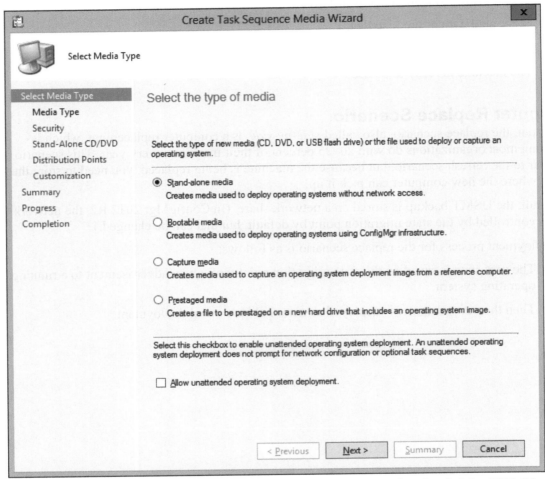

Creating standalone media using the Task Sequence Media Wizard in ConfigMgr 2012 R2.

Chapter 5

MDT 2013 Lite Touch – Technical Drilldown

In the Chapter 3, you learned about the ViaMonstra environment. It is now time to start drilling into the MDT 2013 Lite Touch deployment solution. This is also where you start setting up the MDT 2013 deployment server (MDT01) used in this book. In this chapter, you learn about MDT 2013 Lite Touch, as well as the following step-by-step configurations:

- Installing and configuring MDT 2013

- Setting Active Directory permissions

- Setting up the deployment share

- Adding operating system images, drivers, and applications

- Creating task sequences

- Configuring the rules (Bootstrap.ini and CustomSettings.ini)

- Configuring Windows Deployment Services (WDS)

- Deploying the Windows 8.1 client

Step-by-Step Guide Requirements

If you want to run the step-by-step guide in this chapter, you need a lab environment configured as outlined in Chapter 3 and Appendix A. In this chapter, you are using the following virtual machines:

DC01

MDT01

The VMs used in this chapter.

You also need to have downloaded the following software:

- Microsoft Deployment Toolkit (MDT) 2013

- System Center 2012 R2 Configuration Manager Toolkit

- 7-Zip 9.20 x64

- Adobe Reader 11.0

- Windows 8.1 Enterprise x64

- The book sample files (http://stealingwithpride.com)

Overview – MDT 2013

MDT 2013 is a free deployment solution built by the Enterprise Client Management organization at Microsoft. The core team members and their roles for the MDT 2013 release were:

- **Aaron Czechowski.** Program Manager

- **Cameron King.** Program Manager

- **Jason Githens.** Program Manager Lead

- **Kiran Alli.** Software Development Engineer

- **Jason Brinkle.** Software Development Engineer

- **Sangeetha Visweswaran.** Software Development Engineer Lead

- **Cheng Xu.** Software Development Engineer in Test

- **Randy Xu.** Software Development Engineer in Test

- **Jason Wang.** Software Development Engineer in Test Lead

The UDI team members (for the ConfigMgr 2012 R2 integration) were:

- **Cameron King.** Program Manager

- **Chris Adams.** Program Manager Lead

- Vendors from Wicresoft…

Lite Touch Components

To quickly master MDT 2013 Lite Touch, it's valuable to first learn what the major components are and what they are used for.

Deployment Workbench

The main administrator UI for MDT is called the Deployment Workbench. The Deployment Workbench is a Microsoft Management Console (MMC) 3.0 snap-in that is supported on Windows 7, Windows 8.1, Windows Server 2008 R2, Windows Server 2012, and Windows Server 2012 R2.

We highly recommend that you run the Deployment Workbench on Windows 8.1 or Windows Server 2012 R2, depending on the machine from which you are administering the deployment solution. If you follow the guides in this book, you install MDT 2013 on Windows Server 2012 R2.

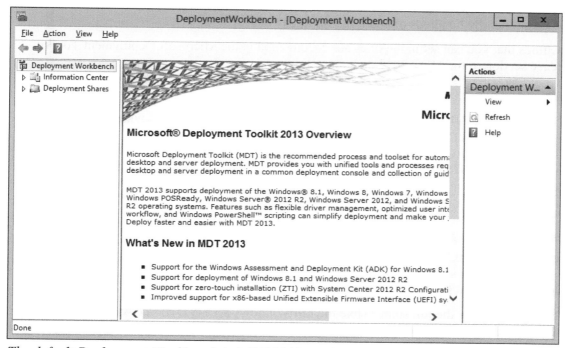

The default Deployment Workbench in MDT 2013, no deployment content added yet.

Deployment Share

One or more shared folders on the server contain all the setup files and scripts needed for the deployment solution. The folder is the deployment share. It also holds the configuration files (called rules) that are gathered when a machine is deployed. These configuration files can reach out to other sources, like a database, external script, or web server to get additional settings for the deployment.

Rules

The rules (CustomSettings.ini and Bootstrap.ini) make up the brain of MDT 2013, the mastermind if you will. The rules control the Windows Deployment Wizard on the client and, for example, can provide the following settings to the machine being deployed:

- Computer name
- Domain to join, and OU in Active Directory to hold the computer object
- Whether to enable BitLocker
- Regional settings
- And literally hundreds of additional settings

The settings that you can set in the rules are documented in the Microsoft Deployment Toolkit Reference section of the MDT 2013 documentation.

Boot Images

Boot images are the WinPE 5.0-based images that are used to start the deployment. They can be started from a CD/DVD, an ISO file, a USB device, or over the network using a PXE server. The boot images connect to the deployment share on the server and start the deployment. Whereas the previous version, MDT 2012 Update, supported WinPE 3.0, WinPE 3.1, and WinPE 4.0 boot images, MDT 2013 supports only WinPE 5.0 boot images when used as a standalone deployment solution.

Operating Systems

Using the Deployment Workbench, you import the operating systems you want to deploy. In this book, we use Windows 8.1, but MDT 2013 also supports deploying Windows 7, Windows 8, Windows Server 2008 R2, Windows Server 2012, and Windows Server 2012 R2.

You can import either the full source (like the full Windows 8.1 DVD) or a custom image that you have created. The full source operating systems are primarily used to create reference images even though technically they also can be used for normal deployments.

Applications

Using the Deployment Workbench, you also add the applications you want to deploy. MDT supports virtually every executable Windows file type. It can be a standard .exe file with command-line switches for an unattended install; it also can be a Windows Installer (MSI) package, a batch file, a VBScript, or a PowerShell script. In fact, it can be just about anything that can be executed unattended. MDT also supports deploying the new Windows 8 applications.

> **Real World Note:** You cannot add an application just anywhere in the task sequence. It needs to be in the state restore phase (or after). We get quite a number of emails from people who tried to install the application during the WinPE phase, and that doesn't work.

Drivers Repository

You also use the Deployment Workbench to import the drivers your hardware needs into a drivers repository that lives on the server, not in the image. The default behavior in MDT 2013 Lite Touch is to do a PnP ID scan when deploying a computer, match that list with the drivers in the repository, and then inject the matching drivers during deployment.

Real World Note: For most deployments, we recommend that you disable the default method for driver injection and instead use the optional "total control" option in MDT 2013 for drivers. For more information about that, see this blog post: http://tinyurl.com/MDT2013Drivers.

Packages

With the Deployment Workbench, in the Packages node, you can add any Microsoft packages that you want to use. The most commonly added packages are language packs, but you also can add security and other updates this way. However, we generally recommend that you use WSUS for operating system updates because package administration in MDT is close to a nightmare. The rare exceptions are critical hotfixes that may not be available via WSUS, or packages for the boot image.

Real World Note: In Windows 8.1, unlike Windows 7, all editions now support using multiple language packs.

Task Sequences

Task sequences are the heart and soul of the deployment solution. When creating a task sequence, you need to select a template. The templates are located in the Templates folder in the MDT installation directory, and they determine which default actions are present in the sequence.

You can think of a task sequence as a list of actions that need to be executed in a certain order. Each action also can have conditions. Some example actions follow:

- **Gather.** Reads configuration settings from the deployment server.

- **Format and Partition.** Creates the partition(s) and formats them.

- **Inject Drivers.** Finds out which drivers the machine needs and downloads them from the drivers repository in MDT.

- **Apply Operating System.** Runs ImageX to apply the operating system image.

- **Windows Update.** Connects to a WSUS server and updates the machine.

Real World Note: You also can create your own task sequence templates. As long as you store them in the Templates folder, they will be available when you create a new task sequence.

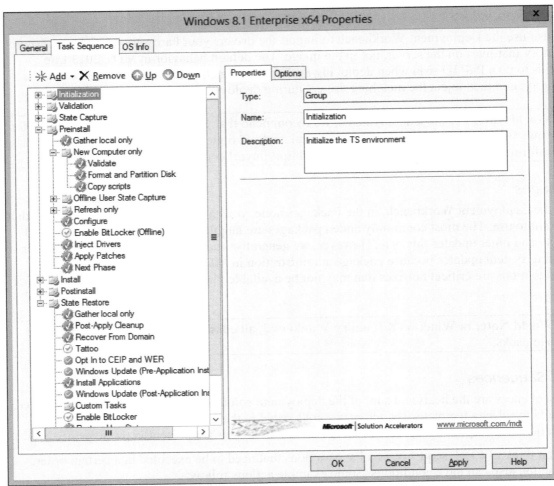

A task sequence that will deploy a Windows 8.1 Enterprise x64 image.

Selection Profiles

Available in the Advanced node, selection profiles provide a generic way in MDT to filter content in the workbench.

Logging

MDT 2013 uses a lot of log files during operating system deployments. By default the logs are client side, but by configuring the server settings (named SLSHARE), you can have MDT 2013 store them on the server, as well.

Monitoring

On the deployment share, you also can enable monitoring. After doing that, you will see all running deployments in the Monitor node in the Deployment Workbench. The cool thing about this monitoring is that it supports ConfigMgr 2012 R2, as well as the Remote Connection feature in DaRT 8.1 (part of MDOP 2013 R2). You learn more about deployment monitoring in Chapter 13.

Creating the MDT 2013 Infrastructure

This section provides a step-by-step tutorial, during which you install the necessary prerequisites, create the shared folders you need, and configure security permissions in the files system and in Active Directory.

Review the MDT 2013 Service Accounts

We use a role-based model when configuring permissions for the various service accounts we use for MDT 2013. It's now time to review the accounts and organizational units the hydration solution created for you:

1. On **DC01**, log on as **VIAMONSTRA\Administrator** using a password of **P@ssw0rd**

2. Using **Active Directory User and Computers**, in the **corp.viamonstra.com** domain level, select the **ViaMonstra** OU. In this OU, you find the following sub OUs:

    o   **Security Groups**

    o   **Servers**

    o   **Service Accounts**

    o   **Software Groups**

    o   **Users**

    o   **Workstations**

3. Select the **Service Accounts** OU, where you find the following accounts related to MDT 2013.

    o   **MDT_BA.** The MDT 2013 Build Account.

    o   **MDT_JD.** The MDT 2013 Join Domain Account.

Note: There are more accounts in the Service Accounts OU, but they are used for ConfigMgr 2012 R2 and Orchestrator 2012 R2.

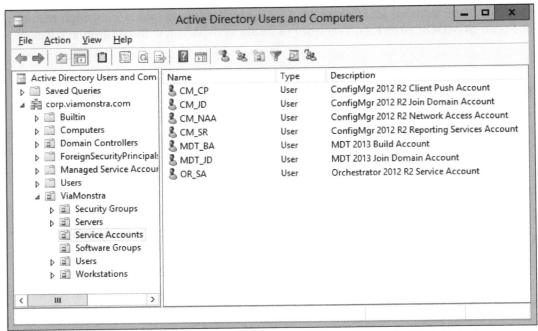

Active Directory Users and Computers listing the Service Accounts.

Set Permissions on the Servers and Workstations OUs

To have the machines join the domain, you need to allow the join account (MDT_JD) permissions to manage computer accounts in the ViaMonstra / Server and the ViaMonstra / Workstations OUs. In this guide, we assume you have downloaded and extracted the book sample files to C:\Setup on DC01.

1. On **DC01**, in an elevated (run as Administrator) **PowerShell** command prompt, configure **Execution Policy** in PowerShell by running the following command:

    ```
    Set-ExecutionPolicy -ExecutionPolicy RemoteSigned -Force
    ```

> **Real World Note:** In Windows Server 2012 R2 the default execution policy is already set to RemoteSigned, but the hydration process hardens that policy, so it needs to be configured.

2. Grant permissions for the **MDT_JD** account to the **ViaMonstra / Workstations** OU by running the following command:

    ```
    C:\Setup\Scripts\Set-OUPermissions.ps1 -Account MDT_JD
    -TargetOU "OU=Workstations,OU=ViaMonstra"
    ```

3. Grant permissions for the **MDT_JD** account to the **ViaMonstra / Servers** OU by running the following command:

    ```
    C:\Setup\Scripts\Set-OUPermissions.ps1 -Account MDT_JD
    -TargetOU "OU=Servers,OU=ViaMonstra"
    ```

The Set-OUPermissions.ps1 script grants the minimum permissions needed to create and update computer objects in the OU that is specified. The permissions granted by the script are:

- **This object and all descendant objects.** Create Computer objects, and Delete Computer objects.

- **Descendant Computer objects.** Read All Properties, Write All Properties, Read Permissions, Modify Permissions, Change Password, Reset Password, Validated write to DNS host name, and Validated write to service principal name.

Install MDT 2013

These steps assume that you have the MDT01 member server configured per the proof-of-concept environment outlined in Chapter 3 and Appendix A, as well as that you have downloaded MDT 2013 to the D:\Setup\MDT 2013 folder on MDT01.

1. On **MDT01**, log on as **VIAMONSTRA\Administrator** using a password of **P@ssw0rd**.

2. Install **MDT 2013** (D:\Setup\MDT 2013\MicrosoftDeploymentToolkit2013_x64.msi) using the default settings.

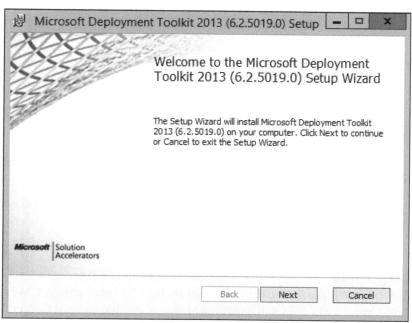

Installing MDT 2013.

Create and Share the Logs Folder

By default MDT 2013 only stores the log files locally on the client, but you enable server-side logging later in this chapter. For that you need to have a folder in which to store the logs:

1. On **MDT01**, create and share the **D:\Logs** folder by running the following commands in an elevated **PowerShell** prompt (pressing **Enter** after each command):

```
New-Item -Path D:\Logs -ItemType directory

New-SmbShare –Name Logs$ –Path D:\Logs -ChangeAccess
EVERYONE

icacls D:\Logs /grant '"MDT_BA":(OI)(CI)(M)'
```

Note: There are no spaces between (OI)(CI)(M) in the preceding command.

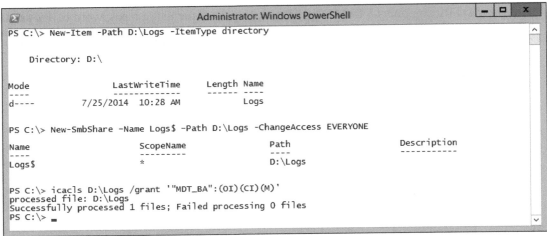

Sharing the D:\Logs folder on MDT01.

2. Verify that the share was created by running the following command:

```
Get-SmbShare
```

Use CMTrace to Log Files

The log files in MDT 2013 Lite Touch are formatted to be read by the CMTrace utility. CMTrace is available as part of System Center 2012 R2 Configuration Manager and the System Center 2012 R2 Configuration Manager Toolkit (also named ConfigMgr 2012 Toolkit R2).

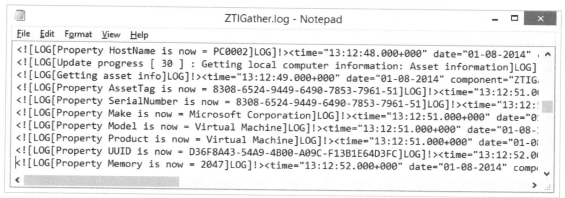

One of the MDT log files opened in Notepad.

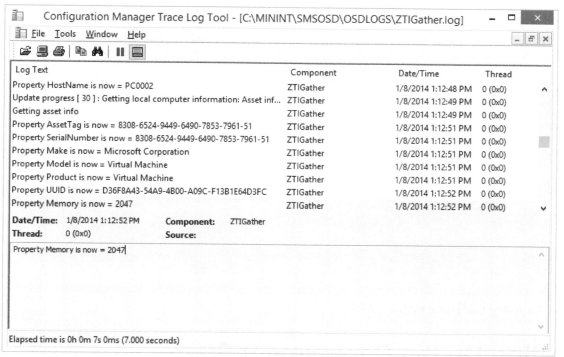

The very same log file opened in CMTrace is much easier to read.

Install ConfigMgr 2012 Toolkit R2

These steps assume that you have downloaded ConfigMgr 2012 Toolkit R2 (System Center 2012 R2 Configuration Manager Toolkit) to the D:\Setup\ConfigMgr 2012 Toolkit R2 folder on MDT01.

1. On **MDT01**, install **ConfigMgr 2012 Toolkit R2 (ConfigMgrTools.msi)** with the default settings.

2. Using **File Explorer**, navigate to the **C:\Program Files (x86)\ConfigMgr 2012 Toolkit R2\ClientTools** folder, start **CMTrace.exe**, and select **Yes** to make it the default viewer for log files.

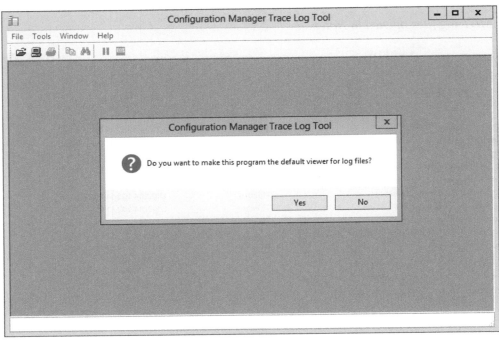

Associating CMTrace with log files.

Setting Up the Deployment Share

In this book, you use a single deployment share for your developments and customizations. For production deployment servers, you normally have at least two deployment shares, one for building reference images and one for production deployments; but to follow the guides in this book, you need only one. Also, in a production deployment share, you normally add a lot of applications and drivers, but for the guides in this book, you don't need to add much of that.

Create the MDT Production Deployment Share

In these steps, you create a deployment share in the D:\MDTProduction folder on MDT01.

1. On **MDT01**, using the **Deployment Workbench** (available on the Start screen), right-click **Deployment Shares** and select **New Deployment Share**.

2. In the **New Deployment Share Wizard**, on the **Path** page, configure the following and click **Next**:

   Deployment share path: **D:\MDTProduction**

3. On the **Share** page, configure the following and click **Next**:

   Share name: **MDTProduction$**

4. On the **Descriptive Name** page, configure the following and click **Next**:

   Deployment share description: **MDT Production**

5. On the **Options** page, accept the default settings and click **Next**.

6. On the **Summary** page, review the information and click **Next**.

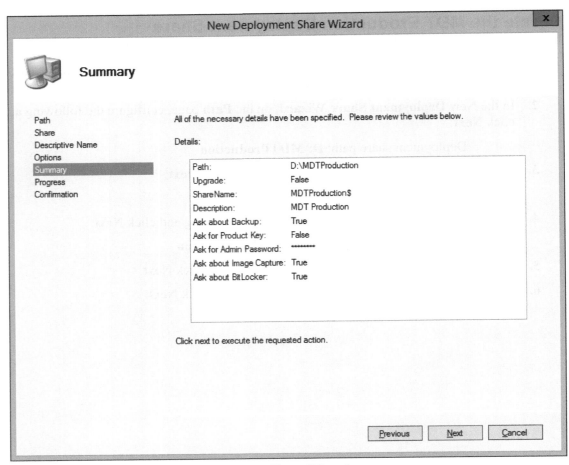

The Summary page in the New Deployment Share Wizard.

7. On the **Confirmation** page, click the **View Script** button.

8. Review the PowerShell script that was generated for you, and then close **Notepad**.

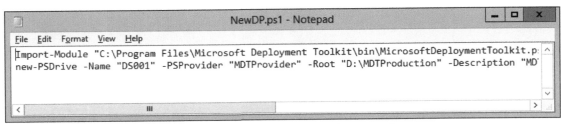

The PowerShell commands that would create a new deployment share.

Real World Note: Not all scripts that Deployment Workbench generates are complete. For example, the preceding script doesn't share the folder, something that you need to add if you want to script the creation of a deployment share.

9. On the **Confirmation** page, click **Finish**.

10. Using **File Explorer**, verify that you can access the **\\MDT01\MDTProduction$** share.

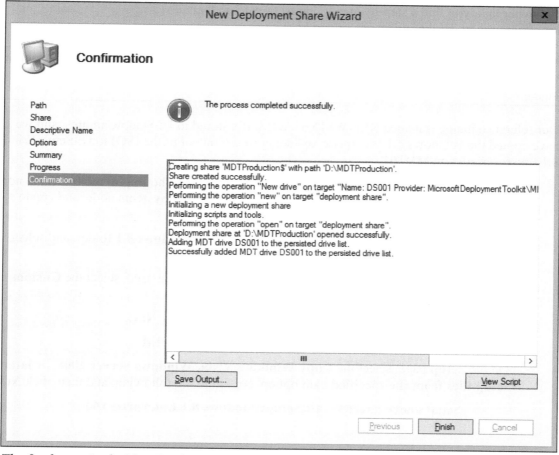

The final page in the New Deployment Share Wizard, showing the View Script button.

Adding Operating System Images

Once the deployment share is created, you can start adding operating systems images, as well as the other setup files you need. When adding images to a deployment share, even a custom Windows 8.1 image, we still recommend you to copy the Windows 8.1 setup files (an option in the wizard). This is because Windows 8.1 stores additional components in the Sources\SxS folder which is outside the image.

Real World Note: Due to the Windows limits on path length, we are purposely keeping the operating system destination directory short: Using the folder name W81X64, rather than a more descriptive name like Windows 8.1 Enterprise x64.

Add the Windows 8.1 Enterprise x64 Reference Image

In this guide, we assume you have a custom reference image of the Windows 8.1 Enterprise x64 image available. Creating reference images is outside the scope of this book, but if you go to the following link, you find a step-by-step guide on how to do that: http://tinyurl.com/BuildingReferenceImages.

> **Note:** For lab and test purposes, you of course can use the default INSTALL.WIM file from the Windows 8.1 Enterprise x64 media, but we strongly encourage you to build a "real" reference image.

Our reference image is named REF-W81X64.WIM. It's stored in D:\Setup\Captures, and we also have copied the Windows 8.1 Enterprise x64 setup files (content of the ISO) to D:\Setup\Windows 8.1 Enterprise x64 on MDT01.

1. On **MDT01**, using the **Deployment Workbench**, expand the **Deployment Shares** node, and then expand **MDT Production**; select the **Operating Systems** node, and create a folder named **Windows 8.1**.

2. Expand the **Operating Systems** node, right-click the **Windows 8.1** folder, and select **Import Operating System**.

3. In the **Import Operating System Wizard**, on the **OS Type** page, select the **Custom image file option**, and click **Next**.

4. On the **Image** page, configure the following, and then click **Next**:

    Source file: **D:\Setup\Captures\REF-W81X64.WIM**

5. On the **Setup** page, select the **Copy Windows Vista, Windows Server 2008, or later setup files from the specified** path option, configure the following, and then click **Next**:

    Setup source directory: **D:\Setup\Windows 8.1 Enterprise x64**

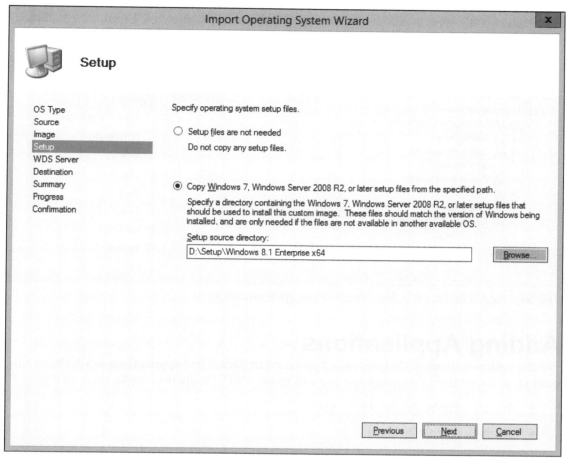

Copying the setup files for the custom Windows 8.1 image.

6. On the **Destination** page, configure the following, and then click **Next**.

    Destination directory name: **W81X64**

7. On the **Summary** page, review the details, and then click **Next**.

8. On the **Confirmation** page, once the image and setup files are added, click **Finish**.

9. After adding the operating system, in **Deployment Workbench**, double-click the added operating system name in the **Operating Systems / Windows 8.1** node and change the operating system name to match the following:

    Windows 8.1 Enterprise x64

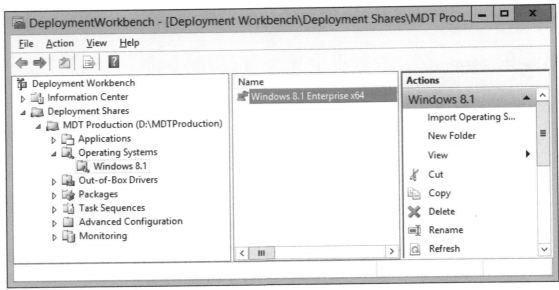

The imported Windows 8.1 operating system after renaming.

Adding Applications

For the customizations in Chapters 8–12 you need to have a few applications available. In this section, you create the following applications in the MDT Production deployment share:

- Install - Adobe Reader 11.0 - x86

- Install - 7-Zip 9.20 - x64

Create the Install - Adobe Reader 11.0 - x86 Application

In these steps, we assume that you have downloaded Adobe Reader 11.0 (AdbeRdr11000_en_US.msi) to D:\Setup\Adobe Reader 11.0 on MDT01.

1. On **MDT01**, using the **Deployment Workbench**, expand the **MDT Production** node, and navigate to the **Applications** node.

2. Right-click the **Applications** node, and create a new folder named **Adobe**

3. Expand the **Applications** node, right-click the **Adobe** folder and select **New Application**.

4. Use the following settings for the **New Application Wizard**:

    a. **Application with source files**

    b. Publisher: **<blank>**

    c. Application name: **Install - Adobe Reader 11.0 - x86**

    d. Version: **<blank>**

    e. Source Directory: **D:\Setup\Adobe Reader 11.0**

    f.   Specify the name of the directory that should be created:
       Install - Adobe Reader 11.0 - x86

    g.   Command Line: **msiexec /i AdbeRdr11000_en_US.msi /q**

    h.   Working directory: **<default>**

> **Real World Note:** Because MDT 2013 does not have a full application model like ConfigMgr 2012 R2 does, you can use VBScript or PowerShell wrappers to provide additional checks or installation processes to the application setup. A wrapper is not needed for MDT, you can just provide the unattended setup switches directly on the command line, but when doing more advanced setup, using a wrapper can be very useful. You find some sample wrappers in Chapter 9, "MDT Scripting Guidelines."

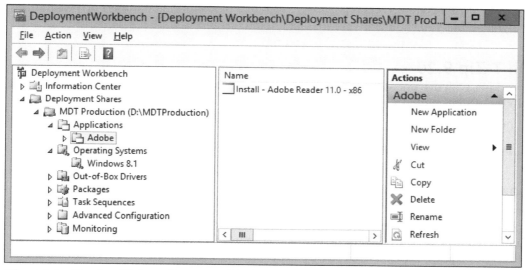

The Adobe Reader 11.0 application added.

Create the Install - 7-Zip 9.20 - x64 Application

In this guide, we assume you have downloaded the 7-Zip 9.20 x64 installation file (7z920-x64.msi) to D:\Setup\7-Zip 9.20 on MDT01.

1.   On **MDT01**, using the **Deployment Workbench**, right-click the **Applications** node, and create a new folder named **Utilities**.

2.   Right-click the **Utilities** folder and select **New Application**. Use the following settings for the **New Application Wizard**:

    a.   **Application with source files**

    b.   Publisher: **<blank>**

    c.   Application name: **Install - 7-Zip 9.20 - x64**

    d.   Version: **\<blank\>**

    e.   Source Directory: **D:\Setup\7-Zip 9.20**

    f.   Specify the name of the directory that should be created:

              Install - 7-Zip 9.20 - x64

    g.   Command Line: **msiexec /i 7z920-x64.msi /qb**

    h.   Working directory: **\<default\>**

Adding Drivers

The key to successful management of drivers for MDT 2013, as well as any other deployment solution, is to have a good drivers repository. From this repository, you import drivers into MDT for deployment, but you should always maintain the repository source for future use.

Install 7-Zip 9.20

When working with drivers, it helps to have a good extractor utility at hand, and our favorite is 7-Zip. In these steps, you use the previously downloaded 7-Zip 9.20.

1. On **MDT01**, navigate to the **D:\Setup\7-Zip 9.20** folder.

2. Install **7-Zip 9.20** (7z920-x64.msi) using the default settings.

Prepare the Drivers Repository

For Windows 7 and Windows 8.1 deployments, you need drivers both for the boot images and for the actual operating system. In this section, you add drivers for the boot image and Windows 8.1 operating systems drivers for one of the hardware models ViaMonstra is supporting: the Dell Latitude E7440 laptop.

1. On **MDT01**, using **File Explorer**, create the **D:\Drivers** folder.

2. In the **Drivers** folder, create the following folder structure:

       WinPE x86
       WinPE x64
       Windows 8.1 x64

3. In the new **Windows 8.1 x64** folder, create the following subfolder:

       Latitude E7440

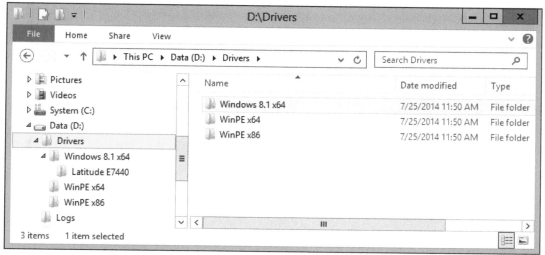

The D:\Drivers structure.

Create the Logical Driver Structure in MDT 2013

When importing drivers to the MDT 2013 driver repository, MDT will create a single instance folder structure based on driver class names. However, you can, and should, mimic the driver structure of your driver source repository in the Deployment Workbench. This is done by creating logical folders in the Deployment Workbench.

1.   On **MDT01**, using **Deployment Workbench**, select **the Out-of-Box Drivers** node.

2.   In the **Out-Of-Box Drivers node**, create the following folder structure:

> **WinPE x86**
> **WinPE x64**
> **Windows 8.1 x64**

3.   In the **Windows 8.1 x64** folder, create the following subfolder:

> **Latitude E7440**

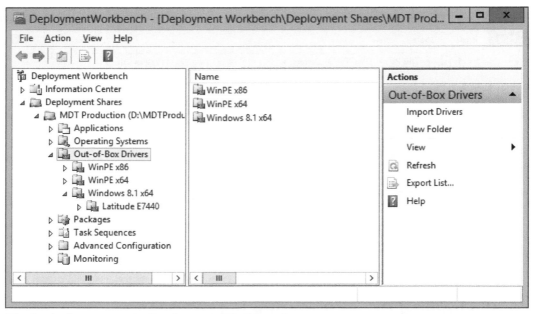

The logical structure in Deployment Workbench.

Create the Selection Profiles for Boot Image Drivers

By default, MDT 2013 will add any storage and network driver that you import to the boot images. You want to have more control than that. You should add only the drivers that are actually needed to the boot image, and the way you can control that is by using selection profiles.

1. On **MDT01**, using the **Deployment Workbench**, in the **MDT Production** node, expand the **Advanced Configuration** node, right-click the **Selection Profiles** node, and select **New Selection Profile**.

2. In the **New Selection Profile Wizard**, create a selection profile with the following settings:

   a. Selection Profile name: **WinPE x86**

   a. Folders: Select the **WinPE x86** folder in **Out-of-Box Drivers**.

3. Again, right-click the **Selection Profiles** node, and select **New Selection Profile**.

4. In the **New Selection Profile Wizard**, create a selection profile with the following settings:

   a. Selection Profile name: **WinPE x64**

   b. Folders: Select the **WinPE x64** folder in **Out-of-Box Drivers**.

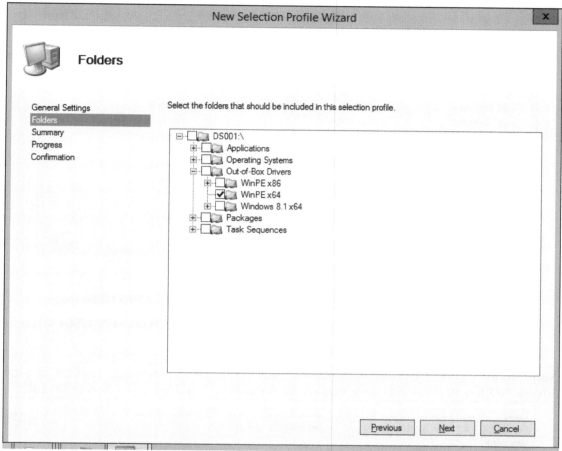

Creating the WinPE x64 selection profile.

Extract and Import Drivers for the x64 Boot Image

WinPE 5.0 already supports the Dell Latitude E7440 model we are using as an example, but here you learn to add boot image drivers, anyway. Who knows, you might have other hardware that need additional drivers. In this example, you add Intel network drivers to the x64 boot image. In these steps, we assume you have downloaded version 19.1 of PROWinx64.exe from intel.com and saved it to a temporary folder.

1. Extract the **PROWinx64.exe** to a temporary folder—in this example, to **D:\Temp\ProWinx64**.

Real World Note: Use 7-Zip 9.20 to extract the file. Even if the PROWinx64.exe file supports a switch for silent extraction (/s), it will fail unless you run it on an operating system with the same architecture.

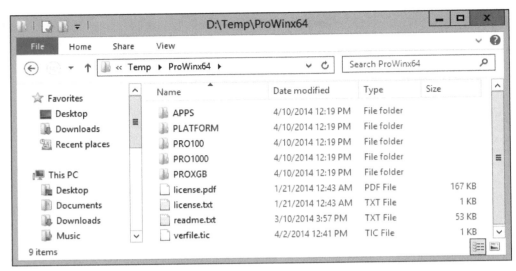

The extracted ProWinx64 drivers.

2. Using **File Explorer**, create the **D:\Drivers\WinPE x64\Intel PRO1000** folder.

3. Copy the content of the **D:\Temp\PROWinx64\PRO1000\Winx64\NDIS64** folder to **D:\Drivers\WinPE x64\Intel PRO1000**.

Note: Network Driver Interface Specification (NDIS) is just a programming interface for network drivers. NDIS 6.40 (NDIS64) is the version for Windows 8.1 and Windows Server 2012 R2.

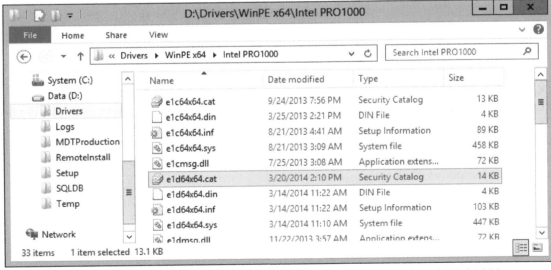

The NDIS64 (Windows 8.1) drivers copied to D:\Drivers\WinPE x64\Intel PRO1000.

4. Using **Deployment Workbench**, expand the **Out-of-Box Drivers** node, right-click the **WinPE x64** node, and select **Import Drivers**. Use the following setting for the **Import Drivers Wizard**:

Driver source directory: **D:\Drivers\WinPE x64\Intel PRO1000**

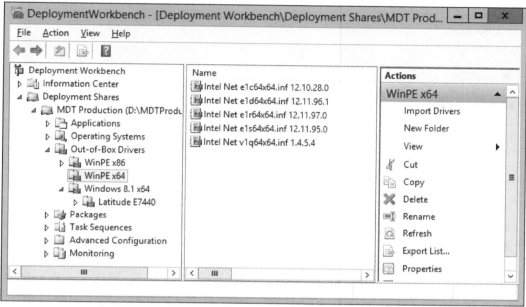

Deployment Workbench showing the imported Intel PRO1000 drivers.

Download, Extract, and Import Drivers for Latitude E7440

For the Dell Latitude E7440 model, you use the ready-made Dell Driver CAB file. The easiest way to get the Dell Driver CAB file is via the Dell TechCenter web site. In these steps, we assume you have downloaded E7440-win8.1-A01-Y7TY2.CAB to D:\Temp on MDT01.

> **Note:** Dell updates their driver CAB files every once in a while, so if the A01 version is not available, just grab the latest version.

1. On **MDT01**, using **7-Zip**, extract the **E7440-win8.1-A01-Y7TY2.CAB** to the **D:\Temp** folder.

2. Using **File Explorer**, navigate to **D:\Temp\E7440\win8.1\x64** and copy the content to the **D:\Drivers\Windows 8.1 x64\Latitude E7440** folder.

> **Real World Note:** Again, make sure to always keep the drivers repository intact. Don't delete these folders to save disk space on the server. You never know when you need start fresh again with drivers.

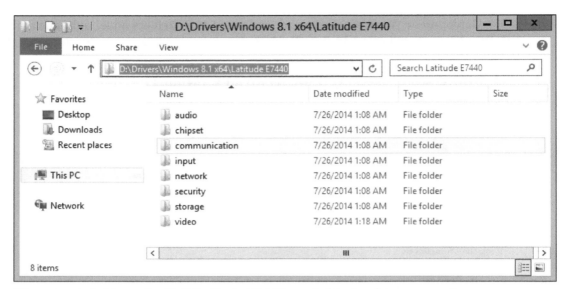

The extracted drivers for Dell Latitude E7440, copied to the drivers repository.

3. Using the **Deployment Workbench**, in the **MDT Production** node, expand the **Out-Of-Box Drivers** node, and expand the **Windows 8.1 x64** node.

4. Right-click the **Latitude E7440** folder, select **Import Drivers**, and use the following settings for the **Import Driver** wizard:

    Driver source directory: **D:\Drivers\Windows 8.1 x64\Latitude E7440**

> **Note:** You don't need to worry about the warnings during driver import; MDT simply does a validation of the drivers and does not import drivers that are flagged with an incorrect platform.

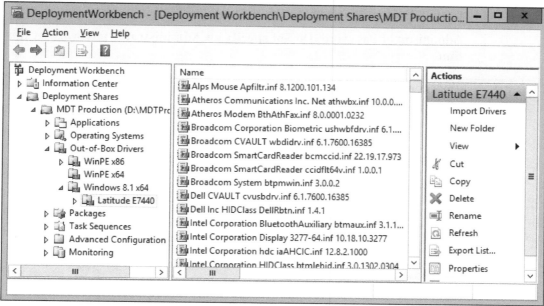

The imported drivers for Dell Latitude E7440.

Creating the Deployment Task Sequence

It is now time to create the task sequence for your production image. Once it is created, you then need to customize it, enabling Windows Update and configuring the driver injection action.

Create the Windows 8.1 Enterprise x64 Task Sequence

1. On **MDT01**, using the **Deployment Workbench**, select **Task Sequences** in the **MDT Production** node, and create a folder named **Windows 8.1**.

2. Expand the **Task Sequences** node, right-click the new **Windows 8.1** folder, and select **New Task Sequence**. Use the following settings for the **New Task Sequence Wizard**:

    a. Task sequence ID: **W81-X64-001**

    b. Task sequence name: **Windows 8.1 Enterprise x64**

    c. Task sequence comments: **Production Image**

    d. Template: **Standard Client Task Sequence**

    e. Select OS: **Windows 8.1 Enterprise x64**

    f. Specify Product Key: **Do not specify a product key at this time.**

    g. Full Name: **ViaMonstra**

    h. Organization: **ViaMonstra**

i. Internet Explorer home page: **about:blank**

j. Administrator Password: **Do not specify an Administrator password at this time.**

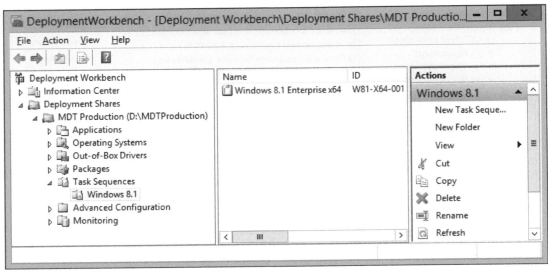

The Windows 8.1 Enterprise x64 task sequence created.

Edit the Windows 8 Task Sequence

1. Right-click the **Windows 8.1 Enterprise x64** task sequence, and select **Properties**.

2. On the **Task Sequence** tab, configure the **Windows 8.1 Enterprise x64** task sequence with the following settings:

   a. Preinstall. After the **Enable BitLocker (Offline)** action, add a **Set Task Sequence Variable** action with the following settings:

      - Name: **Set DriverGroup001**

      - Task Sequence Variable: **DriverGroup001**

      - Value: **Windows 8.1 x64\%Model%**

   b. Preinstall. Configure the **Inject Drivers** action with the following settings:

      - Choose a selection profile: **Nothing**

      - **Install all drivers from the selection profile**

> **Real World Note:** This way of configuring drivers is called "total control" and is a well proven method for working with drivers. If you are working with hardware that does not have useful model names (like Lenovo), you might want to add additional logic via the userexit script, something you learn about in Chapter 9, "MDT Scripting Guidelines."

     c.   State Restore. Enable the **Windows Update (Pre-Application Installation)** action.

     d.   State Restore. Enable the **Windows Update (Post-Application Installation)** action.

3.   Click **OK**.

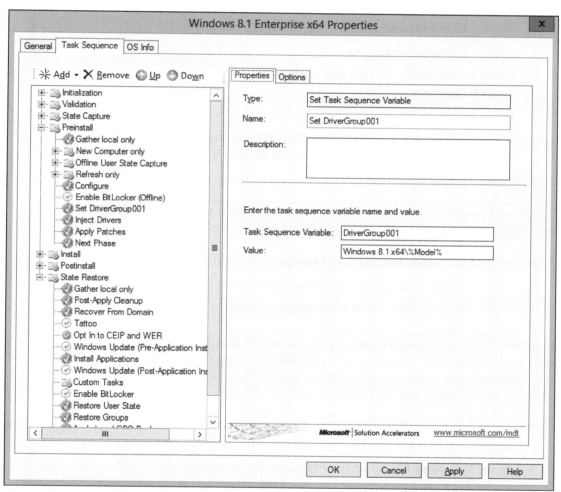

The task sequence for production deployment.

Configuring the Deployment Share

After adding setup files and applications to the deployment share, you need to configure the deployment share rules (Boostrap.ini and CustomSettings.ini) and boot image settings.

Configure Rules and Boot Image Settings

In these steps, we assume you have downloaded and extracted the book sample files to D:\Setup on MDT01.

1. On **MDT01**, using **File Explorer**, copy the following files from **D:\Setup\ MDTProduction\Control** folder to **D:\MDTProduction\Control**. Overwrite the existing files.

   o **Bootstrap.ini**

   o **CustomSettings.ini**

2. Using **Deployment Workbench**, right-click the **MDT Production** deployment share and select **Properties**.

3. In the **Windows PE** tab, in the **Platform** drop-down list, make sure **x86** is selected.

4. In the **General** sub-tab, in the **Windows PE Customizations** area, set the **Custom background bitmap file** to: **D:\Setup\Branding\ViaMonstraBackground.bmp**

5. Click **Apply**.

Real World Note: The console has a tendency of crashing when you change the custom background image. That's why you save the changes before continuing.

6. In the **Lite Touch Boot Image Settings** area, configure the following settings:

   o Image description: **MDT Production x86**

   o ISO file name: **MDT Production x86.iso**

Real World Note: Because you are going to use PXE later to deploy the machines, you don't really need the ISO file; however, we recommend creating ISO files because they are very useful when troubleshooting deployments and for quick tests. Also, because WinPE 5.0, unlike previous versions, automatically sets the scratch space size, you don't need to configure it.

7. In the **Drivers and Patches** sub-tab, select the **WinPE x86** selection profile and select the **Include all drivers from the selection profile** option.

8. In the **Windows PE** tab, in the **Platform** drop-down list, select **x64**.

9. In the **General** sub-tab, in the **Windows PE Customizations** area, set the **Custom background bitmap file** to: **D:\Setup\Branding\ViaMonstraBackground.bmp**.

10. Click **Apply**.

Real World Note: Again, the console has a tendency of crashing when you change the custom background image. That's why you save the changes before continuing.

11. In the **Lite Touch Boot Image Settings** area, configure the following settings:

- Image description: **MDT Production x64**

- ISO file name: **MDT Production x64.iso**

12. In the **Drivers and Patches** sub-tab, select the **WinPE x64** selection profile and select the **Include all drivers from the selection profile** option.

13. Click **OK**.

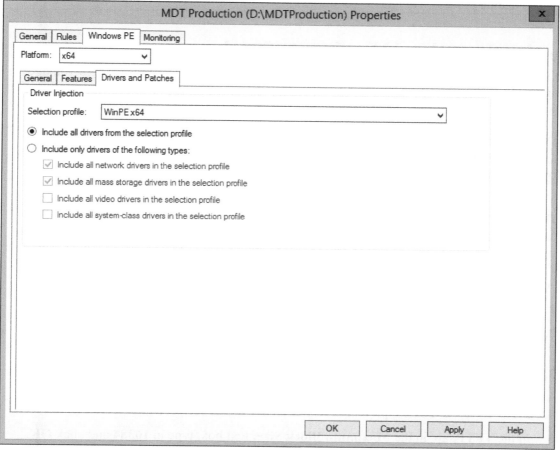

The Drivers and Patches sub-tab for the x64 boot image.

Update the Deployment Share

The deployment share needs to be updated after it has been configured. Again, this is the process when the WinPE 5.0 boot images are created.

1. On **MDT01**, using **Deployment Workbench**, right-click the **MDT Production** deployment share and select **Update Deployment Share**.

2. Use the default options for the **Update Deployment Share** wizard.

Note: The update process will take 5–10 minutes.

Deploying the Windows 8.1 Image

In this section, you use the previously created task sequence to deploy the Windows 8.1 image through a fully automated process. First, you need to add the boot image to Windows Deployment Services (WDS) and then start the deployment.

Real World Note: Depending on your deployment, you might need both x86 and x64 boot images. You don't need it for the samples in this book, but you may need it to support all deployment scenarios in a production environment.

Configure Windows Deployment Services (WDS)

You need to add the MDT Production Lite Touch x64 boot image to WDS in preparation for the deployment. You also configure the TFTP block size, which will decrease the time it takes to boot WinPE 5.0 over the network. For the following steps, we assume that Windows Deployment Services has already been installed on MDT01 according to the instructions in Appendix A.

1. On **MDT01**, using **Server Manager**, select **Tools / Windows Deployment Services**.

2. In the **Windows Deployment Services** console, expand **Servers / MDT01.corp.viamonstra.com**, right-click **Boot Images**, and select **Add Boot Image**.

3. Browse to the **D:\MDTProduction\Boot\LiteTouchPE_x64.wim** file and add the image with the default settings.

4. Right-click **MDT01.corp.viamonstra.com**, and select **Properties**.

5. In the **TFTP** tab, in the **Maximum Block Size:** text box, type in **16384** and click **OK**.

Note: If you experience any problems after increasing the TFTP block size, try setting it to a lower value, like 8192 or 4096. Do not set it higher than 16384.

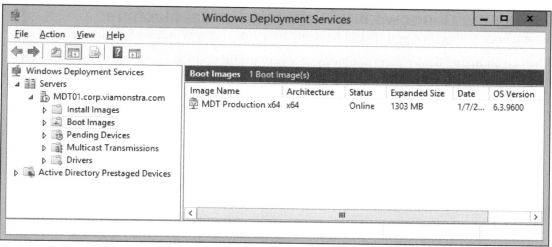

The x64 boot image added to the WDS console.

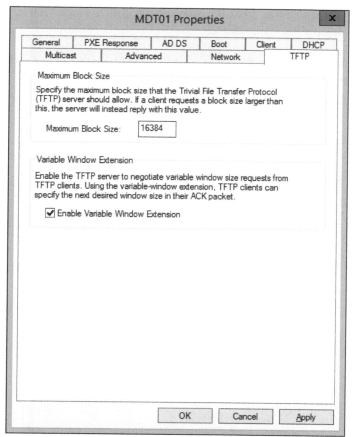

Configuring the TFTP block size to speed up WinPE boot time.

Deploy the Windows 8.1 Client to a Virtual Machine

Great work! At this time you should be ready for deploying a Windows 8.1 client.

When customizing deployment solutions, it's very useful to do as many tests as possible on virtual machines (unless you are customizing settings for drivers that need real physical hardware). This is simply because you can always rule out hardware issues when testing and/or troubleshooting, and you also can take advantage of snapshots (checkpoints) in the virtual machine platform.

1. On the **Host PC**, create a virtual machine with the following settings:

   a. Name: **PC0003**

   b. Location: **C:\VMs**

   c. Memory: **2048 MB**

   d. Network: The virtual network for the New York site

   e. Hard disk: **60 GB** (dynamic disk)

> **Note:** If you are using Hyper-V in Windows Server 2012 R2 or Windows 8.1, the new Generation 2 VMs can PXE boot without using a legacy network adapter.

2. Start the **PC0003** virtual machine, and press **Enter** to start the PXE boot. (If using earlier Hyper-V versions, you need to press F12.)

```
WDS Boot Manager version 0000
Client IP: 192.168.1.100
Server IP: 192.168.1.210
Server Name: MDT01.corp.viamonstra.com

Press ENTER for network boot service.
```

The initial PXE boot process of PC0003 when using a Generation 2 (UEFI) VM.

3. After WinPE has booted, complete the **Windows Deployment Wizard** using the following setting:

   a. Password: **P@ssw0rd**

   b. Select a task sequence to execute on this computer: **Windows 8.1 Enterprise x64**

   c. Computer Name: **PC0003**

   d. Applications: Select both applications

4. The setup will eventually complete and do the following:

   a. Install the Windows 8.1 Enterprise operating system.

   b. Install the selected applications.

5. When the setup is completed, log in to **PC0003** and using **Disk Management**, review the UEFI disk layout.

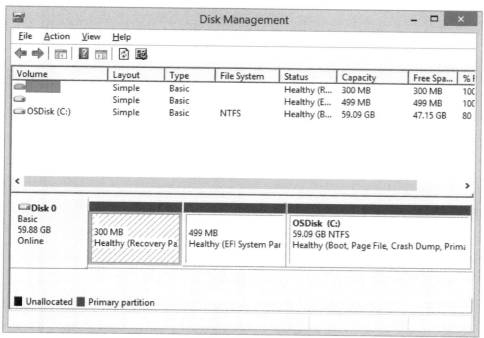

The disk layout after deploying PC0003 (UEFI).

Chapter 6

ConfigMgr 2012 R2 OSD – Technical Drilldown

This chapter is a technical drilldown to OSD in ConfigMgr 2012 R2. This is also where you start setting up the ConfigMgr 2012 R2 infrastructure. In this chapter, you learn about the OSD components in ConfigMgr 2012 R2 and do the following configurations:

- Configure discovery methods and create boundary groups
- Configure the Network Access account
- Adding the reporting services point
- Setup ConfigMgr 2012 R2 integration with MDT 2013
- Create the ConfigMgr 2012 R2 OSD structure
- Create boot images
- Add operating system images and adding applications
- Add drivers
- Create task sequences
- Configure rules, distribute content, and deploy task sequences
- Deploying Window 8.1 using PXE

Step-by-Step Guide Requirements

If you want to run the step-by-step guide in this chapter, you need a lab environment configured as outlined in Chapter 3 and Appendix A. In this chapter, you are using the following virtual machines:

DC01

CM01

The VMs used in this chapter.

You also need to have downloaded the following software:

- Microsoft Deployment Toolkit (MDT) 2013

- ConfigMgr 2012 R2 CU2 (KB 2970177)

- 7-Zip 9.20 x64

- Adobe Reader 11.0

- Windows 8.1 Enterprise x64

- The book sample files (http://stealingwithpride.com)

ConfigMgr 2012 R2 OSD Components

Operating system deployment with ConfigMgr 2012 R2 is basically part of the normal software distribution infrastructure, but there are additional components used, as well. For example, OSD in ConfigMgr may use the State Migration Point role, which is a role that is not used by normal application deployment in ConfigMgr. This section describes the components involved with software distribution, including OSD, in ConfigMgr 2012 R2.

State Migration Point (SMP)

The state migration point is used to store user-state migration data during computer replace scenarios. The state migration point encrypts each backup with a unique password key and keeps track of the mapping between the old computer and the new computer.

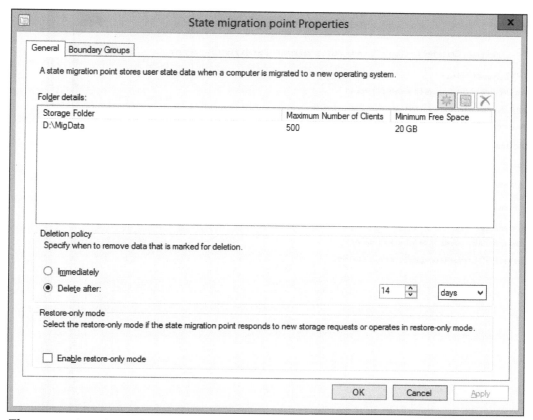

The state migration point properties.

Distribution Point (DP)

The distribution point is used for all packages in ConfigMgr, including all the OSD-related packages. However, there are two settings in the DP properties that are unique to operating system deployment and those are PXE boot and Multicast. Both PXE and Multicast require that the DP is running on a server operating system, and the Multicast protocol requires the DP to run on Windows Server 2008 or later. We recommend using Windows Server 2012 R2 for your distribution points.

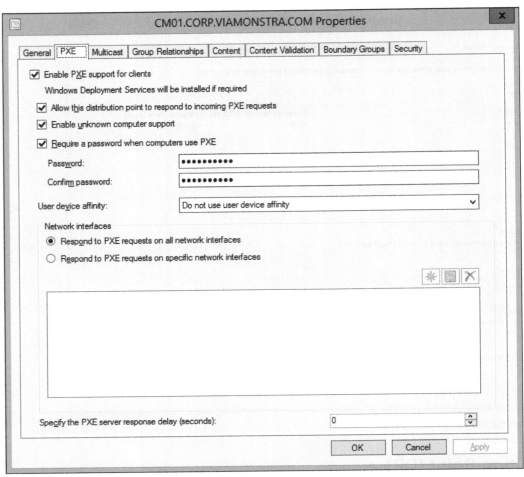

Enabling PXE on a local distribution point.

Software Update Point (SUP)

The software update point, which is normally used to deploy updates to existing machines, also can be used to update an operating system as part of the deployment process. In the default task sequence used for OSD, there is an action named Install Software Updates that will do just that.

Real World Note: The Install Software Updates action is known for having an issue (breaking) when there is too many updates to deploy at the same time. The fix is easy, however; you simply make sure your reference image is fairly up to date. Something you should do anyway. ☺

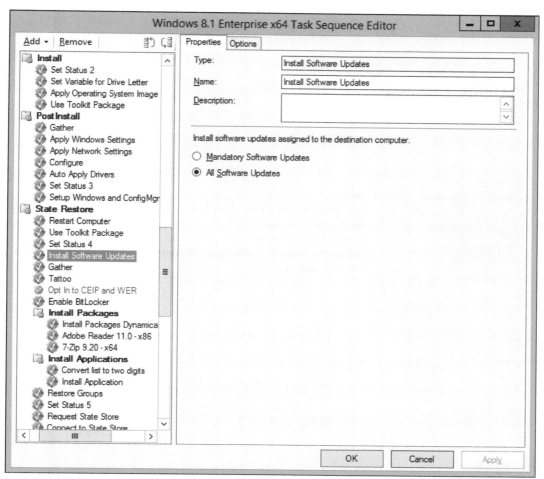

The task sequence action that installs software updates during deployment.

Reporting Services Point

During OSD, the task sequence reports progress back to the ConfigMgr server that can be reviewed in the ConfigMgr reports. There are quite a few reports in ConfigMgr related to OSD, divided into categories like deployment status, deployment, progress, and references.

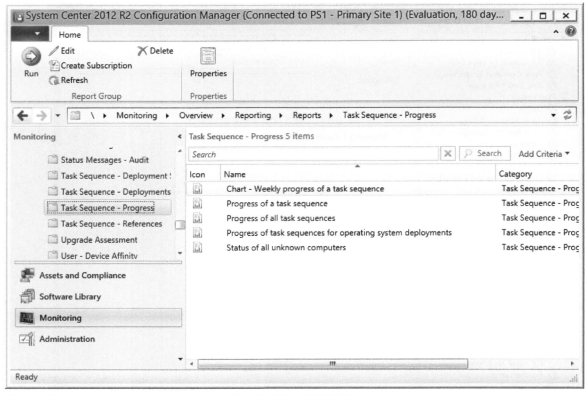

The task sequence progress reports in ConfigMgr 2012 R2.

Boot Images

The boot images in ConfigMgr 2012 R2 are based on Windows PE 5.0 and, as with MDT 2013 Lite Touch, they are used to start the deployment. A boot image package in ConfigMgr 2012 R2 consists of two files, one template and one file that contains the updated version of the boot image with all the drivers and other tools. The boot image packages are replicated to distribution points.

You also can, and should, create custom WinPE images in ConfigMgr 2012 R2. This is because the native ConfigMgr 2012 R2 boot images are missing support for both HTA and ADO (Active Data Objects, SQL Server support). We find that these features are too valuable not to include in a boot image used for deployments. The MDT 2013 integration requires these features and will help you create that boot image.

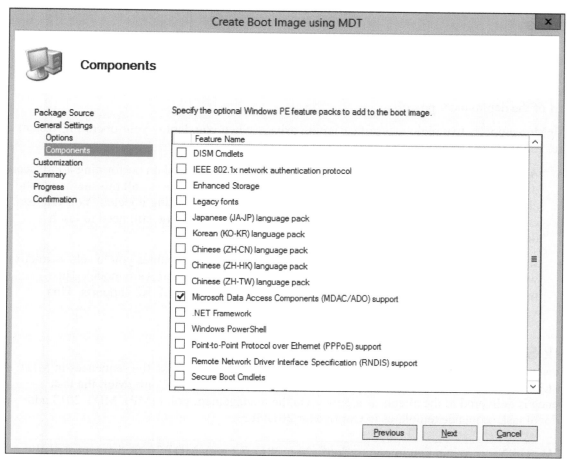

Adding components when creating custom WinPE 5.0 boot images for ConfigMgr 2012 R2.

Operating System Images

The OS Image package contains only one file, the custom .wim image. This is typically the production deployment image. The OS Image package is deployed (behind the scenes) by the OSDApplyOS.exe component in ConfigMgr, which has a very useful feature: it can use a single x86 boot image to deploy both x86 and x64 operating system images. This means that for most hardware you need to maintain only a single boot image with drivers. The exception is when you are deploying UEFI based machines; in that case, you need to boot on the correct architecture.

Operating System Installers

The OS Installers (which used to be named OS Install package in ConfigMgr 2007) was originally added to create reference images using ConfigMgr. Please don't do that. We recommend that you use MDT 2013 Lite Touch to create your reference image.

Drivers

Like MDT 2013 Lite Touch, ConfigMgr 2012 R2 also provides a repository (catalog) of managed device drivers. In ConfigMgr they are located in the Drivers and Driver Packages nodes in the ConfigMgr console. The purpose of a central repository is that it allows you to have a "generic worldwide image" that you can deploy to any hardware, and ConfigMgr injects the correct drivers as part of the deployment process.

ConfigMgr supports two main ways of assigning drivers when you deploy your operating system image, Auto Apply Drivers and Apply Driver Package:

- **Auto Apply Drivers**. This is the default method, and it is based on performing a PnP scan during deployment and then injecting matching drivers. We like to call this method "total chaos" because it's quite difficult to know which drivers are being injected. You can use categories to help filter down the drivers that are applied, but you still need to test a deployment and see which drivers PnP assigns for you.

- **Apply Driver Package**. The method we recommend, which enables you to select exactly which drivers are being injected when you deploy to a given hardware model. This method works with all types of deployment that ConfigMgr 2012 R2 supports. This variant of the method we call "total control."

Task Sequences

The task sequences in ConfigMgr 2012 R2 look and feel pretty much like the sequences in MDT 2013 Lite Touch, and they are used for the same purpose. However, in ConfigMgr, the task sequence is delivered to the clients as a policy via the management point (MP). MDT 2013 adds additional task sequence templates to ConfigMgr 2012 R2.

Real World Note: When you integrate ConfigMgr 2012 R2 with MDT 2013, there are actually two types of task sequence templates in ConfigMgr: the built-in task sequence templates, which are used when you select New / Task Sequence, and the MDT-based task sequences, which are used when you select Create Microsoft Deployment Task Sequence.

The task sequence templates added by MDT 2013 are the following:

- **Client Task Sequence.** A task sequence for deploying operating system images to client computers. This is the main task sequence used for Windows client deployments.

- **Client Replace Task Sequence.** A task sequence that by default captures a user state with the USMT ScanState tool. If enabled via the rules, it also creates a full data .wim of the system and does a reasonably secure wipe of the disk (by running the format command with the /P:3 switch, which zeroes every sector on the volume three times).

- **Microsoft Deployment Custom Task Sequence.** A custom task sequence that does not install an operating system. It only adds three actions, with the purpose of being a starting point when you want to deploy one or more applications in a task sequence.

- **Server Task Sequence.** A task sequence for deploying operating system images to server computers. The main difference from the standard Client Task Sequence is that the server sequence does not do user state capture and restore.

- **User Driven Installation Task Sequence.** A task sequence used to support the UDI scenarios that MDT 2013 adds to ConfigMgr 2012 R2. UDI is explained in Chapter 12.

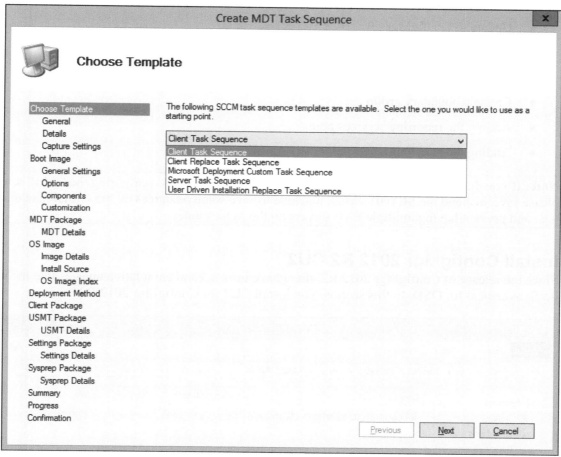

Selecting templates in the Create MDT Task Sequence wizard.

User-State Migration

For the computer refresh and computer replace scenarios in ConfigMgr, the User State Migration Tool (USMT) is used by default. USMT is basically the command-line, enterprise version, of the Windows Easy Transfer utility built into Windows 7 and Windows 8.1.

The purpose of USMT is to allow you to back up and restore user data and settings as part of your deployment process. USMT is also highly customizable, meaning you can select exactly which data you want to back up and restore. In ConfigMgr 2012 R2, USMT 6.3 is used by default.

Setting Up the ConfigMgr 2012 R2 Infrastructure

In this section, you set up a base ConfigMgr 2012 R2 server for software distribution. In these guides, you use the CM01 virtual machine you configured as part of the hydration kit. The base configuration involves the following:

- Update to ConfigMgr 2012 R2 CU2
- Configure Active Directory group membership
- Configure discovery methods
- Create a boundary group
- Adding the reporting services point
- Adding the state migration point

Note: If you did the guides in the previous chapter, before you start configuring the CM01 server, please save/suspend the MDT01 virtual machine to save some resources on the virtual machine host and prevent having multiple PXE servers on the same subnet.

Install ConfigMgr 2012 R2 CU2

Since the release of ConfigMgr 2012 R2, there have been several cumulative updates that include hotfixes critical for OSD. In this section, you install CU2 for ConfigMgr 2012 R2.

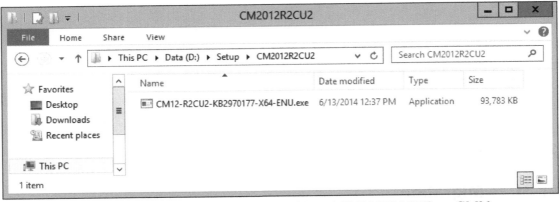

The CU2 update (KB 2970177) downloaded to D:\Setup\CM2012R2CU2 on CM01.

In these steps, we assume you have downloaded the KB 2970177 update to D:\Setup\CM2012R2CU2 on CM01.

1. On **CM01**, log in as **VIAMONSTRA\Administrator** using a password of **P@ssw0rd**.
2. Make sure the **ConfigMgr console** is closed before continuing.

3. Install **ConfigMgr 2012 R2 CU2** (CM12-R2CU2-KB2970177-X64-ENU.exe) with the default settings.

> **Note:** If the setup warns you about an earlier software installation that still has outstanding file rename operations pending, cancel the CU2 setup, restart the server, and then start the CU2 setup again.

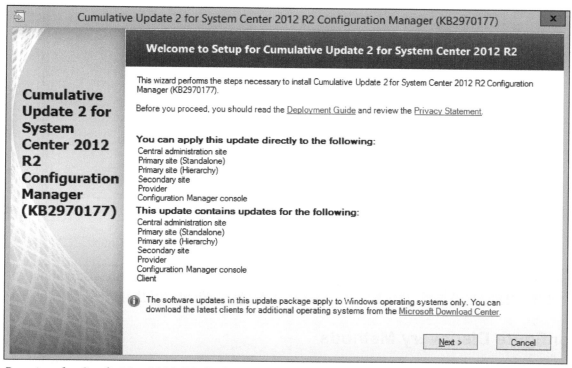

Running the ConfigMgr 2012 R2 CU2 setup.

Create Software Groups

One common way to assign deployments in ConfigMgr 2012 R2 is to use groups in Active Directory. In these steps, you create a few software groups and add the Johan and Maik users as members.

1. On **DC01**, log in as **VIAMONSTRA\Administrator** using a password of **P@ssw0rd**.

2. Using **Active Directory User and Computers**, in the **ViaMonstra / Software Groups** OU, create the following global security groups:

    o   **7-Zip 9.20 - x64**

    o   **Adobe Reader 11.0 - x86**

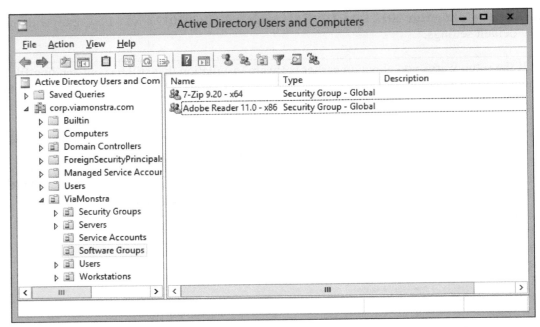

The software groups created.

3. Add the **Johan** and **Maik** user accounts as members to the preceding groups.

Real World Note: When you create groups that are going to be used for software distribution, they need to contain at least one member for the ConfigMgr group discovery process to find them.

Configure Discovery Methods

1. On **CM01**, log in as **VIAMONSTRA\Administrator** using a password of **P@ssw0rd**.

2. From the **Start screen**, select the **Configuration Manager Console**.

3. In the **Administration** workspace, expand **Hierarchy Configuration / Discovery Methods**.

4. Enable **Active Directory Forest Discovery** and then select the settings to automatically create Active Directory site and IP address range boundaries. When prompted, run the discovery.

Configuring Active Directory Forest Discovery.

5. Using **CMTrace** (located in D:\Program Files\Microsoft Configuration Manager\tools), review the **D:\Program Files\Microsoft Configuration Manager\Logs\ADForestDisc.log** file.

Real World Note: In the log you may see the following error: Discovered subnet 192.168.1.0/24 in AD site NewYork in forest corp.viamonstra.com was not saved in the database. But don't worry, it's a known issue, and the boundary will be created anyway.

6. Still in the **Administration** workspace, select the **Boundaries** node and review the boundaries that were created.

7. In the **Discovery Methods** node, enable **Active Directory System Discovery**. Add the following OUs by clicking the * button and clicking **Browse**.

   o   Domain Controllers

   o   ViaMonstra / Servers

   o   ViaMonstra / Workstations

The three OUs added in Active Directory System Discovery.

8. Using **CMTrace**, review the **D:\Program Files\Microsoft Configuration Manager\Logs\adsysdis.log** file.

9. In the **Assets and Compliance** workspace, select **Device Collections**. Press **F5** or click the **Refresh** button to refresh the view. You should now see 9 or 10 members in the **All Systems** collection (depending on whether you deployed the optional OR01 server).

Note: It may take a while for the collection to refresh; you can view progress via the colleval.log file. If you want to speed up the process, you can manually update membership on the All Systems collection by right-clicking the collection and selecting Update Membership.

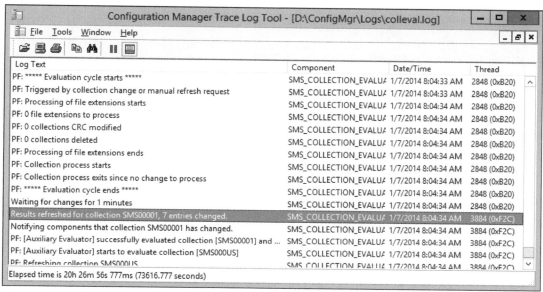

The colleval.log displaying info about resources added.

10. In the **Administration** workspace, in the **Discovery Methods** node, enable **Active Directory User Discovery**, add the **ViaMonstra / Users** OU, and run the discovery.

11. Using **CMTrace**, review the **D:\Program Files\Microsoft Configuration Manager\Logs\adusrdis.log** file.

12. In the **Assets and Compliance** workspace, select **Users**. Press **F5** or click the **Refresh** button to refresh the view. You should now see two members.

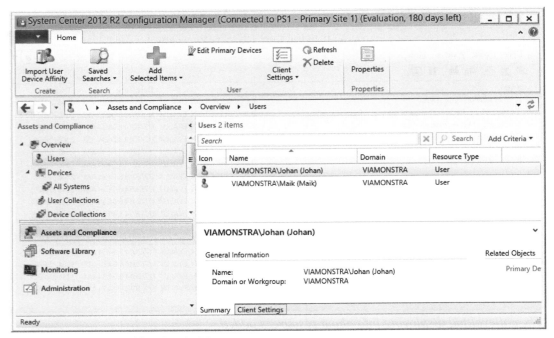

The users discovered by ConfigMgr.

13. In the **Discovery Methods** node, enable **Active Directory Group Discovery**, add the **ViaMonstra / Software Groups** OU as the location, name it **Software Groups**, and run the discovery.

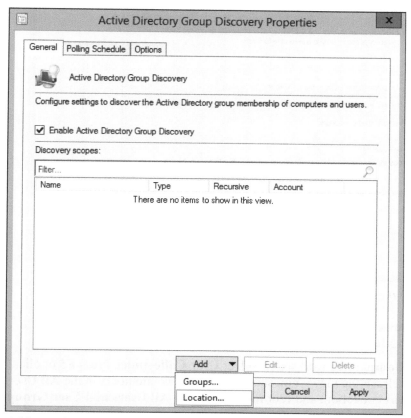

Adding a location when enabling Active Directory Group Discovery.

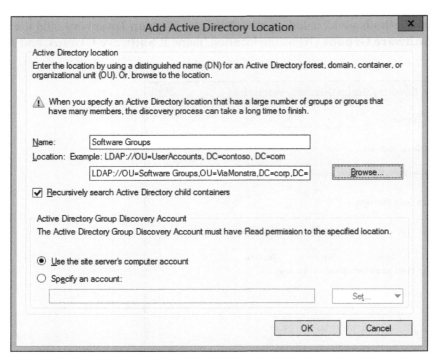

More details on adding the location for Active Directory Group Discovery.

14. Using **CMTrace**, review the **D:\Program Files\Microsoft Configuration Manager\Logs\adsgdis.log** file.

15. In the **Assets and Compliance** workspace, select **User Collections**. Press **F5** or click the **Refresh** button to refresh the view. You should now see two members in the **All Users** and **All User Groups** collection, and four members in the **All Users and User Groups** collection.

Note: Again, it may take a while for the collection to refresh, and as for the device collection, you can view progress via the colleval.log file. If you want to speed up the process, you can manually update membership on the collections by right-clicking on a collection and selecting Update Membership.

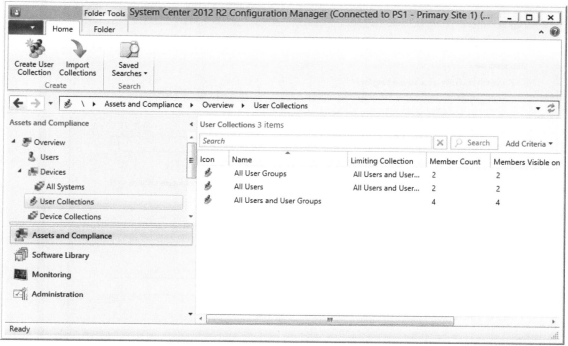

The User Collections node after the discovery methods have been configured.

Create a Boundary Group

To make sure clients can locate content on the distribution point and find the management point, you configure a boundary group.

1. Using the **ConfigMgr console**, in the **Administration** workspace, select **Boundary Groups**.

2. Create a boundary group using the following settings:

   a. In the **General** tab

      - Name: **HQ Assignment**

      - Boundaries: Add the **NewYork** and **192.168.1.1 – 192.168.1.254** boundaries.

   b. In the **References** tab

      - Site assignment area: Select the **Use the boundary group for site assignment** check box.

      - Content location area: Add the **CM01** distribution point.

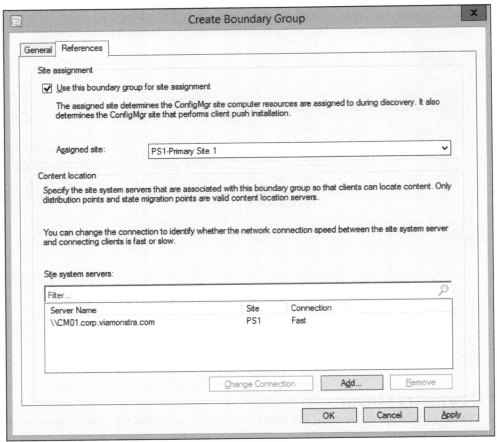

Creating the HQ Assignment boundary group.

Add the Reporting Services Point

Reports in ConfigMgr are very useful for keeping track of deployments, both for applications and task sequences. You also can create custom reports if needed.

1. Using the **ConfigMgr console**, in the **Administration** workspace, expand **Site Configuration** and select **Sites**.

2. On the ribbon, select **Add Site System Roles**, and use the following settings for the **Add Site System Roles Wizard**:

   a. General: **<default>**

   b. Proxy: **<default>**

   c. System Role Selection: **Reporting services point**

      d.   Reporting Services Point: Click **Verify**.

      e.   User name: Add a new account:

           ▪   User name: **VIAMONSTRA\CM_SR**

           ▪   Password: **P@ss0wrd**

      f.   Summary: **<default>**

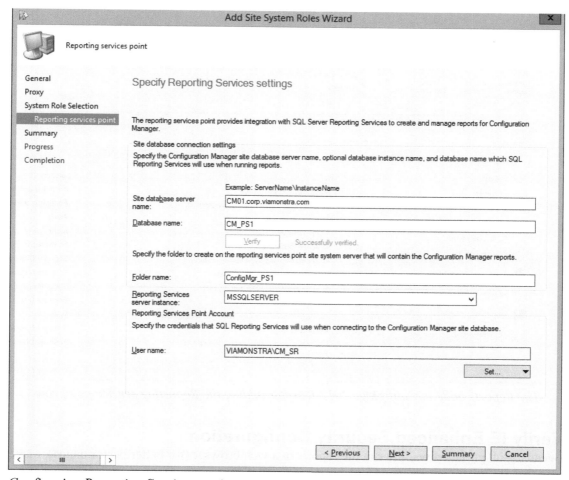

Configuring Reporting Services settings.

3.   Using **CMTrace**, review the **D:\Program Files\Microsoft Configuration Manager\Logs\srsrpsetup.log** and **D:\Program Files\Microsoft Configuration Manager\Logs\srsrp.log** files.

> **Note:** It will take a short while for the log files to appear. Wait until all reports have been deployed before continuing. You don't need to worry about the red lines in the log; the target folder contains the word error in the name so you see many red lines. Anyway, this is a good time to take a quick break. ☺

4.   In the **ConfigMgr console**, in the **Monitoring** workspace, expand the **Reporting / Reports** node, select the **Reports** node, and then review the reports available.

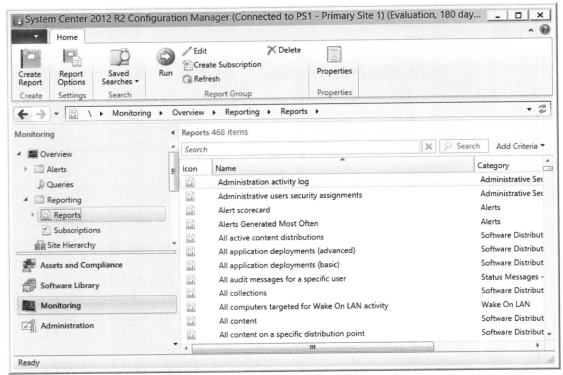

The Reports node in ConfigMgr 2012 R2 after adding the Reporting service point role.

Verify IE Enhanced Security Configuration

Because you probably want to run the reports in a web browser (for better performance), make sure that IE Enhanced Security Configuration is disabled.

1.   On **CM01**, using the **Server Manager**, select **Local Server**.

2.   In the **PROPERTIES for CM01** pane, make sure the **IE Enhanced Security Configuration** is set to **Off**.

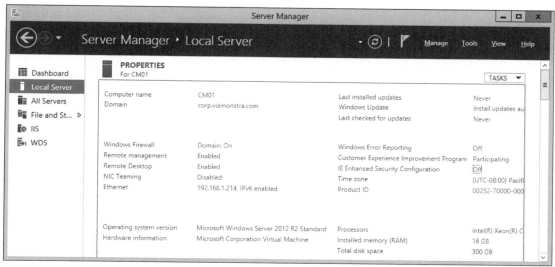

Making sure IE Enhanced Security Configuration is disabled.

Preparing for OSD and MDT 2013 Zero Touch

In this section, you integrate ConfigMgr 2012 R2 with MDT 2013, as well as make other preparations needed for OSD. Preparing for MDT 2013 Zero Touch involves the following:

- Review the service accounts
- Configure Active Directory permissions
- Create the folder structure
- Create a new ConfigMgr client package
- Integrate MDT 2013 with ConfigMgr 2012 R2
- Configure the Network Access account
- Configure Client Agent settings
- Enable PXE on the distribution point
- Speed up PXE

The ConfigMgr 2012 R2 Service Accounts

As you learned in Chapter 5, we use a role-based model when configuring permissions for the various service accounts we use. For ConfigMgr 2012 R2 we use the following service accounts.

- **CM_CP.** The ConfigMgr 2012 Client Push Account
- **CM_JD.** The ConfigMgr 2012 Join Domain Account
- **CM_NAA.** The ConfigMgr 2012 Network Access Account
- **CM_SR.** The ConfigMgr 2012 Reporting Services Account

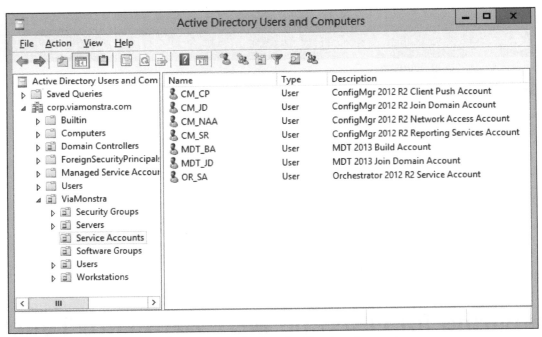

Active Directory Users and Computers listing the Service Accounts.

Set Permissions on the Servers and Workstations OUs

Like the deployments using MDT 2013 Lite Touch, ConfigMgr 2012 deployments also need permissions to join machines in Active Directory. In this guide, you allow the join account used for ConfigMgr 2012 R2 (CM_JD) permissions to manage computer accounts in the ViaMonstra / Server OU and the ViaMonstra / Workstations OU. In this guide, we assume you have downloaded and extracted the book sample files to C:\Setup on DC01.

1. On **DC01**, in an elevated (run as Administrator) **PowerShell** command prompt, configure **Execution Policy** in PowerShell by running the following command (if you already did this in Chapter 5 when configuring MDT 2013 Lite Touch, you can skip this step and continue on to step 2):

   ```
   Set-ExecutionPolicy –ExecutionPolicy RemoteSigned -Force
   ```

2. On **DC01**, grant permissions for the **CM_JD** account to the **ViaMonstra / Workstations** OU by running the following command:

   ```
   C:\Setup\Scripts\Set-OUPermissions.ps1 –Account CM_JD
   -TargetOU "OU=Workstations,OU=ViaMonstra"
   ```

3. Grant permissions for the **CM_JD** account to the **ViaMonstra / Servers** OU by running the following command:

```
C:\Setup\Scripts\Set-OUPermissions.ps1 -Account CM_JD
-TargetOU "OU=Servers,OU=ViaMonstra"
```

Create the ConfigMgr 2012 R2 OSD folder structure

When doing OSD with ConfigMgr one of the key factors of success is making sure you have good folder structure for all your packages. In this guide we assume you have downloaded and extracted the books sample files to D:\Setup on CM01.

1. On **CM01**, in an **elevated PowerShell** prompt (run as Administrator), run the following command:

```
D:\Setup\Scripts\Create-ConfigMgrFolders.ps1
```

2. The preceding script creates the following folder structure and also shares the **D:\Logs** folder as **Logs$** and the **D:\Sources** folder as **Sources**.

> **D:\MigData**
>
> **D:\Logs**
>
> **D:\Sources**
>
> **D:\Sources\OSD**
>
> **D:\Sources\OSD\Boot**
>
> **D:\Sources\OSD\DriverPackages**
>
> **D:\Sources\OSD\DriverSources**
>
> **D:\Sources\OSD\MDT**
>
> **D:\Sources\OSD\OS**
>
> **D:\Sources\OSD\Settings**
>
> **D:\Sources\Software**
>
> **D:\Sources\Software\Adobe**
>
> **D:\Sources\Software\Microsoft**
>
> **D:\Sources\Software\Utilities**

Add the State Migration Point

When doing computer replace scenarios, the state migration point is used by default to keep track of the backups stored on the server.

1. Using the **ConfigMgr console**, in the **Administration** workspace, expand **Site Configuration** and select **Sites**.

2. On the ribbon, select **Add Site System Roles** and use the following settings for the **Add Site System Roles Wizard**:

   a. General: **<default>**

   b. Proxy: **<default>**

   c. System Role Selection: **State migration point**

   d. Specify state migration point settings: Add a new folder (using the button that looks like an asterisk):

      ▪ Storage Folder: **D:\MigData**

      ▪ Maximum Number of Clients: **500**

      ▪ Minimum Free Space: **20 GB**

      ▪ Deletion policy: **14 days**

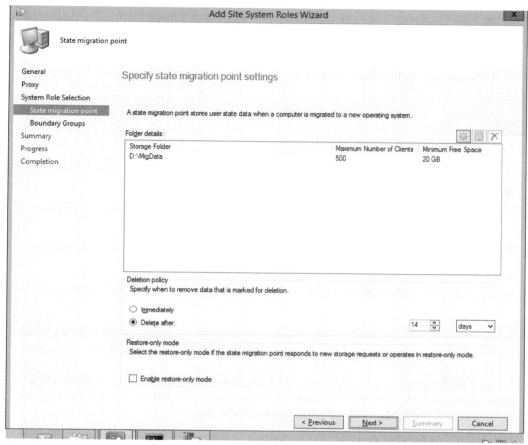

Configuring the state migration point.

    e. On the **Associate boundary groups with this system** page, make sure the **HQ Assignment** boundary group is added.

3. Using **CMTrace**, in the **D:\Program Files\Microsoft Configuration Manager\Logs** folder, review the following files:

    o **smpmgr.log**

    o **smpMSI.log**

Create a New ConfigMgr Client Package

Even without the installed update, we recommend that you create a custom ConfigMgr client package for better distribution control. However, because CU2 also has updates for the ConfigMgr 2012 R2 client, it makes even more sense to create a new package. In these steps, you create a new ConfigMgr client package that includes the client update.

1. On **CM01**, in the **D:\Sources** folder, create a subfolder named **ConfigMgr Client with Hotfixes**.

2. Using **File Explorer**, copy the contents of **D:\Program Files\Microsoft Configuration Manager\Client** to the newly created folder (D:\Sources\ConfigMgr Client with Hotfixes).

3. In **D:\Sources\ConfigMgr Client with Hotfixes**, create a folder named **Hotfix**.

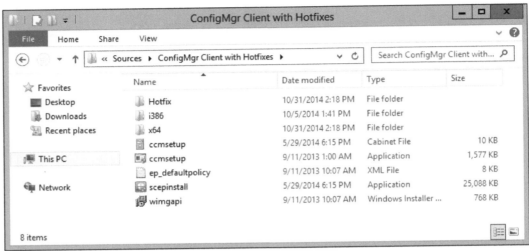

The new D:\Sources\ConfigMgr Client with Hotfixes folder, after copying the client files.

4. Using **File Explorer**, navigate to the **D:\Program Files\Microsoft Configuration Manager\hotfix\KB2970177\Client** folder and copy the **i386** and **x64** subfolders to **D:\Sources\ConfigMgr Client with Hotfixes\Hotfix**.

5. Using the **ConfigMgr console**, in the **Software Library** workspace, create a new package with the following settings:

   o Name: **ConfigMgr Client with Hotfixes**

   o Source folder: **\\CM01\Sources\ConfigMgr Client with Hotfixes**

   o Select **Do not create a program**.

6. Make a note of the new Package ID. In our environment it was **PS10000A**.

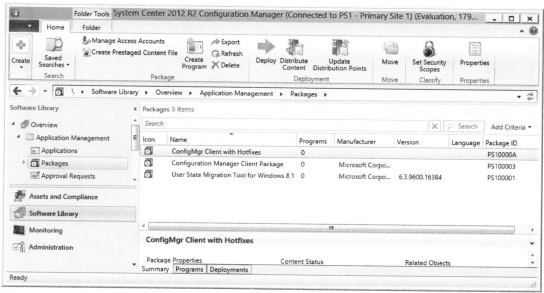

The new ConfigMgr client package, with its Package ID.

7. Distribute the new **ConfigMgr Client with Hotfixes** package to the **CM01** distribution point by selecting the **Packages** node, right-clicking the **ConfigMgr Client with Hotfixes** package, and selecting **Distribute Content**. Use the following setting for the **Distribute Content Wizard**:

    Content Destination: Add the **CM01** distribution point.

Set Up ConfigMgr 2012 R2 Integration with MDT 2013

To extend the ConfigMgr console with the new MDT options, you need to run the Configure ConfigMgr Integration wizard that is installed together with MDT 2013. In this guide, we assume that you have downloaded MDT 2013 to the D:\Setup\MDT 2013 folder on CM01.

1. On **CM01**, close the **ConfigMgr console** before continuing.

2. Install **MDT 2013** (D:\Setup\MDT 2013\MicrosoftDeploymentToolkit2013_x64.msi) using the default settings.

3. From the **Start screen**, run the **Configure ConfigMgr Integration** application with the following settings:

    o   Site Server Name: **CM01.corp.viamonstra.com**

    o   Site code: **PS1**

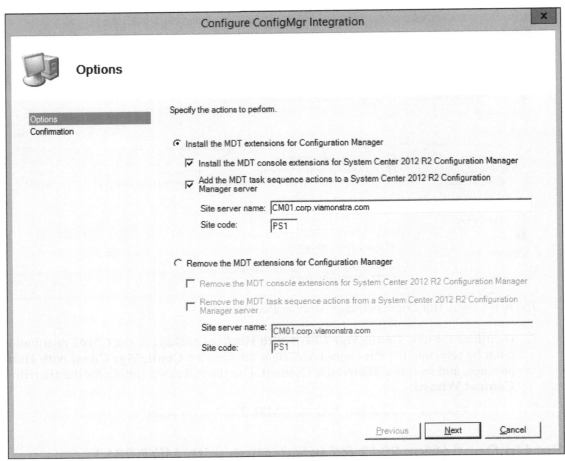

Running the MDT 2013 integration with ConfigMgr 2012 R2.

Configure the Network Access Account

1. On **CM01**, using the **ConfigMgr console**, in the **Administration** workspace, expand **Site Configuration** and select **Sites**.

2. Right-click the **PS1 – Primary Site 1**, and select **Configure Site Components / Software Distribution**.

3. In the **Network Access Account** tab, select the **Specify the account that accesses network locations** option, click the **New** button (which looks like an asterisk), and then select **New Account**.

4. In the **Windows User Account** dialog box, configure the **VIAMONSTRA\CM_NAA** user account (select New Account) as the Network Access account (the password is **P@ssw0rd**). Then use the **Verify** option to verify that the account can connect to **\\DC01\sysvol** network share.

Configuring the Network Access account and verifying the connection.

Configure the Client Settings

In these steps, you configure the organization name in Client Agent settings. This name will be visible in the task sequence progress bar when you deploy the Windows 8.1 Enterprise x64 image later in this chapter.

1. On **CM01**, using the **ConfigMgr console**, in the **Administration** workspace, select **Client Settings**.

2. Right-click **Default Client Settings**, and select **Properties**.

3. In the **Computer Agent** node, in the **Organization name displayed in Software center** text box, type in **ViaMonstra** and click **OK**.

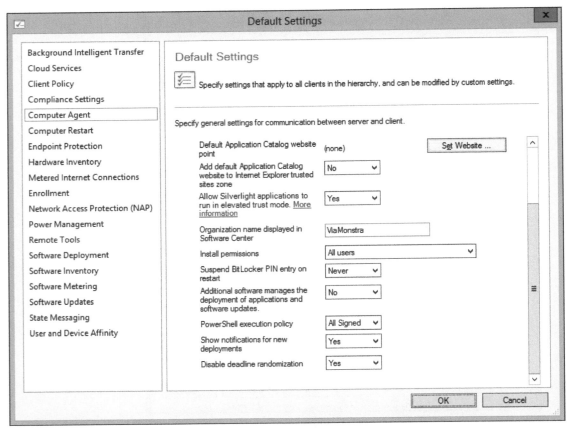

Configuring Client settings.

Enable PXE on the CM01 Distribution Point

In this section, you configure the CM01 for PXE support and also enable unknown computer support. Having PXE enabled is not a requirement for OSD or MDT, but being able to start deployments via PXE is very useful.

1. On **CM01**, using the **ConfigMgr console**, in the **Administration** workspace, select **Distribution Points**.

2. Right-click the **CM01.CORP.VIAMONSTRA.COM** distribution point and select **Properties**.

3. In the **PXE** tab, enable the following settings:

    o   Enable PXE support for clients

    o   Allow this distribution point to respond to incoming PXE requests

    o   Enable unknown computer support

    o   Require a password when computers use PXE

Password and Confirm password: **P@ssw0rd**

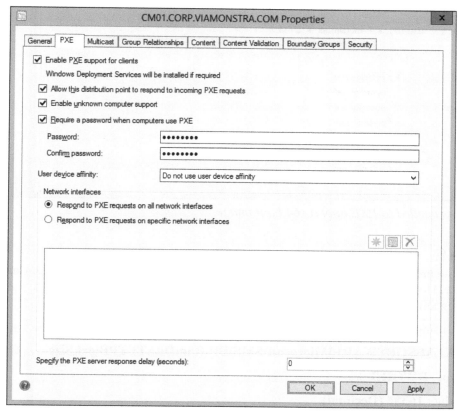

Enabling PXE on the CM01 distribution point.

4. Using **CMTrace**, review **the D:\Program Files\Microsoft Configuration Manager\Logs\distmgr.log** file, and look for the line **ConfigurePXE**.

5. Using **File Explorer**, verify that you have seven files in the **D:\RemoteInstall\SMSBoot\x86** and **D:\RemoteInstall\SMSBoot\x64** folders.

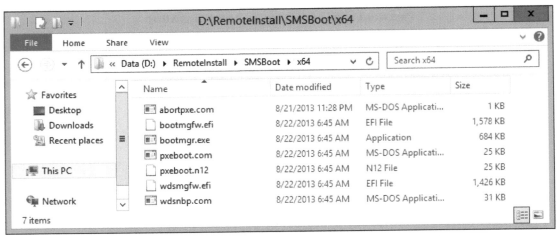

The netboot files needed to PXE boot a x64 boot image.

Speed Up PXE

As you learned in the preceding chapter, you can decrease the WinPE boot time by configuring the TFTP block size. However, when using ConfigMgr 2012 R2, you can't use the WDS console. You have to use Regedit instead.

1. On **CM01**, using the **Regedit**, create this in the registry:

    a. **HKLM\SOFTWARE\Microsoft\SMS\DP\RamDiskTFTPBlockSize**

    b. Type: **DWORD**

    c. Value: **16384 (Decimal)**

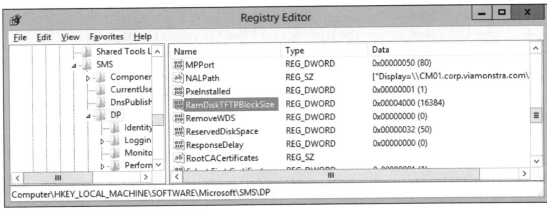

Creating the RamDiskTFTPBlockSize DWORD in the registry.

2. Restart the **Windows Deployment Service** (WDS).

> **Note:** Again, if you experience any problems after increasing the TFTP block size, try setting it to a lower value, like 8192 or 4096. Do not set it higher than 16384.

Creating Boot Images

After the preparations are done, you start creating all the various packages the task sequence needs, and the first package you create is the custom WinPE 5.0 boot image.

Create a Custom x64 Boot Image (WinPE 5.0)

1. On **CM01**, using the **ConfigMgr console**, in the **Software Library** workspace, expand **Operating Systems**.

2. Right-click **Boot Images**, select **Create Boot Image using MDT**, and create a new boot image package using the following settings:

    a. Package source folder to be created (UNC Path):
        \\CM01\Sources\OSD\Boot\Zero Touch WinPE 5.0 x64

> **Note:** You need to type the preceding path, the final folder (Zero Touch WinPE 5.0 x64) because it does not yet exist. It will be created by the wizard.

    b. Name: **Zero Touch WinPE 5.0 x64**

    c. Platform: **x64**

    d. Scratch Space: **<default>**

> **Note:** As you learned in the preceding chapter, WinPE 5.0 allocates the scratch space dynamically, meaning there is no point in setting a default value. The only time a default value is used is when you have less than 1 GB of RAM in the machine, and if you do, you should not deploy Windows at all to that machine. ☺

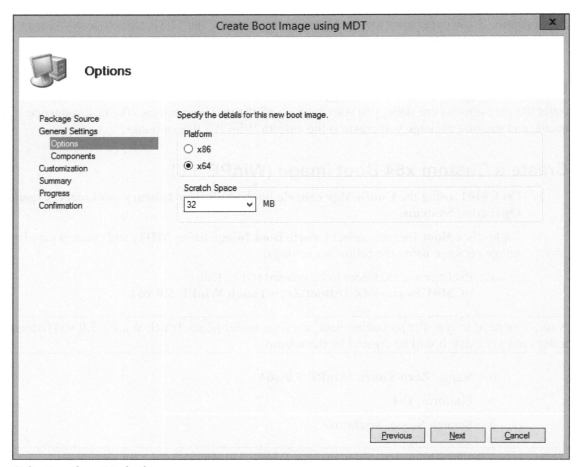

Selecting the x64 platform.

    e.   Components: **<default>**

    f.   **Enable command support (F8)**

Real World Note: The most common reason a boot image creation fails is because of antivirus software. If you have antivirus software running on your ConfigMgr server, make sure to exclude dism.exe from processes that are scanned by the antivirus software, or disable the antivirus software while creating your boot image.

3.   Distribute the boot image to the **CM01** distribution point by selecting the **Boot images** node, right-clicking the **Zero Touch WinPE 5.0 x64** boot image, and selecting **Distribute Content**. Use the following setting for the **Distribute Content Wizard**:

    Content Destination: Add the **CM01** distribution point.

4. Using **CMTrace**, review the **D:\Program Files\Microsoft Configuration Manager\Logs\distmgr.log** file. Do not continue until you can see the boot image is distributed. Look for the line with **STATMSG: ID=2301**....

5. Using the **ConfigMgr console**, right-click the **Zero Touch WinPE 5.0 x64** boot image and select **Properties**.

6. In the **Data Source** tab, select the **Deploy this boot image from the PXE-enabled distribution point** check box and click **OK**.

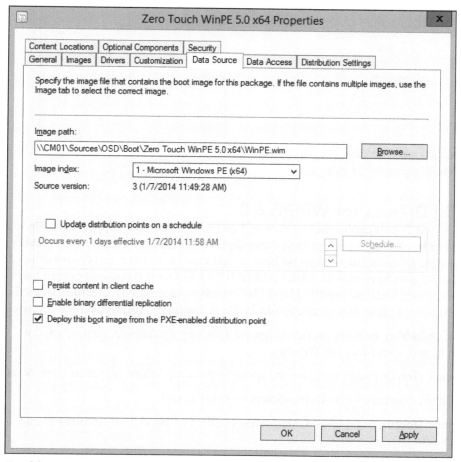

Enabling the WinPE 5.0 x64 boot image for PXE.

7. Using **CMTrace**, review the **D:\Program Files\Microsoft Configuration Manager\Logs\distmgr.log** file. Look for the line **Expanding <Package ID> to D:\RemoteInstall\SMSImages**.

8. Using **File Explorer**, review the **D:\RemoteInstall\SMSImages** folder. There should be three subfolders containing boot images.

Real World Note: For this environment, you only need an x64 boot image (because you only have a x64 image of Windows 8.1). However, if you want to support both x86 and x64 operating system images (and you are not deploying to UEFI hardware), you can instead add an x86 boot image that can deploy both x86 and x64 operating systems.

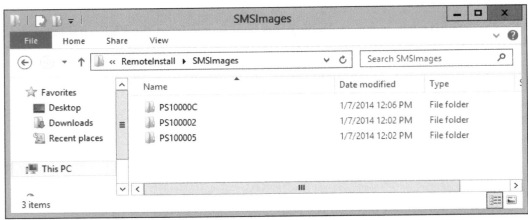

D:\RemoteInstall\SMSImages folder after configuring the boot image for PXE.

Optional - Add Drivers for WinPE 5.0

Like the MDT 2013 Lite Touch deployment solution, ConfigMgr 2012 R2 supports an easy way to add drivers for your boot image. For the Dell Latitude E7440 model you don't need drivers for the boot image, but here follows instructions on how to add new or updated drivers when needed. In this guide we assume you have downloaded updated Intel Pro x64 drivers, and copied them to the D:\Sources\OSD\DriverSources\WinPE x64 folder (needs to be created). Detailed steps for downloading and extracting these drivers are found in the "Chapter 5, Adding drivers" section.

1. Using the **ConfigMgr console**, in the **Software Library** workspace, right-click the **Drivers** node and select **Import Driver**.

2. On the **Locate Driver** page configure the following source folder, and then click **Next**:

   \\CM01\Sources\OSD\DriverSources\WinPE x64

3. On the **Driver Details** page, click **Categories**, create a category named **WinPE x64**, and then click **Next**.

4. On the **Add Driver to Packages** page, accept the default settings and click **Next**.

5. On the **Add Driver to Boot Images** page, select the **Zero Touch WinPE 5.0 x64** boot image, and select the **Update distribution points when finished** check box. Click **Next** twice, and when the update is completed, click **Close**.

Real World Note: The Updating Boot Image part of the wizard will appear to hang when displaying "Done", but no worries after (quite) a while it will complete.

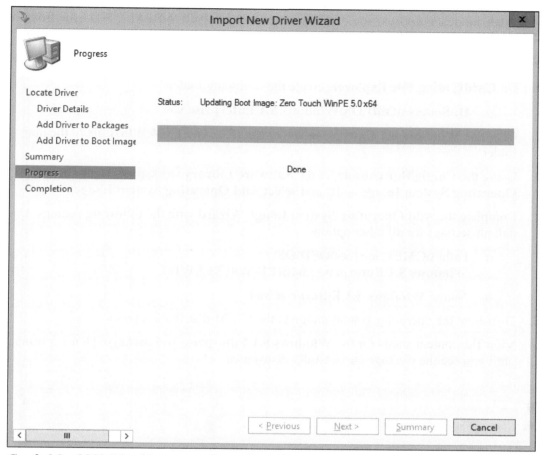

ConfigMgr 2012 R2 taking a nap (but still working in the background).

Adding Operating System Images

ConfigMgr 2012 R2 supports two methods for deploying Windows: applying a single WIM file via the operating system image method, or adding a full set of source files using the operating system installer method. The operating system image method is what you should be using because it prevents possible conflicts between Windows PE and Windows setup versions. The operating system installer method is mainly available for backwards compatibility reasons. Using the operating system image method simply provides a more consistent deployment experience.

Add a Windows 8.1 Operating System Image

In this example, we assume you have a custom reference image of Windows 8.1 Enterprise x64 image available. Again, creating reference images is outside the scope of this book, but if you go to the following link, you find a step-by-step guide on how to do that: http://tinyurl.com/BuildingReferenceImages. In this example, our reference image is named REF-W81X64.WIM.

Note: For lab and test purposes, you of course can use the default INSTALL.WIM file from the Windows 8.1 Enterprise x64 media, but we strongly encourage you to build a "real" reference image.

1. On **CM01**, using **File Explorer**, create the following folder:

   D:\Sources\OSD\OS\Windows 8.1 Enterprise x64

2. Copy the **Windows 8.1 Enterprise x64** image (REF-W81X64.WIM) file to the new folder.

3. Using the **ConfigMgr console**, in the **Software Library** workspace, right-click the **Operating System Image** node, and select **Add Operating System Image**.

4. Complete the **Add Operating System Image Wizard** with the following settings. Use default settings for all other options.

   a. Path: **\\CM01\Sources\OSD\OS\
      Windows 8.1 Enterprise x64\REF-W81X64.WIM**

   b. Name: **Windows 8.1 Enterprise x64**

5. Distribute the operating system image to the **CM01** distribution point.

6. View the content status for the **Windows 8.1 Enterprise x64** package. Don't continue until you see the package successfully distributed.

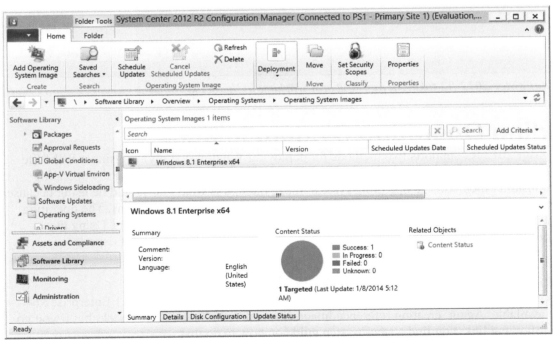

Content status for the Windows 8.1 Enterprise x64 image in the ConfigMgr console.

Creating Packages and Programs

Packages still exist in ConfigMgr 2012 R2, and that is the preferred way to install applications as part of an OSD task sequence. Applications are supported for that as well, but packages have proven to be more reliable for OSD. Also, when deploying a package as part of a task sequence, you can select the program. When deploying applications, you can't specify the deployment type.

In this section, you create the following packages in ConfigMgr 2012 R2:

- Adobe Reader 11.0 - x86

- 7-Zip 9.20 - x64

Create the Adobe Reader 11.0 - x86 Package

In this guide we assume that you have downloaded Adobe Reader 11.0 (AdbeRdr11000_en_US.msi) to D:\Setup\Adobe Reader 11.0 on CM01.

1. On **CM01**, using **File Explorer**, navigate to the **D:\Sources\Software\Adobe** folder and create the **Adobe Reader 11.0 - x86** subfolder.

Real World Note: In ConfigMgr 2012 R2, we normally don't specify the "Install - " prefix for packages or applications (like we did in Chapter 5 for MDT). Instead we are using features in ConfigMgr 2012 R2 application model or packages/programs to run install or uninstalls.

2. Copy the **Adobe Reader 11.0** installation file (AdbeRdr11000_en_US.msi) to the following folder:

D:\Sources\Software\Adobe\Adobe Reader 11.0 - x86

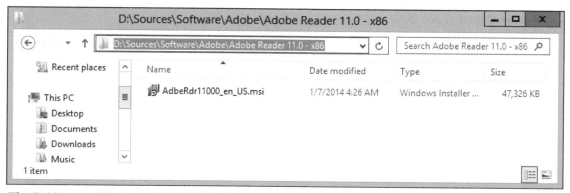

The D:\Sources\Software\Adobe\Adobe Reader 11.0 - x86 folder.

3. Using the **ConfigMgr console**, right-click **Packages** and select **Create Package**. Use the following settings for the **Create Package and Program Wizard**.

   a. Package

      ▪ Name: **Adobe Reader 11.0 - x86**

      ▪ Source folder: **\\CM01\Sources\Software\Adobe\ Adobe Reader 11.0 - x86**

   b. Program Type

      Standard program

   c. Standard Program

      ▪ Name: **Install**

      ▪ Command line: **msiexec /i AdbeRdr11000_en_US.msi /q**

      ▪ Program can run: **Whether or not a user is logged on**

   d. Requirements:

      <default>

   e. Summary:

      <default>

4. In the **Packages** node, select the **Adobe Reader 11.0 - x86** package, click the **Programs** tab, right-click the **Install** program, and select **Properties**.

5. In the **Install Properties** window, select the **Advanced** tab, and then select the **Allow this program to be installed from the Install Package task sequence without being deployed** check box.

6. Click **OK**.

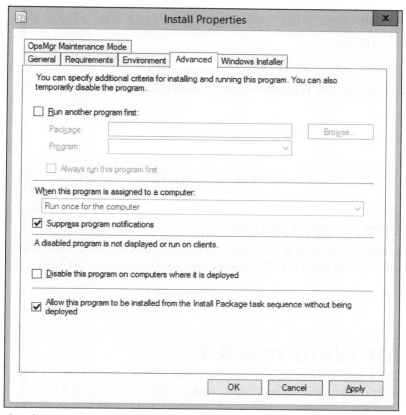

Configuring the Install program for the Adobe Reader 11.0 - x86 package.

Create the 7-Zip 9.20 - x64 Package

In this guide we assume you have downloaded the 7-Zip 9.20 x64 installation file (7z920-x64.msi) to D:\Setup\7-Zip 9.20 on CM01.

1. On **CM01**, using **File Explorer**, navigate to the **D:\Sources\Software\Utilities** folder and create the **7-Zip 9.20 - x64** subfolder.

2. Copy the **7-Zip 9.20 - x64** installation file (**7z920-x64.msi**) to the following folder:

   D:\Sources\Software\Utilities\7-Zip 9.20 - x64

3. Using the **ConfigMgr console**, right-click **Packages** and select **Create Package**. Use the following settings for the **Create Package and Program Wizard**.

   a. Package

      - Name: **7-Zip 9.20 - x64**
      - Source folder: **\\CM01\Sources\Software\Utilities\7-Zip 9.20 - x64**

   b. Program Type

      Standard program

     c.   Standard Program

- Name: **Install**
- Command line: **msiexec /i 7z920-x64.msi /qb**
- Program can run: **Whether or not a user is logged on**

     d.   Requirements:

         <default>

     e.   Summary:

         <default>

4. In the **Packages** node, select the **7-Zip 9.20 - x64** package, click the **Programs** tab, right-click the **Install** program, and select **Properties**.

5. In the **Install Properties** window, select the **Advanced** tab, and then select the **Allow this program to be installed from the Install Package task sequence without being deployed** check box.

6. Click **OK**.

Add Drivers for Windows 8.1

Like when configure MDT 2013 Lite Touch for drivers in Chapter 5, you need to have a good drivers repository. From this repository, you import drivers into ConfigMgr 2012 R2 for deployment, but you should always maintain the repository source for future use.

Install 7-Zip 9.20

Again, when working with drivers, it helps to have a good extractor utility at hand, and our favorite is 7-Zip. In these steps, you use the previously downloaded 7-Zip 9.20.

1. On **CM01**, navigate to the **D:\Sources\Software\Utilities\7-Zip 9.20 - x64** folder.

2. Install **7-Zip 9.20** (7z920-x64.msi) using the default settings.

Prepare the Drivers Repository

In this section, you add drivers for the boot image and Windows 8.1 operating systems drivers for one of the hardware models ViaMonstra is supporting: the Dell Latitude E7440 laptop.

1. On **CM01**, using **File Explorer**, in the **D:\Sources\OSD\DriverSources** folder, create the following subfolder:

       Windows 8.1 x64

2. In the new **Windows 8.1 x64** folder, create the following subfolder:

       Latitude E7440

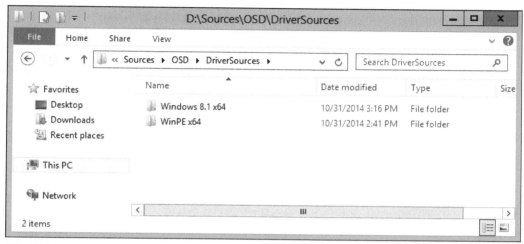

The D:\Sources\OSD\DriverSources structure on CM01.

Download, Extract, and Import Drivers for Latitude E7440

For the Dell Latitude E7440 model, you use the ready-made Dell Driver CAB file. The easiest way to get the Dell Driver CAB file is via the Dell TechCenter web site. In these steps, we assume you have downloaded E7440-win8.1-A01-Y7TY2.CAB to D:\Temp on CM01.

> **Note:** Again, Dell updates their driver CAB files every once in a while, so if the A01 version is not available, just grab the latest version.

1. On **CM01**, using **7-Zip**, extract the **E7440-win8.1-A01-Y7TY2.CAB** to the **D:\Temp** folder.

2. Using **File Explorer**, navigate to **D:\Temp\E7440\win8.1\x64** and copy the content to the **D:\Sources\OSD\DriverSources\Windows 8.1 x64\Latitude E7440** folder.

3. Using the **ConfigMgr console**, right-click the **Drivers** folder and select **Import Driver**.

4. In the **Import New Driver Wizard**, on the **Specify a location to import driver** page, below the **Import all drivers in the following network path (UNC)** option, browse to the **\\CM01\Sources\OSD\DriverSources\Windows 8.1 x64\Latitude E7440** folder and click **Next**.

5. On the **Specify the details for the imported driver** page, click **Categories**, create a category named **Windows 8.1 x64 - Latitude E7440**, and then click **Next**.

6. On the **Select the packages to add the imported driver** page, click **New Package**, use the following settings for the package, and then click **Next**:

   a. Name: **Windows 8.1 x64 - Latitude E7440**

   b. Path: **\\CM01\Sources\OSD\DriverPackages\Windows 8.1 x64\ Latitude E7440**

> **Note:** The package path does not yet exist, so you have to type it in. The wizard will create the new package in that folder.

7. On the **Select drivers to include in the boot image** page, don't select anything, and click **Next** twice. After the package has been created, click **Close**.

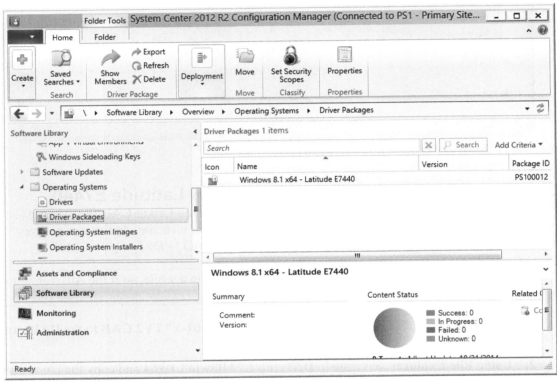

The Dell driver package created in the ConfigMgr console.

Creating Task Sequences

To use the new task sequence templates that MDT 2013 adds to ConfigMgr 2012 R2, you select "Create MDT Task Sequence" instead of "Create Task Sequence" when creating new task sequences.

> **Real World Note:** Unfortunately, there are a few known bugs in the MDT task sequence templates, which means that you need to edit the task sequences and do a few additional configurations after the task sequence is created.

Create a Task Sequence

In these steps, you create a task sequence that deploys your Windows 8.1 Enterprise x64 image.

1. Using the **ConfigMgr console**, in the **Software Library** workspace, expand **Operating Systems** and select **Task Sequences**.

2. On the ribbon, select **Create MDT Task Sequence** and create a new task sequence using the following settings:

   a. Choose Template

   > Template: **Client Task Sequence**

   b. General

   - Task sequence name: **Windows 8.1 Enterprise x64**
   - Task sequence comments: **Production image**

   c. Details

   > **Join a Domain**

   - Domain: **corp.viamonstra.com**
   - Account: **VIAMONSTRA\CM_JD**
   - Password: **P@ssw0rd**

   d. Windows Settings

   - User name: **ViaMonstra**
   - Organization name: **ViaMonstra**
   - Product key: **<blank>**

   e. Capture Settings

   > **This task sequence will never be used to capture an image**

   f. Boot Image

   - **Specify an existing boot image package**
   - Select the **Zero Touch WinPE 5.0 x64** boot image package.

   g. MDT Package

   - **Create a new Microsoft Deployment Toolkit Files package**
   - Package source folder to be created (UNC Path): **\\CM01\Sources\OSD\MDT\MDT 2013**

   h. MDT Details

   > Name: **MDT 2013**

    i.   OS Image

- **Specify an existing OS image**
- Select the **Windows 8.1 Enterprise x64** package.

    j.   Deployment Method

        Perform a "Zero Touch Installation" OS Deployment, with no user interaction

    k.   Client Package

- **Specify an existing ConfigMgr client package**
- Select the **ConfigMgr Client with Hotfixes** package.

    l.   USMT Package

- **Specify an existing USMT package**
- Select the **Microsoft Corporation User State Migration Tool for Windows 8 6.3.9600.17237** package.

    m.   Settings Package

- **Create a new settings package**
- Package source folder to be created (UNC Path): **\\CM01\Sources\OSD\Settings\Windows 8.1 x64 Settings**

    n.   Settings Details

        Name: **Windows 8.1 x64 Settings**

    o.   Sysprep Package

        No Sysprep Package is required

Edit the Task Sequence

In addition to basic operatings like adding driver packages to the task sequence, the MDT standard client task sequences unfortunately have the following known issues that needs to be addressed before it can be used:

- Issue #1. UEFI deployments does not work (at all).

- Issue #2. The local Administrator account is set to blank.

- Issue #3. The image is install to the E: drive instead of the C: drive.

- Issue #4. The backup is never restored in replace scenarios.

- Issue #5. Dynamically changing OU don't work.

- Issue #6. You cannot logon the first time when deploying Windows 8.1 (KB 2976660)

In the following guide, you edit the task sequence to address the preceding issues.

1. Using the **ConfigMgr console**, select **Task Sequences**, right-click the **Windows 8.1 Enterprise x64** task sequence, and select **Edit**.

2. In the **Execute Task Sequence** group, add a Set Task Sequence Variable action with the folloing settings:

   a. Name: **Restart machine after task sequence when completed**

   b. Task Sequence Variable: **SMSTSPostAction**

   c. Vaulue: **shutdown /r /t 0**

3. In the **Initialization** group, select the first **Format and Partition Disk (UEFI)** action, and in the **Volume** list, delete the first three volumes.

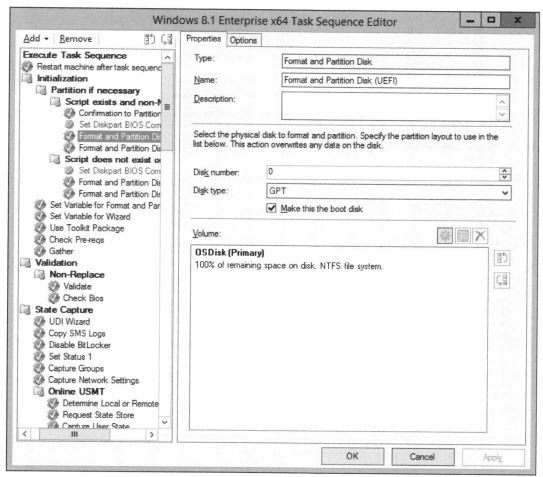

Removing the partitions from the first UEFI action.

4. In the **Initialization** group, select the second **Format and Partition Disk (UEFI)** action, and in the **Volume** list, delete the first three volumes.

> **Real World Note:** Without these changes, the task sequence will fail when deploying to UEFI machines.

5. In the **Install** group, select **Set Variable for Drive Letter** and configure the following:

    OSDPreserveDriveLetter: **True**

> **Real World Note:** If you do not change this value, your Windows installation will end up in E:\Windows instead of C:\Windows.

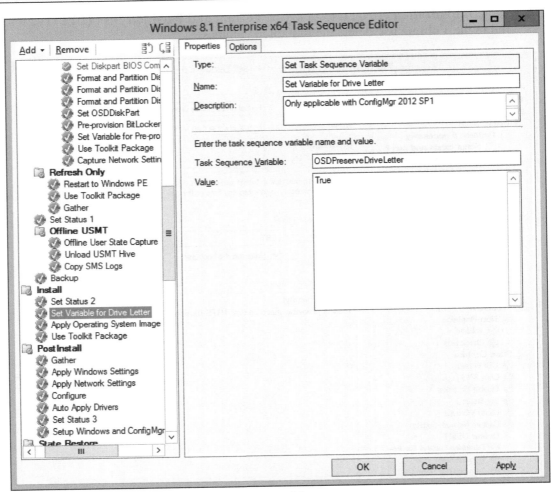

Configuring the OSDPreserveDriveLetter variable.

6. In the **Post Install** group, select **Apply Windows Settings** and configure the following:

    o   Select the **Enable the account and specify the local administrator** option, and assign a password of **P@ssw0rd**.

  o Time zone: Select the same time zone as the CM01 server is using.

> **Real World Note:** The default task sequence assigns a blank administrator password which is really bad. You need to set a password for the UDI components to work. This was a changed introduced in MDT 2013 when the standard client task sequence was merged with the UDI task sequence.

7. In the **Post Install** group, select **Apply Network Settings** and configure the **Domain OU** value to use the **ViaMonstra / Workstations** OU (browse for values).

> **Real World Note:** You need to set the Domain OU value to something. If it's left blank, the rules cannot overwrite it.

8. In the **PostInstall** group, disable the **Auto Apply Drivers** action. (Disabling is done by selecting the action and, in the Options tab, selecting the Disable this step check box.)

9. After the disabled PostInstall / Auto Apply Drivers action, add a new group name **Drivers**.

10. After the PostInstall / Drivers group, add an **Apply Driver Package** action with the following settings:

  o Name: **Latitude E7440**

  o Driver Package: **Windows 8.1 x64 - Latitude E7440**

  o Options: Add a Query WMI condition with the following query:

  > **SELECT * FROM Win32_ComputerSystem WHERE Model LIKE '%Latitude E7440%'**

  o Click **Test query** to verify the syntax. It should return "contains valid syntax".

11. In the **Post Install** group, select **Setup Windows and ConfigMgr**, and in the **Installation properties**, type in the following. (Remember: The Package ID for the ConfigMgr Client with Hotfixes is PS10000A in our example.)

  > **PATCH="C:_SMSTaskSequence\OSD\PS10000A\Hotfix\x64\ configmgr2012ac-r2-kb2970177-x64.msp"**

> **Real World Note:** If you also create a task sequence for x86 editions of Windows 8.1, you need to change the PATCH property to use the x86 update (configmgr2012ac-r2-kb2970177-i386.msp).

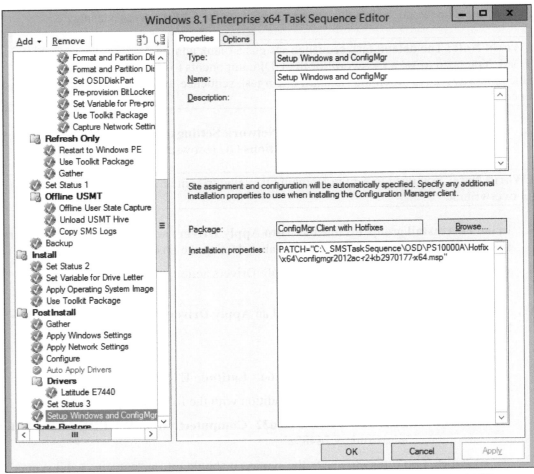

Configuring the task sequence to install the ConfigMgr client update (KB 2970177).

12. In the **State Restore** group, after the **Set Status 5** action, add a **Request State Store** action with the following settings:

    a. **Restore state from another computer**

    b. Select the **If computer account fails to connect to state store, use the Network Access account** check box.

    c. Options: select the **Continue on error** check box.

    d. Options / Condition: Add the following condition:

        Task Sequence Variable

            USMTLOCAL not equals **True**

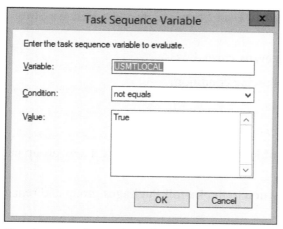

Configuring the options for the Request State Store action.

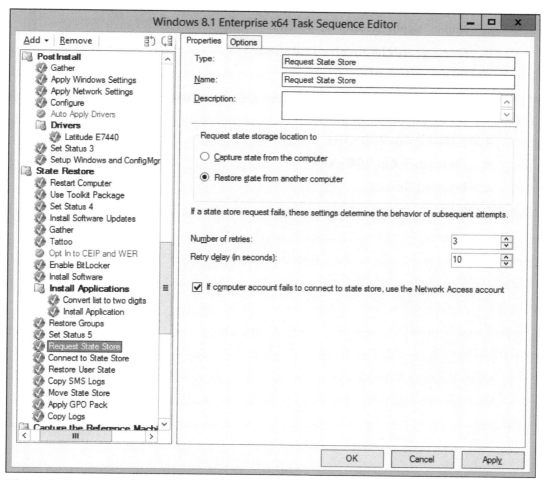

The task sequence, after adding the missing Request State Store action.

13. In the **State Restore** group, after the **Restore User State** action, add a **Release State Store** action with the following settings:

    a. Options: select the **Continue on error** check box.

    b. Options / Condition: Add the following condition:

    Task Sequence Variable

    USMTLOCAL not equals **True**

14. In the **State Restore** group, after the **Enable BitLocker** action, create a new group named **Install Packages**.

15. Move up the existing **Install Software** action to the **Install Packages** group and rename it to **Install Packages Dynamically**.

16. After the **Install Packages Dynamically** action, add a new **Install Package** action with the following settings:

    a. Name: **Adobe Reader 11.0 - x86**

    b. Package: **Adobe Reader 11.0 - x86**

    c. Program: **Install**

17. After the **Adobe Reader 11.0 - x86** action, add a new **Install Package** action with the following settings:

    a. Name: **7-Zip 9.20 - x64**

    b. Package: **7-Zip 9.20 - x64**

    c. Program: **Install**

18. Click **OK**.

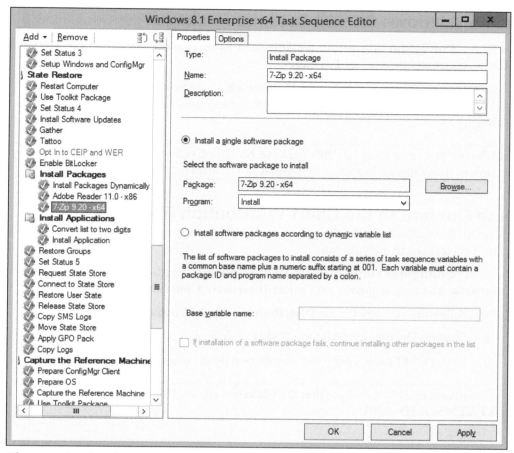

The completed task sequence.

Configuring the Rules, Distributing Content, and Deploying Task Sequences

When the task sequence is completed, you need to distribute all the packages it reference, as well as deploy the actual task sequence. In addition, since the task sequence will take instructions from the settings package (the rules), they need to be configured to match the environment.

Configure the Rules (the Windows 8.1 x64 Settings Package)

This section assumes you have copied the book sample files to D:\Setup.

1. On **CM01**, using **File Explorer**, navigate to the **D:\Setup\Windows 8.1 Settings** folder.

2. Copy the **CustomSettings.ini** file to the following folder (replace the existing file):

    D:\Sources\OSD\Settings\Windows 8.1 x64 Settings

Update the Windows 8.1 x64 Settings Package

1. Using the **ConfigMgr console**, in the **Software Library** workspace, expand **Application Management** and then select **Packages**.

2. Update the distribution points for the **Windows 8.1 x64 Settings** package by right-clicking the **Windows 8.1 x64 Settings** package and selecting **Update Distribution Points**.

Real World Note: You need to update this package because ConfigMgr 2012 R2 always stores the first version in the content library (even if you don't distributed the package yet).

Distribute Content to the CM01 Distribution Point

In ConfigMgr 2012, Microsoft added the option of distributing all packages (and applications) that a task sequence references in a single run.

1. Using the **ConfigMgr console**, select **Task Sequences**, right-click the **Windows 8.1 Enterprise x64** task sequence, and select **Distribute Content**.

2. Use the following settings for the **Distribute Content Wizard**:

    a. Content Destination: Add the **CM01** distribution point.

    b. Using **CMTrace**, verify the distribution by reviewing the **distmgr.log** file.

Note: Do not continue until you can see that the packages are distributed. Again, look for the lines containing **STATMSG: ID=2301**.

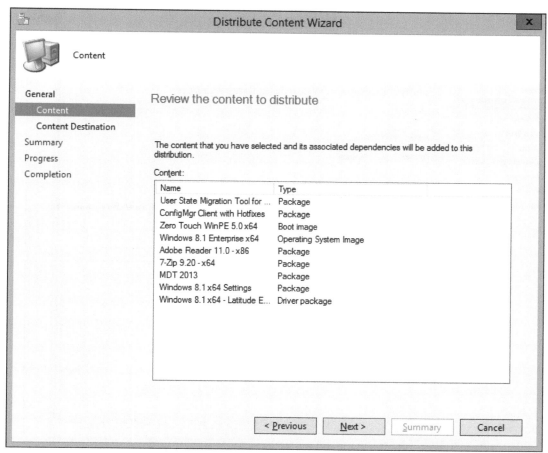

Distributing all the packages the Windows 8.1 Enterprise task sequence needs.

Create a Deployment for the Task Sequence

In these steps, you deploy the Windows 8.1 Enterprise x64 task sequence to the All Unknown Computers collection.

1. Using **ConfigMgr console**, select **Task Sequences**, right-click the **Windows 8.1 Enterprise x64** task sequence, and then select **Deploy**.

2. Use the following settings for the **Deploy Software Wizard**:

   a. General

      Collection: **All Unknown Computers**

   b. Deployment Settings

      ▪ Purpose: **Available**

      ▪ Make available to the following: **Configuration Manager clients, media and PXE**

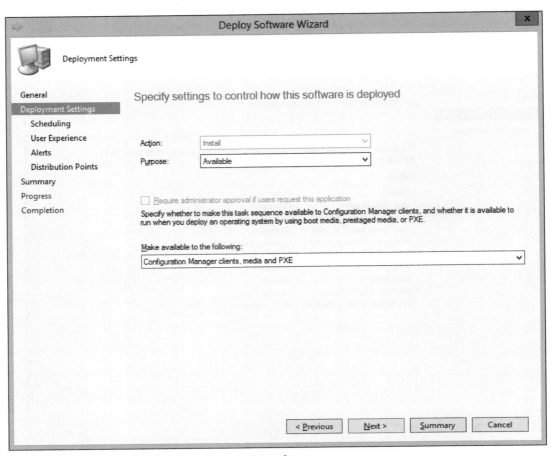

Deploying the Windows 8.1 Enterprise x64 task sequence.

    c.   Scheduling

               <default>

    d.   User Experience

               <default>

    e.   Alerts

               <default>

    f.   Distribution Points:

               <default>

Deploying Window 8.1 Using PXE

In these steps, you do a network deployment of your Windows 8.1 Enterprise task sequence. Since you are doing PXE deployments, please make sure MDT01 VM is not running (if you completed the guides in the preceding chapter). Having two PXE servers running on the same subnet never ends well. ☺

Deploy the Windows 8.1 Image

1. On the **Host PC**, create a virtual machine with the following settings:

    a. Name: **PC0004**

    b. Location: **C:\VMs**

    c. Memory: **2048 MB**

    d. Network: The virtual network for the New York site

    e. Hard disk: **60 GB** (dynamic disk)

> **Note:** Again, if you are using Hyper-V in Windows Server 2012 R2, the new Generation 2 VMs can PXE boot without the need of using a legacy network adapter.

2. Start the **PC0004** virtual machine, and press **Enter** to start the PXE boot (or press **F12** if you are using an earlier Hyper-V version). Then complete the **Task Sequence Wizard** using the following settings:

    a. Password: **P@ssw0rd**

    b. Select a task sequence to execute on this computer:
        Windows 8.1 Enterprise x64

3. The task sequence will now run and do the following:

    a. Install the Windows 8.1 operating system

    b. Install the ConfigMgr Client

    c. Join it to the domain

    d. Install the two added packages (applications)

> **Real World Note:** During the PXE boot process, you can review the SMSPXE.log on the DP (CM01 in this case) to see the communication between the client, the ConfigMgr PXE provider, and the ConfigMgr database.

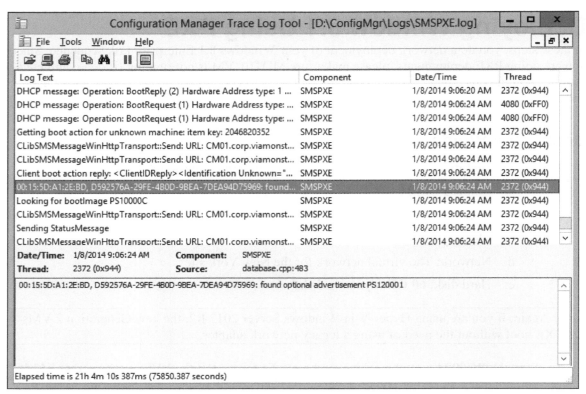

The SMSPXE.log showing that PC0004 had an optional deployment.

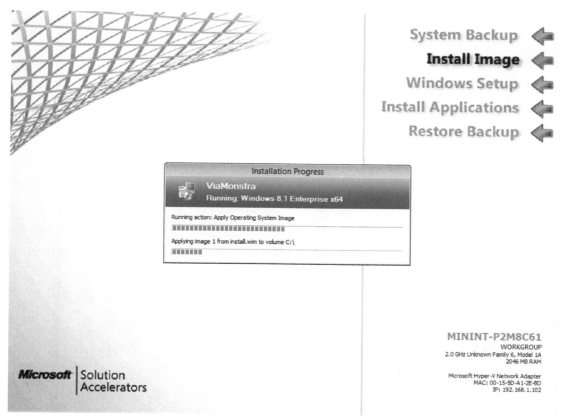

Deploying PC0004, displaying the organization name you configured in Client Settings.

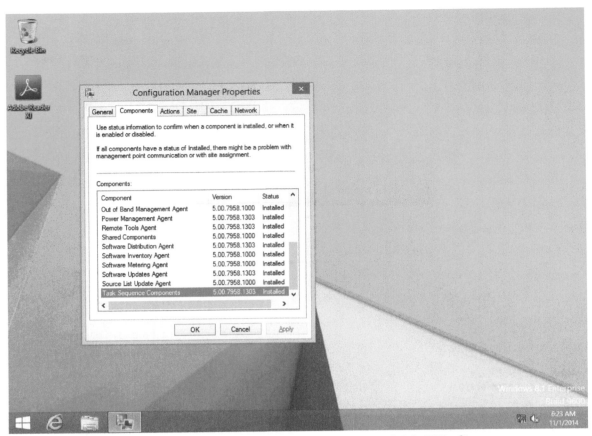

The completed deployment, showing the updated ConfigMgr 2012 R2 CU2 client.

Chapter 7

Customization Guidelines – Tips and Tricks for the IT Pro

This chapter will give you some general customization guidelines for the development process when you customize your deployment. In this chapter, you learn about the parts of the development process that you should set up before starting to implement any changes and also get an introduction to using a version control system, including:

- Identifying the different components of a version control system
- Installing all required components
- Creating and handling different projects
- Handling and tracking changes

Step-by-Step Guide Requirements

If you want to follow the step-by-step guides in this chapter, you need a lab environment configured as outlined in Chapter 3 and Appendix A. In this chapter, you are using the following virtual machines:

DC01

VC01

PC0001

The VMs used in this chapter.

You also need to have downloaded the following software:

- VisualSVN Server 2.7.3
- TortoiseSVN 1.8.8
- The book sample files (http://stealingwithpride.com)

The Development Process

Before you start creating and implementing any customizations in your OSD solution, you should take a moment and think about some processes and standards for your project.

Setting standards and creating processes to be followed during your development efforts might sound a bit over-complicated if you are just "tweaking" a script to your needs. But implementing such standards and processes at the very beginning will help you achieve higher and much more consistent quality throughout your project, shorten the time it takes to get your changes into production, and save you a lot of time in the long run.

We recommend that you implement at least the following aspects into your development process. However, as each of these aspects literally requires a book of its own, as there are many different ways to implement them, we can only raise your awareness of their importance and provide with a basis for further exploration.

Documentation

Documentation is probably the most often mentioned and at the same time most often ignored advice. Document what you are doing, while you are doing it. And document it in a way that it's possible to hand it over to someone else who can then continue the work based on your documentation.

There are typically different types of documentation with regards to software:

- **Requirements.** Statements that identify certain characteristics of a system
- **Architecture/design.** General overview, including relations to the environment
- **Technical.** Documentation of the code, algorithm, interfaces, and so forth.
- **User.** Manuals for the end user, system administrator, and support staff

Some of these may not be required or could even be overkill for small projects. But at a bare minimum, the technical documentation should be available. And this technical documentation doesn't necessarily need to be in a separate document. It's often enough to just add some meaningful comments directly in the code, script, wizard page, and so on. As mentioned before, document what you are doing, while you are doing it.

Backup

Superheroes need it, police rely on it, and everyone who uses a computer should use some form of it. As you are working in the IS business, doing backups should be a regular process in your day-to-day work.

So there is nothing really new here, but take a moment and make sure you have a strategy to back up your current deployment environment, including all the customizations and changes you have implemented. And make sure you are able to restore it to a certain state. Otherwise all the time spent already might be lost.

Structure and Naming Conventions

The intent of naming conventions is to allow useful information to be deduced from the names based on regularities. At first glance, naming conventions don't seem all that important. Again, they might sound over-complicated for something as small as tweaking a deployment solution or creating an additional wizard page.

However, implementing (preferably the same) naming conventions even in very small projects makes it significantly easier to understand what a system is doing and how to fix or extend it for new business needs.

Even in this book certain naming conventions and structural elements have been implemented to increase readability and ease understanding.

Change Control

It's very important to keep track on your changes, especially if you start customizing the default MDT solution, as those changes might need to be added or updated, or they even might interfere with newer releases.

Change or version control probably isn't something that comes to mind when you start thinking about customizing or extending your OSD solution. It's something typically related to "real" programming, huge projects, and the like. But the idea of change control will actually bring some benefit to all your efforts.

A version control system is a combination of technologies and practices for tracking and controlling changes. This does not relate only to source code; it also relates to any project-related files like documentation. Having something under version control allows you to keep track of changes, compare different versions, roll back unwanted changes to older versions, break bigger changes into smaller chunks and incorporate them later into the main project again, and more.

If you start working with change control, it might feel like "just another backup solution," but change control is more than just restoring a file (or set of files) to a certain state.

Separate Environments

Each change that is introduced into a system has the potential to break other parts of the system, no matter whether it's by the addition of new features, removal of bugs or errors, or even making changes that are meant to be only cosmetic.

So at least have separate test and production environments, where the test environment is a copy of the production environment so you can test all changes properly. If they don't match, all your testing is useless. And here the other aspects we've discussed about the development process tie in. To keep those environments in sync, you need to make sure you keep track of all changes, have them properly documented, and have processes in place to move those changes between the environments.

Version Control

You have learned already that it's very important to keep track of your changes throughout your projects. We will now dig into a specific way in which change control can be implemented, that is, by using a version control system (VCS).

Throughout the book, we primarily use VisualSVN Server as a version control system. VisualSVN Server is a free Windows-based implementation of Subversion, which is a free, open-source version control system. To access the repository, we use the TortoiseSVN Windows shell extension. It hooks directly into File Explorer and gives access to the repository by simple right-click actions.

In addition to Subversion, another often used open-source VCS is Git. The main difference between Subversion and Git is that Subversion uses a central repository and users just check out individual parts of it to make changes. To make them available globally, changes have to be committed back to the central repository, which then keeps track of them. This differs from Git, in which every user has a clone of the repository. Changes are committed to the local clone of the repository and then can be pushed or pulled between different repositories. In our scenario, we prefer the central repository over the flexibility, but also complexity, of having multiple clones of the repository.

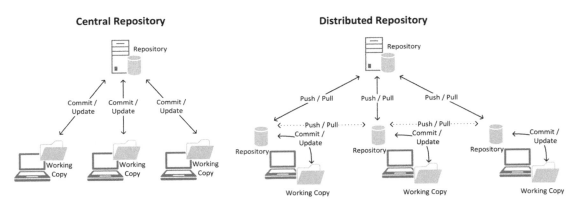

Central vs. distributed repository.

With Microsoft Visual Studio Team Foundation Server Express 2013, Microsoft also offers a free (for up to five users) version control system with a central repository that nicely integrates into Visual Studio, including the Express versions. However, to access the repository, one is required to use Microsoft Visual Studio (Express). As most of the typical administrative work is done using tools other than Microsoft Visual Studio, we prefer the Subversion-based solution over the Team Foundation Server one.

Because a version control system isn't often used during the administration of systems, we will now go through some basic terms and definitions and also cover some typical tasks using VisualSVN Server in combination with the TortoiseSVN extension. However, as version control isn't the primary purpose of this book, we cover only some basic functionality required for daily usage.

Terminology

In this section, you learn about the core functions and terminology of version control.

Repository

The *repository* is simply the root of everything you would like to keep track of. You can have several repositories, e.g. one per project, or several projects within one repository. Think of it as a container for everything you would like to keep together.

To keep the management requirements to a minimum, our recommendation is to use one single repository to store everything related to your work. Having, for example, development, test, and production sections within a single repository allows you to keep the history of all your changes and easily transfer changes from one environment to the other.

Project

A *project* is a logical group of files you are working on and that belong together. We recommend separating all your deployment, customization, and other work into different projects. A typical project as used in this book can be a custom wizard pane, a custom script, some or modification to a script, but also the complete configuration of a deployment share.

However, as projects are just mapped to folders within the repository, the definition of a project is not as strict as you might think. Something becomes a project by convention instead of some specific configuration and is meant to enable you to structure your deployment work.

By Subversion convention, each project has three default subfolders:

- Trunk

- Branches

- Tags

Whereas not all of them may be necessary for every project, we recommend sticking to this convention.

If you only have a few projects, each project is typically located at the root of the repository. However, if you have several projects, or are storing projects from different environments in a single repository, you might want to group and create a structure for those projects.

Trunk, Branches, and Tags

The *trunk* is more or less your individual project. It's the main source from the start of your project until the present. By definition, a trunk always contains the latest working version of your project.

A *branch* can be seen as a copy of the trunk that you are working on. As mentioned, the trunk should always contain the latest working version of your project. If you now need to change something in this project that either will take a longer period of time to implement and/or has the potential to break something in the project or with the components with which it's being used, you should create a branch of your trunk. Branches are also used often if it's uncertain whether a particular change will ever be integrated into a trunk or maybe leads to a separate project.

Now all required changes are applied to this branch, and the trunk stays unchanged and usable during that time. Changes to the trunk like small updates or fixes can easily be applied to the branch, as they have the same origin and the repository "knows" about this and is able to transfer these changes on request.

If all work on a branch has been finished and verified as working, a branch can be re-integrated into the trunk. Again, the repository knows about the differences between files in the branch and the trunk, as they have the same origin, and is able to transfer them from the branch over to the trunk.

A *tag* is almost identical to a branch. It's also a copy of the trunk, but it's more like a snapshot at a specific point in time. By convention, you don't change anything after you have created a tag. These "tagged" copies are typically created if you publish or release a version. That allows you to easily support and test your projects on specific versions.

Working Copy

The *working copy* is simply what it says. It's the local copy of the project you are currently working on. While the original files are hosted on the VCS server (even if the server is installed locally), you need to copy them to your computer to work on them. This is also often called "checkout." In the case of Subversion, checkout really means taking a copy. It's not locking the file(s) or marking them somehow. It's just a copy. And at any time you can query the server for updates or publish (*commit*) your updated file(s) to the server.

Because a working copy is just a copy of one of your projects with references to the source, it is stored in a local folder. You can have multiple working copies of different or even from the same project. And several people can have working copies of the same project, allowing them to make changes in parallel.

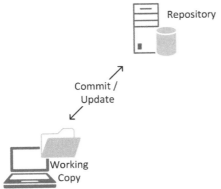

Using a working copy within the VCS

VisualSVN Server

VisualSVN Server is a free Windows-based implementation of Subversion, which again is a free, open-source version control system.

Install VisualSVN Server

In this guide we assume you have downloaded VisualSVN Server 2.7.3 from http://www.visualsvn.com/server/download to D:\Setup on VC01.

1. On **VC01**, log in as **VIAMONSTRA\Administrator** using a password of **P@ssw0rd**.

2. Start the **VisualSVN Server** setup (VisualSVN-Server-2.7.3.msi).

3. On the **Welcome to the VisualSVN Server 2.7.3 Setup Wizard** page, click **Next**.

4. On the **End-User License Agreement** page, accept the license agreement, and click **Next**.

5. On the **Select Components** page, select the **VisualSVN Server and Management Console** option. Leave the other settings at default values, and click **Next**.

6. On the **VirtualSVN Server Editions** page, select **Standard Edition**, and click **Next**.

7. On the **Initial Server Configuration** page, use **D:\Repositories** as path for the repositories, clear the **Use secure connection (https://)** check box, and click **Next**.

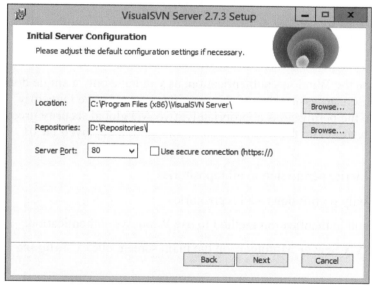

VisualSVN Server configuration.

8. On the **Ready to Install** page, click **Install**.

9. On the **Completing the VisualSVN Server 2.7.3 Setup Wizard** page, accept the default settings and click **Finish** to close the wizard and start VirtualSVN Server Manager.

Real World Note: Throughout this book you use HTTP connections on port 80 to the Subversion server and the repositories to avoid the additional complexity that comes with the usage of certificates and the corresponding PKI as that is out of scope for this book. However, we highly recommend that you use secure connections (https://) in production environments and add a proper SSL certificate to the VisualSVN Server to encrypt the traffic.

Configure Security

By default, new repositories are configured to give read and write access to all users. But that's definitely not the preferred configuration, as the repositories might also store some critical information that isn't supposed to be accessed by everyone.

So before you start creating the repositories, you have to configure the authentication method that you are going to use and also set up appropriate groups that you are going to use for authorization.

VisualSVN Server supports two authentication methods:

- Subversion authentication
- Windows authentication

The most commonly used authentication method is Windows authentication, but the Subversion authentication method might be the preferred solution if you have only a few users accessing the repository, or if users are accessing the repository from different domains/forests without trust.

Real World Note: Be aware that the user names and passwords are **case sensitive** if you use the Subversion authentication, which is quite uncommon for most Windows-focused users.

Throughout this book, you will use the Windows authentication, as you have only a single domain for corp.viamonstra.com and all users accessing the repository will have an Active Directory account in this domain. To handle the permissions appropriately, two AD global security groups have been created already if you have set up the hydration environment and deployed DC01 according to Appendix A:

- **VCS Users.** For read and write permission to all repositories
- **VCS Readers.** For read-only permission to all repositories

First, you need to change the default authentication method to use Windows authentication.

1. On **VC01**, using **VisualSVN Server Manager**, on the main screen, click **Configure authentication options**.

2. In the **Authentication** tab, select the **Use Windows authentication** option and then select **Basic authentication**.

3. Click **OK**.

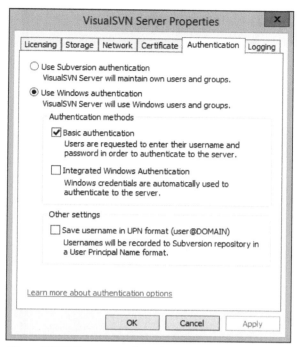

VisualSVN Server authentication settings.

Real World Note: The free version of VisualSVN Server only supports basic authentication. There is an enterprise version available that also supports integrated Windows authentication and some additional logging options. However, for the scenarios covered in this book, the free version perfectly fits our needs.

To configure the default groups:

1. On **VC01**, using **VisualSVN Server Manager**, in the main screen, right-click the **Repositories** node and select **Properties**.

2. Click **Add** and add the following groups:

   o **VCS Users**

   o **VCS Readers**

3. Select **Read / Write** permission for the **VCS Users** group.

4. Select **Read Only** permission for the **VCS Readers** group.

5. Click **OK**.

VisualSVN Server repositories security settings.

Create the Repositories

After you have installed and configured the VisualSVN Server, you need to set up the repositories. Per our recommendation, you set up two repositories. One called **Main** that will store all your deployment-related data for the development, test, and production environments. Within this repository, you create subsections for each environment and create further subsections beneath for each project.

The second repository you create is called **Sandbox**. That repository is used mainly for training and experimenting purposes. You can use this repository to get used to the typical tasks of version control as described in this chapter without having any side effects on the production repository.

To create the two default repositories used in this book:

1. On **VC01**, using **VisualSVN Server Manager**, in the main screen, click **Create new repository**. Use the following settings:

    a. Repository Name: **Main**

    b. Select **Empty repository**.

    c. Select **No specific permissions** to configure the repository to use the global permissions that we just configured.

d. Click on **Create** and verify that the repository has been successfully created. Note the **Repository URL**, which is used in the following guides.

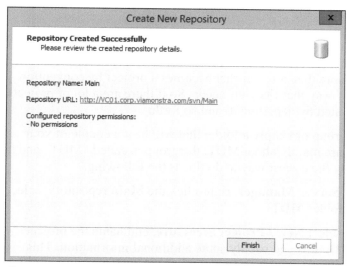

Create new repository in VisualSVN Server

2. Repeat **step 2** using the repository name **Sandbox**.

Installing TortoiseSVN

After you have installed and configured VisualSVN Server and set up your repositories, you need something on the client side of things to be able to access the repositories. For this task, you use the TortoiseSVN client.

TortoiseSVN is a free, open-source Subversion client, implemented as a Microsoft Windows shell extension. This has the nice benefit that it hooks into File Explorer and you can use the context menu to have access to your version control system.

In these steps we assume you have downloaded the TortoiseSVN 1.8.8 x64 client from http://tortoisesvn.net/downloads.html to C:\Setup on PC0001.

1. On **PC0001**, log in as **VIAMONSTRA\Administrator** using a password of **P@ssw0rd**.

2. Run the installer (TortoiseSVN-1.8.8.25755-x64-svn-1.8.10.msi) for **TortoiseSVN** using the default settings.

Common Tasks

In this section, you learn about the most common tasks when using version control.

Creating a Project

The fundamental elements for all future work are *projects*. A project does not necessarily need to be large. It can even be only a couple of administrative scripts you have written for your work. As the project in Subversion is nothing more than a folder that becomes a project by convention, you are free to use and implement it in any way that fits your needs. So if there are a lot of projects, they could be grouped by topic, separated by department, and so forth.

Start with this idea and first create a group or simply a folder that will host a couple of your projects. As the samples in this book are mainly about MDT, the group is called "MDT" and hosts all the MDT-related projects. Probably the easiest way to do this is the following:

1. On **VC01**, using **VisualSVN Server Manager**, right-click the **Main** repository, select **New / Folder**, and name the folder **MDT**.

2. Right-click the **MDT** folder, select **New / Project Structure**, and name the project **LocationSelection** and click **Details** and supply some additional information. This message will show up later in the log and help to identify what happened during different revisions. We will get to this shortly.

3. Expand the nodes for **Main / MDT / LocationSelection** and verify that VisualSVN has created the structure for the branches, tags and trunk.

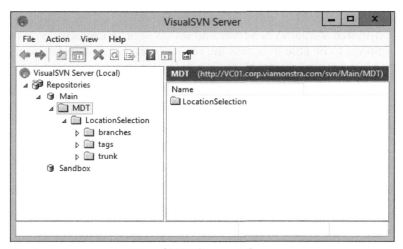

Project structure in VisualSVN Server Manager.

Real World Note: The project and its structure also could be created using the Repository Browser from the TortoiseSVN client. However, we recommend using the VisualSVN Server Manager, as this requires only a single step and enforces the usage of the same structure for every project.

Opening a Repository

The VisualSVN Server is installed, and the repositories and a project have been created. Now it's time to connect to the repository so you can browse through its content.

> **Real World Note:** Before you do anything, we recommend creating a folder on the root of one of your drives that acts as a container for (almost) all your working copies. This will make it easier to handle different projects or versions. Throughout this book, you use **C:\Working** as this root.

In this guide we assume you have downloaded the books sample files.

1. On **PC0001**, using **File Explorer**, create the **C:\Working** folder.

2. Right-click **C:\Working** and select **TortoiseSVN / Repo-Browser**.

3. Use the URL **http://VC01.corp.viamonstra.com/svn/Main**.

Repository URL.

> **Real World Note:** To get the correct URL for a repository or an individual project, you can use the VisualSVN Server Manager.

4. Use **VIAMONSTRA\Maik** and a password of **P@ssw0rd** in the **Username** and **Password** for the domain, and select the **Save authentication** check box.

> **Real World Note:** Again, the standard version of VisualSVN Server doesn't support Windows integrated authentication, so the username and password have to be supplied manually.

This opens the Repository Browser from the TortoiseSVN client, which you can use to browse through a repository, show the log of individual files/folders, create new folders, export a project, and so forth. Most of the tasks can be done in either the Repository Browser or the TortoiseSVN context menu.

Checking Out a Project

To be able to work on a project, it needs to be checked out from the repository.

During a *checkout*, the *content* of a folder/project in the repository is copied to a local folder. Additionally, a hidden folder is created locally that stores additional information and is required to keep track of the changes to the files and subfolders and acts as a reference to the repository.

A checkout is typically based on the most recent version of a folder/project; however, it can be based on an older version, as well, such as files from an older date that are required for a specific support case. That's what tags are normally used for. If you check out files based on an older version and need to make changes to them, you are required to create a new branch based on that version.

Real World Note: Be aware that the folders and files that are checked out aren't locked for any modifications by other users. By default, several users can have the same set of folders and files checked out and work on them concurrently, as all changes are made to the local copy.

To check out a project, you need to know the appropriate URL. You can get this URL from the VisualSVN Server Manager on VC01 or by using the Repository Brower as explained previously. Most dialog boxes in TortoiseSVN give you the option to open the Repository Browser from there, as well.

1.   On **PC0001**, using **File Explorer**, right-click **C:\Working** and select **SVN Checkout**.

2.   Use the following settings for the chcekout:

   a.   URL of repository:
        http://VC01.corp.viamonstra.com/svn/Main/MDT/LocationSelection/trunk

   b.   Checkout Directory: **C:\Working\LocationSelection**

   c.   Click **OK** twice.

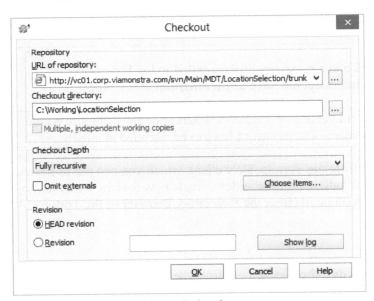

The TortoiseSVN Checkout dialog box.

Real World Note: One might expect the folder that has been selected to be checked out, but only the content of the folder in the repository is checked out to the selected local folder! If the target folder does not exist, it is created. If it exists, the checkout will overwrite files and folders if they have the same names as the ones from the repository.

After a project has been checked out, it can be modified locally. However, the changes won't be reflected in the repository until they have been committed.

Committing Changes

The working copy can be changed as often and for as long as necessary. Files can be updated, new files added, or existing ones deleted. However, all those changes are local only and not reflected in the repository automatically. Updating the repository with the changes made to the working copy is called *committing* the changes.

Real World Note: Changes can be committed only if the working copy is up to date. When working with several users on the same repository or working on several projects at the same time, the revision in the repository may be newer than the revision of the working copy. As a best practice, we recommend that you always update the working copy first, before you commit changes.

For this example, you use the files that we created for Chapter 12 to create a new wizard pane that allows the selection of a location. In this guide we assume you have downloaded the book sample files to C:\Setup on PC0001.

To commit the changes from the working copy:

1. On **PC0001**, copy the content of the **C:\Setup\LocationSelection** folder to the **C:\Working\LocationSelection** folder

2. Using **File Explorer**, right-click the **C:\Working\LocationSelection** folder, and select **SVN Commit**.

3. In the **Message:** text box, type in a message to show up in the log history for this revision.

4. From the list of **Changes**, select the following non-versioned files:

    o **DeployWiz_LocationSelection.vbs**

    o **DeployWiz_LocationSelection.xml**

    o **DeployWiz_LocationSelectionDef.xml**

5. Click **OK**.

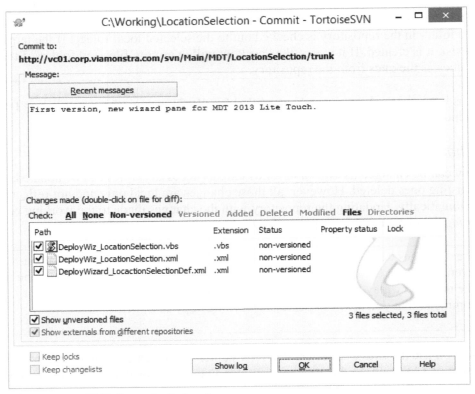

The TortoiseSVN Commit dialog box.

6. Verify that the three files have been added successfully, and click **OK**.

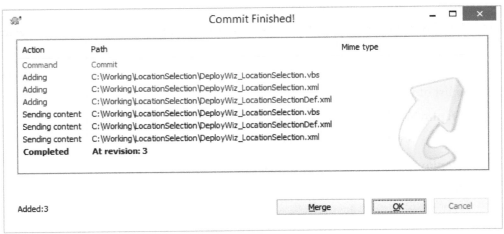

The TortoiseSVN Commit summary.

It's up to you how often you commit your changes. We recommended doing this at least every couple hours if you are continuously working on it. But at the latest, if you finish your work for the day, it's a good time to commit all changes so far. If you are unsure what to do, just commit once more. It doesn't hurt. ;-)

> **Real World Note:** If you want to delete or rename a file or folder, the recommended way is to use the TortoiseSVN context menu. It's recommended for files but actually is a necessity for folders. The corresponding methods from the context menu make sure that the repository is aware of this change, e.g. that the folder is still the same, just with a different name now, and keeps the history. Whereas, for example, renaming a folder directly in File Explorer causes the repository to see this as one folder being deleted and a new one being created. In that case, all history information about changes so far are lost.

Updating a Working Copy

In cases you are not the only one working on a specific project or you have several working copies of the same project, there might be changes in the repository that a working copy is missing. If the repository is newer than the working copy, it's not possible to commit any changes. So we recommend checking for updates regularly and applying them to the working copy.

To update your working copy:

1. On **PC0001**, using **File Explorer**, right-click the **C:\Working\LocationSelection** folder and select **SVN Update**.

2. Confirm the updates if there were any.

Tagging a Version

Every time a version of the project is released, you should make a read-only copy of this project for reference purposes. This copy is called a *tag*. It's read-only by convention. Subversion itself does not limit anyone from actually making changes to it. But this convention has a couple good reasons for it, so we recommend sticking with it.

The biggest advantage of tagging versions is that it helps to easily get all files of a project at a specific point in time, for example, in case there is some support required for a specific version released.

For this example, you tag the current revision of the LocationSelection pane as Version 1.

1. On **PC0001**, using **File Explorer**, right-click **C:\Working\LocationSelection** (your working copy) and select **TortoiseSVN / Branch/tag**.

2. In the **To path:** text box, type in **/MDT/LocationSelection/tags/Version 1**.

3. Type in a short message that describes the change.

4. Click **OK** twice.

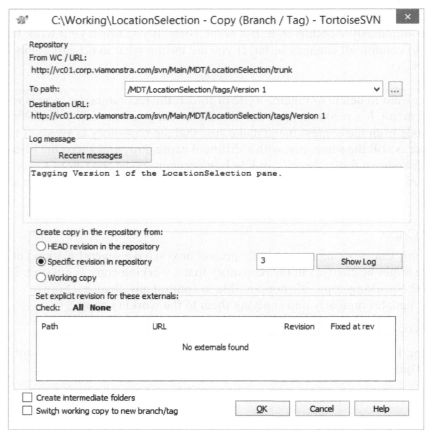

The TortoiseSVN Copy dialog box.

The tag typically is created based on the current revision of the working copy. As the revision is incremented on any commit to the repository and you might have several projects within the repository that you or others are working on, the latest revision of the repository doesn't necessarily match the latest revision of the working copy. If you are unsure what revision to use, check the log.

Real World Note: As the tag is being created within the repository, make sure that you commit all changes of the working copy first so that the repository is in sync.

You should avoid selecting the option to create intermediate folders when creating a tag or branch. This option is disabled by default to avoid typos. For example, if you type the target path as /MDT/LocationSelection/tag/Version 1 instead of /MDT/LocationSelection/tags/Version 1, you end up with a folder tags and a folder tag.

By definition, a tag is a read-only copy, so the option to switch the working copy to the new tag shouldn't be used.

Create a Branch

Whenever you need to make major changes to a project, it is helpful not to work directly on the main project, the trunk itself. It's better to make a copy of the current project and implement your changes on this copy. This copy is called a *branch*. The process is almost identical to creating a tag as shown in the preceding section.

1. On **PC0001**, using **File Explorer**, right-click the **C:\Working\LocationSelection** folder and select **TortoiseSVN / Branch/tag**.

2. In the **To path:** text box, type in **/MDT/LocationSelection/branches/Version 2**.

3. Add a short message that describes this change.

4. To immediately start working on the newly created branch, select the **Switch the working copy to the new branch\tag** check box.

5. Click **OK** twice.

> **Real World Note:** If you don't select this option, the working copy will still point to the original location, i.e. to the trunk. Every change will still be committed to the trunk and not reflected in the newly created branch.

Verify Current Location

When working with several working copies and/or branches or tags, it might become confusing and one might end up changing information in the wrong copy. So to ensure that the working copy is pointing to the correct location, complete these steps:

1. On **PC0001**, using **File Explorer**, right-click the **C:\Working\LocationSelection** folder and select **Properties**.

2. Select the **Subversion** tab.

3. Verify that the URL is pointing to the correct location.

4. Optionally, click the **Show log** button to see the history of this copy and check whether the revision is the required one.

> **Real World Note:** The Subversion properties contain a lot of additional useful information. However, most of this is outside of the scope of this book and not required in day-to-day work. Please check the TortoiseSVN documentation for further information.

Merging Changes

When working with branches, at some point in time, it becomes necessary to apply those changes to either the trunk or a different branch. This typically happens when the work on a branch has been finished, or at least a certain milestone has been reached, or some important changes from the trunk have to be integrated into the current branch.

Merging Changes from the Trunk

This option is typically used when applying smaller changes, like a hotfix to the trunk that also needs to be merged into the branch.

1. On **PC0001**, using **File Explorer**, right-click the **C:\Working\LocationSelection** folder and select **TortoiseSVN / Merge**.

2. Select **Merge a range of revisions**.

3. Select the **URL** of the trunk as the source for the merge (http://vc01.corp.viamonstra.com/svn/Main/MDT/LocationSelection/trunk).

4. Optionally select a **revision range** to merge. By default, this can be left empty, which merges all revisions.

5. Leave the rest of the settings at the defaults and finish with **Merge**.

6. Verify the merge completed successfully and confirm with **OK**.

> **Real World Note:** Be aware that the changes from the trunk haven't been committed yet! A best practice is to verify now whether the branch with all the changes from the trunk is still working as expected. All errors and problems should be fixed before finally committing this back to the repository. This ensures that the branch itself is still in a usable condition and, in the worst case, can be easily reverted to a previous version.

Merging Changes from a Branch

Merging changes from a branch mostly happens when the development on a certain branch has been finished. This is also called reintegrating a branch back into the trunk. However, it also could be that a branch has reached an important milestone and is ready to be used within the trunk, but additional development work has to continue.

> **Real World Note:** It's important to realize that the target is always the current working copy. So if we have finished all work on the branch and committed the changes, we first need to switch the working copy back to the trunk to be able to merge the changes from the branch.

To merge the changes from a branch back into the trunk:

1. On **PC0001**, using **File Explorer**, right-click the **C:\Working\LocationSelection** folder and select **TortoiseSVN / Switch**.

2. Select the **URL** of the trunk and click **OK** (/MDT/LocationSelection/trunk).

3. Ensure the **working copy** is now using the trunk as a source.

4. Click **OK**.

5. Using **File Explorer**, right-click the folder now containing the working copy of the trunk and select **TortoiseSVN / Merge**.

6. Select **Merge a range of revisions**.

7. Select the **URL** of the branch as the source for the merge
    (http://vc01.corp.viamonstra.com/svn/Main/MDT/LocationSelection/branches/Version 2)

8. Leave the rest of the settings at their defaults and finish with **Merge**.

9. Verify the merge completed successfully and confirm with **OK**.

Real World Note: Be aware that the changes from the branch haven't been committed yet! A best practice is to verify now whether the trunk with all the changes from the branch is still working as expected. All errors and problems should be fixed before finally committing this back to the repository. This ensures that the trunk is always in a usable and working condition and in the worst case can easily be reverted to a previous version.

Importing an Existing Project

As you have just started getting some projects under version control, you probably have a lot of projects that still exist somewhere else. If you need to continue working on them, it might make sense to import them before changing anything. In this example you import one of the book sample projects, the SimpleFrontend project that you learn more about in Chapter 12.

1. On **VC01**, using the **VisualSVN Server Manager**, expand the **Main** repository, right-click the **MDT** folder, select **New / Project Structure**, and name the project **SimpleFrontend**.

2. On **PC0001**, copy the **SimpleFrontend** folder from the book samples files to the **C:\Working** folder.

3. Using **File Explorer**, right-click the **SimpleFrontend** folder and select **SVN Checkout**.

4. Select the **URL** of the trunk subfolder for the project you created in **step 1** (http://vc01.corp.viamonstra.com/svn/Main/MDT/SimpleFrontend/trunk).

5. Verify that the Checkout directory is set to **C:\Working\SimpleFrontend**.

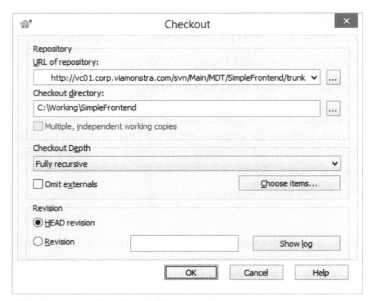

Checking out the SimpleFrontend project.

6. Click **OK**, click **Yes**, and then click **OK** again.

Real World Note: TortoiseSVN will warn you that the target folder is not empty and existing files might be overwritten. As we are checking out an empty folder, this warning can be safely ignored.

7. Using **File Explorer**, right-click the **SimpleFrontend** folder and select **SVN Commit**.

8. All the files and folders within the project will show up as **non-versioned**. Select all the files that shall be put under version control, and in the **Message:** text box, type in a short message for the log and click **OK**.

9. Confirm all the selected files have successfully been added to the repository.

This way you kind of converted a local project into a working copy of a repository and can continue to work on the project, but now you have it under version control and have full control over all changes.

Exporting a Project

Exporting is pretty similar to a checkout. It allows you to create a local copy of a folder/project from the repository based on a specific version. The difference is that an export only copies the files and folders. It does not create and keep any reference to the repository. So there is no change tracking possible with an export.

An export is most often used when the project files will be given to someone who is not actively working on them, or when changes to the copy don't matter. Most often, a specific tag is the source for an export.

1.   On **PC0001**, using **File Explorer**, create the **C:\Export\LocationSelection** folder.

2.   Right-click the **C:\Export\LocationSelection** folder and select **TortoiseSVN / Export**. Use the following settings:

    a.   Select the **URL** of the project you would like to have exported, e.g. **http://VC01.corp.viamonstra.com/svn/Main/MDT/LocationSelection/trunk**.

    b.   Export Directory: **C:\Export\LocationSelection**

3.   Click **OK** twice and confirm that all files and folders have been exported successfully.

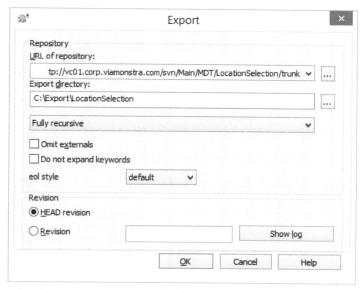

The TortoiseSVN Export dialog box.

Real World Note: A best practice is to export either the trunk or a specific branch or tag only instead of manually selecting a specific revision.

Changing the Version or Undoing Changes

One of the biggest advantages using a version control system is the possibility of changing files or even complete folders/projects to a different version. This allows you to restore the status of a project at almost any point in its history.

Most often this functionality is used either to troubleshoot some problem with a specific version, or revert to the most recent previous version in case some local changes broke the project.

To update a working copy to a specific version:

1. On **PC0001**, using **File Explorer**, right-click the **C:\Working\LocationSelection** folder and select **TortoiseSVN / Update to revision**.

2. Use the **Show Log** button to see the history of the project and select the correct revision.

Real World Note: In case you just need to undo local changes and revert to the latest version from the repository, you can optionally use the **Revert** option from the **TortoiseSVN** context menu. It will show a list of files that have been changed since their last commit. However, this does not undo any changes which have already been committed.

Chapter 8

Bending the Rules – The Gather Process

When using MDT 2013 Lite Touch, or integrating MDT 2013 with ConfigMgr 2012 R2, it's the rules that make most of the magic. The rules make up the background engine that assigns settings used by the deployment. In its most basic form, you can store the settings in a text file, the CustomSettings.ini, but you also can have the rules engine reach out to other scripts, databases, or even web services.

Step-by-Step Guide Requirements

If you want to follow the step-by-step guides in this chapter, you need a lab environment configured as outlined in Chapter 3 and Appendix A. In this chapter, you are using the following virtual machines:

DC01   CM01   PC0002

The VMs used in this chapter.

You also need to have downloaded the following software:

- ConfigMgr 2012 Toolkit R2
- The book sample files (http://stealingwithpride.com)

The Flow

The way MDT and ConfigMgr use the rules is the same. During a deployment there are three key actions that occur: the Gather action, the Configure action, and the Apply Operating System action. Let us give you a simple example.

If you have a CustomSettings.ini file that look like this:

```
[Settings]
Priority=Default

[Default]
MachineObjectOU=ou=Workstations,ou=viamonstra,dc=corp,
dc=viamonstra,dc=com
```

Then the task sequence will do the following during deployment:

1. The Gather action will read the CustomSettings.ini file and store the information as variables, both in memory and on the hard drive so they can survive a reboot. In this example, it stores the MachineObjectOU variable and its value (ou=Workstations,ou=viamonstra,dc=corp,dc=viamonstra,dc=com).

2. The Configure action is called, and it in turn does two things:

    a. It copies the Unattend.xml template from the server to the client hard drive. In MDT 2013 Lite Touch, the template is copied from the task sequence control folder in the deployment share. For ConfigMgr 2012 R2, the template is copied from the settings package the task sequence is configured to use (Windows 8.1 x64 settings in your environment).

    b. It updates the local Unattend.xml with the settings read by the Gather action. In this example, it updates the MachineObjectOU section of the Unattend.xml with the value from the CustomSettings.ini file (ou=Workstations,ou=viamonstra,dc=corp,dc=viamonstra,dc=com).

3. The image is deployed using the now updated Unattend.xml file. MDT 2013 Lite Touch uses DISM to apply it; ConfigMgr simply copies it to the correct location.

Explaining the CustomSettings.ini Rules

As you have seen in the examples in this book, the CustomSettings.ini file contains multiple sections. Sections are used to group settings together, and their priority (the order in which they are read) is controlled by the Priority property. In the following example, the [Init] section is read before the [Default] section.

```
[Settings]
Priority=Init, Default

[Init]
TimeZoneName=Pacific Standard Time

[Default]
MachineObjectOU=ou=Workstations,ou=viamonstra,dc=corp,
dc=viamonstra,dc=com
```

In the preceding example, it doesn't matter in which order the sections are, it's still the Priority property that defines the order.

Conflicting Settings

But what if you have conflicting settings? Say you have one section that sets the computer name (OSDComputerName) to PC00075 and another that sets the computer name to PC00076. Which value will win? Well, for most settings, the first writer will win, which means that if the first section sets the computer name to PC00075, the computer name will be set to PC00075.

First writer wins is true for most settings, but not all. Each built-in property is defined in the ZTIGather.xml, and in there you find a setting for each property, the overwrite setting which tells the rules engine whether a property can be overwritten. For example:

```
<property id="OSDComputerName" type="string" overwrite="false"...
```

159

Using Subsections

You also can nest sections, for example, to detect whether the computers are virtual machines, and for all virtual machines, apply a local policy (GPO Pack).

```
[Settings]
Priority=ByVMType, Default

[Default]
ApplyGPOPack=NO

[ByVMType]
Subsection=IsVM-%ISVM%

[IsVM-True]
ApplyGPOPack=YES
```

Setting Up a Rules Simulation Environment

The best way to learn how the rules engine works is to set up a rules simulation environment. Using this environment, you can test your settings in a few seconds without having to do a full deployment.

The magic is done by calling the ZTIGather.wsf script after first making sure there isn't an existing variables.dat file in the C:\MININT\SMSOSD\OSDLOGS folder that will cause the simulation not to read any changes in your rules. To simply the process, we created a small PowerShell script that deletes any existing C:\MININT folder and runs the ZTIGather.wsf script.

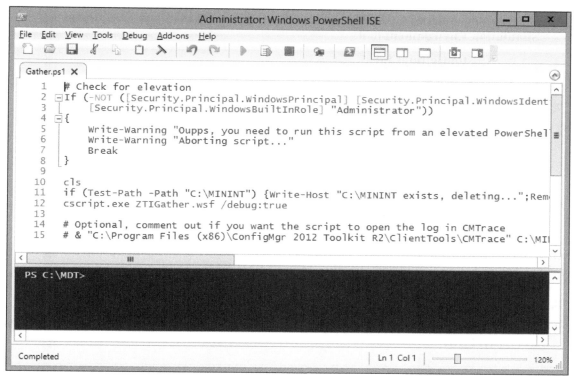

Content of the sample Gather.ps1 script.

Real World Note: A little known fact is that you can use the /inifile: switch to the ZTIGather.wsf script to specify an alternate rules file (.ini file). This is very useful when you are testing multiple configurations.

In this section, we assume you have copied the book sample files and ConfigMgr 2012 Toolkit R2 to C:\Setup on PC0002.

1. On **PC0002**, log on as **VIAMONSTRA\Administrator**.

2. Add the **VIAMONSTRA\CM_NAA** user account to the local **Administrators** group.

3. Log out and log on as **VIAMONSTRA\CM_NAA**.

4. Install **ConfigMgr 2012 Toolkit R2 (ConfigMgrTools.msi)** with the default settings.

5. Using **File Explorer**, navigate to the **C:\Program Files (x86)\ConfigMgr 2012 Toolkit R2\ClientTools** folder, start **CMTrace.exe**, and select **Yes** to make it the default viewer for log files.

6. Create a folder named **C:\MDT**, and copy the following files from **C:\Setup\Rules Simulation Environment** to it:

   o **Customsettings.ini**

   o **Gather.ps1**

7. Copy the following files from **\\CM01\Sources\OSD\MDT\MDT 2013\Scripts** to **C:\MDT**:

   o **ZTIDataAccess.vbs**

   o **ZTIGather.wsf**

   o **ZTIGather.xml**

   o **ZTIUtility.vbs**

Note: If you only installed MDT01 per the instructions in Chapter 5, and didn't complete the guides in Chapter 6, you should copy the files from \\MDT01\MDTProduction$\Scripts instead.

8. In the **C:\MDT** folder, create a subfolder named **x64**.

9. Copy the **\\CM01\Sources\OSD\MDT\MDT 2013\Tools\x64\Microsoft.BDD.Utility.dll** to **C:\MDT\x64**.

Note: Again, if you don't have CM01, you can get the file from \\MDT01\MDTProduction$\Tools\x64.

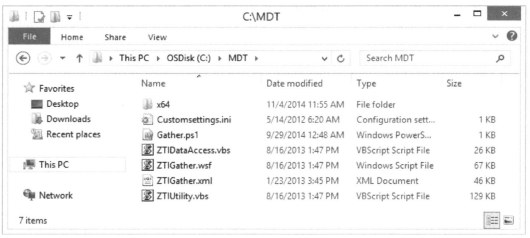

The C:\MDT folder after copying the files.

10. Start an elevated **PowerShell prompt** (run as Administrator), change the working directory to **C:\MDT**, and run the following commands (pressing **Enter** after each):

```
Set-ExecutionPolicy -ExecutionPolicy RemoteSigned -Force
.\Gather.ps1
```

11. Using **CMTrace**, review the **ZTIGather.log** in the **C:\MININT\SMSOSD\OSDLOGS** folder.

12. Review values for the following properties:

- **IPAddress001**
- **MacAddress001**
- **DefaultGateway001**
- **Make**
- **Mode**
- **IsDesktop**
- **VMPlatform**
- **IsOnBattery**

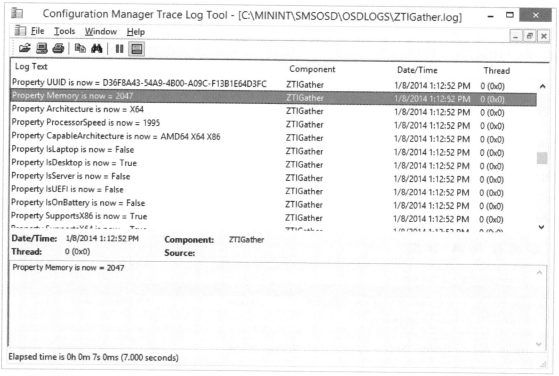

The ZTIGather.log file.

Assigning Settings

In this section, you learn about a few commonly used configurations of the CustomSettings.ini file. The first one is assigning computer names.

Sample #1 – Set Computer Names

Most deployments have a naming standard for computer names. Here is an example that sets the computer name to PC- (prefix) and the serial number.

```
[Settings]
Priority=Default

[Default]
OSDComputerName=PC-%SerialNumber%
```

If you put this example in your CustomSettings.ini file and run the simulation, you see the following (incorrect computer name) in the log file.

ZTIGather.log showing the (incorrect) computer name.

What's the problem here? Well, obviously the computer name is too long. A computer name should have 15 or fewer characters. If you were to run the same simulation on a physical machine (in this example an HP laptop), you would see the following (acceptable) computer name.

ZTIGather.log showing the (acceptable) computer name.

Now, what can you do to make sure the computer name doesn't exceed 15 characters? You can use VBScript functions directly in the CustomSettings.ini file, like this:

```
[Settings]
Priority=Default

[Default]
OSDComputerName=PC-#Right("%SerialNumber%",12)#
```

Now the result is different The preceding change takes the serial number and keeps only the 12 right-most characters, and you have a computer name that is acceptable (and hopefully still unique).

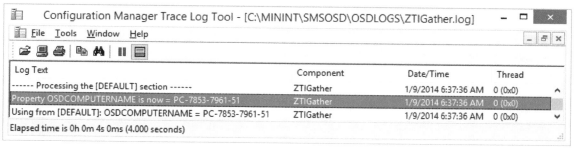

ZTIGather.log displaying the truncated computer name.

Sample #2 – Install Applications in MDT 2013 Lite Touch

Another way to use the CustomSettings.ini file is to assign applications. In MDT 2013 Lite Touch, every application that you add to the deployment workbench get a unique GUID.

In the following figure, you see the properties for the Install - Adobe Reader 11.0 - x86 application you used in Chapter 5. That application has the {04e23691-c504-44a3-96cf-e08bff0c1054} GUID assigned.

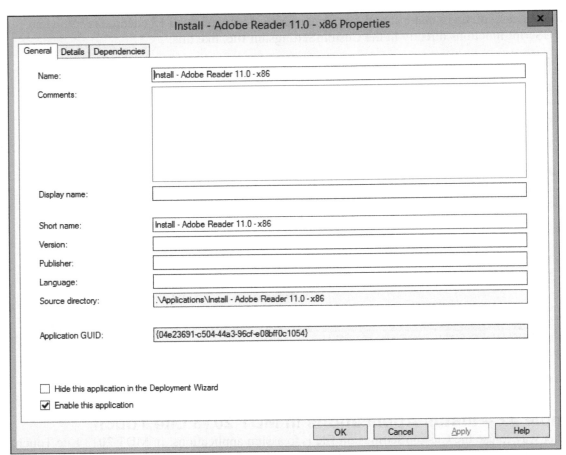

Properties for the Install - Adobe Reader 11.0 - x86 application.

If you want to deploy Adobe Reader by assigning it in the CustomSettings.ini file, you simply set the following:

```
[Settings]
Priority=Default

[Default]
Applications001={04e23691-c504-44a3-96cf-e08bff0c1054}
```

If you want additional applications, you just increase the number (Application002, Application003, and so forth), like this:

```
[Settings]
Priority=Default

[Default]
Applications001={04e23691-c504-44a3-96cf-e08bff0c1054}
Applications002={1f07fa4e-0618-487f-955b-074072b67918}
Applications003={09d25b95-603d-4452-981a-529fd1f7cec0}
```

Sample #3 – Install Applications in ConfigMgr 2012 R2

For ConfigMgr 2012 R2, it's similar to MDT 2013 Lite Touch, but as you learned in Chapter 6, the best way to deploy applications in a task sequence is, in fact, to use packages and not the new application model.

When using packages in ConfigMgr 2012 R2, you need to know the package ID and the program name. In our environment, the Adobe Reader package has a package ID of PS10000E, and the program name is Install. In the CustomSettings.ini file, you put them together, separated by a colon (:), like this:

```
[Settings]
Priority=Default

[Default]
Packages001=PS10000E:Install
```

As in Sample #2, you can have multiple packages:

```
[Settings]
Priority=Default

[Default]
Packages001=PS10000E:Install
Packages002=PS10000F:Install
Packages003=PS10000G:Install
```

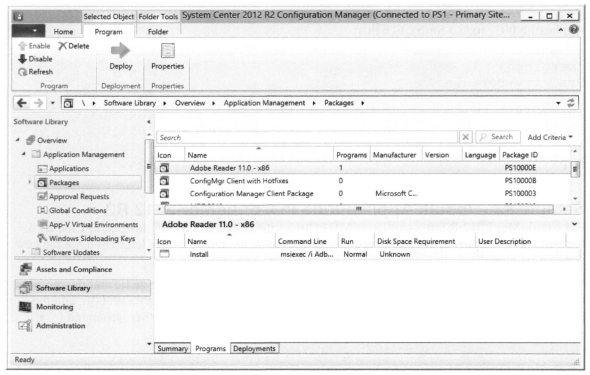

Displaying the package ID and program name for the Adobe Reader package.

Sample #4 – Per Model Settings

Here is an example in which you assign different settings depending on what hardware model you are deploying. The Gather action by default "knows" the model name of your computer, and that means you can do the following in the CustomSettings.ini file:

```
[Settings]
Priority=Model

[HP Elitebook 8540w]
Packages003=PS10000G:Install
```

This example configures the ConfigMgr task sequence to deploy that package, but only if the machine is a HP Elitebook 8540w.

Sample #5 – Per Location Settings

Here is an example in which you assign different settings depending on your machine's location (subnet). The Gather action by default "knows" the default gateway of your computer, and that means you can do the following in the CustomSettings.ini file:

```
[Settings]
Priority=DefaultGateway

[DefaultGateway]
192.168.1.1=New York
192.168.2.1=Stockholm

[New York]
KeyboardLocale=en-US

[Stockholm]
KeyboardLocale=sv-SE
```

This example configures the ConfigMgr task sequence to set the keyboard locale to en-US if the machine is in New York and sv-SE if the machine is in Stockholm.

Sample #6 – Detecting Whether the Machine Is a Virtual Machine

The Gather action also detects whether the machine is a virtual machine and what type of virtual machine it is. And everything that Gather knows, you can use in your rules, like this:

```
[Settings]
Priority=ByVMType

[ByVMType]
Subsection=IsVM-%ISVM%

[IsVM-True]
Packages001=PS100011:Upgrade Hyper-V IS
```

The preceding example installs the Hyper-V Integration Services package if the machine is a virtual machine.

Sample #7 – Laptop, Desktop, or Server

The Gather action also detects whether the machine is a laptop, desktop, or server by querying the chassis type via WMI. You can use this information to assign, for example, different OUs depending on whether the machine is a laptop, desktop, or server:

```
[Settings]
Priority=ByLaptopType, ByDesktopType

[ByLaptopType]
Subsection=Laptop-%IsLaptop%

[ByDesktopType]
Subsection=Desktop-%IsDesktop%

Laptop-True]
MachineObjectOU=ou=laptops,dc=corp,dc=viamonstra,dc=com

[Desktop-True]
MachineObjectOU=ou=desktops,dc=corp,dc=viamonstra,dc=com
```

This example joins a machine to different OUs based on whether it's a laptop or desktop.

Calling UserExit Scripts

If you need to run an external VBScript, for example to set a computer name, you can easily do that via a UserExit. You learn more about creating UserExit script in the next chapter, but here is a short example:

```
[Settings]
Priority=Default

[Default]
OSINSTALL=YES
UserExit=Setname.vbs
```

Calling a SQL Database

In the Gather process, Microsoft also added ready-made routines to read data and call stored procedures from a SQL database. It could be either the free SQL Server Express or a full SQL Server. We think this feature is so important that there is an entire chapter about it, Chapter 10, but here is an example of how to have the Gather action read the ComputerSettings view in a database named MDT (a view is a table as far as MDT is concerned) and retrieve the settings:

```
[Settings]
Priority=CSettings

[CSettings]
SQLServer=CM01
Database=MDT
Netlib=DBNMPNTW
SQLShare=Logs$
Table=ComputerSettings
Parameters=UUID, AssetTag, SerialNumber, MacAddress
ParameterCondition=OR
```

Calling Web Services

The same story holds with web services, as the Gather action knows how to contact a web service. You learn all the gory details about web services in Chapter 11, but here is an example in the CustomSettings.ini file:

```
[Settings]
Priority=Default

[GetOUList]
WebService=http://CM01/SimpleFrontend/ConfigMgr.asmx/GetOUList
```

Chapter 9

MDT Scripting Guidelines

In this chapter, you learn how the MDT scripts are structured, what exists already in the MDT framework, and some more general guidelines that will help you to create your own custom scripts.

In this chapter, you learn the following things about scripting for MDT 2013:

- The structure of MDT scripts
- Using script templates
- Useful classes and objects
- Creating UserExit scripts
- Using the MDT logging engine
- Troubleshooting scripts

Step-by-Step Guide Requirements

If you want to follow the step-by-step guides in this chapter, you need a lab environment configured as outlined in Chapter 3 and Appendix A. In this chapter, you are using the following virtual machines:

DC01

MDT01

PC0001

The VMs used in this chapter.

You also need to have downloaded the following software:

- Notepad++
- The book sample files (http://stealingwithpride.com)

Custom Scripts

MDT comes with a lot of scripts to support your deployment efforts. However, sometimes you need to create a custom script to solve a custom problem. In fact, we highly recommend creating a custom script for almost everything, even if it just executes a small command line. When using a custom script, you can still call functions from the built-in scripts, as that allows you to take advantage of the built-in capabilities with regard to logging, error handling, and existing objects and makes your life easier.

> **Real World Note:** We don't recommend changing the original MDT scripts because all changes might be overwritten when you install a new MDT version. Also Microsoft does not support customized scripts. If you need to make a change to an original MDT script, make a copy first and give it a unique name. In the case of a .wsf file, make sure the class name within the script matches the new file name and then update the steps in the Task Sequence using the original script to use the updated script.

Default Structure

If you need to create a custom scripts, it is best to review how the scripts included with MDT are constructed. The standard MDT script is a .wsf file, written in VBScript, which allows references to be made to functions that are contained in other scripts. Those other scripts are typically VBScript, as well. However, it's technically possible to use other supported scripting languages like JavaScript or JScript.

MDT scripts leverage this functionality by referencing two scripts by default:

- **ZTIUtility.vbs**. Used to initialize the MDT environment and set up classes

- **ZTIDataAccess.vbs**. Includes common database routines, including connecting to and querying databases, and provides a web service interface

We recommend starting with one of the MDT scripts and stripping out the main function code so it can act as a template for all future custom scripts. In the following sections you, find sample templates.

The Pre-MDT 2010 Script Template

With MDT 2010, the MDT team changed the default structure of their scripts, mainly to support some better error handling and ease their internal testing efforts. However, scripts based on this older format are still supported in MDT 2010 and later versions and will work flawlessly. There are even some benefits to creating custom scripts based on this slightly older format. Actually, most of the scripts that are supplied with this book are based on this format.

```
<job id="MDT_Script_Template">
    <script language="VBScript" src="ZTIUtility.vbs"/>
    <script language="VBScript" src="ZTIDataAccess.vbs"/>
    <script language="VBScript">
' //************************************************************
```

```
' // ***** Script Header *****
' //
' // File:       MDT_Script_Template.wsf
' //
' // Purpose:    Template for creating MDT scripts
' //
' // Usage:      cscript MDT_Script_Template.wsf [/debug:true]
' //
' //
' // Customer History:
' //
' //
' // ***** End Header *****
' //****************************************************************

Option Explicit

' //****************************************************************
' //
' // Global constants and variable declarations
' //
' //****************************************************************

Dim iRetVal

' //****************************************************************
' // End declarations
' //****************************************************************


' //****************************************************************
' // Main Routine
' //****************************************************************

On Error Resume Next
iRetVal = ZTIProcess
ProcessResults iRetVal
On Error Goto 0

' //****************************************************************
' // Function: ZTIProcess()
' //
' // Input: None
' //
' // Return: Success - 0
' //         Failure - non-zero
```

175

```
' //
' //Purpose: Perform main ZTI processing
' //
' //***********************************************************
Function ZTIProcess()

    iRetVal = Success

    ZTIProcess = iRetVal

    ' Insert your code here

End Function

    </script>
</job>
```

When you create a script based on this template, your custom code is handled within the function ZTIProcess. All your custom logic should be contained or called from this function. Depending on the success or failure condition of your code, the iRetVal variable should be set appropriately to forward the result properly to MDT and let it act accordingly, such as stopping further execution in case of a failure, ignore, and so forth.

By default, the On Error Resume Next part of the template forces the script to continue even in the case of errors. MDT then evaluates those errors, and logs them properly for further investigation. However, this default error handling might not be appropriate for your script. In that case, you need to add your own error handling and reset the errors before exiting and handing execution back to MDT.

MDT 2010+ Script Template

Since MDT 2010, all versions of MDT use a different template to create the scripts:

```
<job id="MDT_Script_Template">
   <script language="VBScript" src="ZTIUtility.vbs"/>
   <script language="VBScript" src="ZTIDataAccess.vbs"/>
   <script language="VBScript">

' //***********************************************************
' // ***** Script Header *****
' //
' // File:       MDT_Script_Template.wsf
' //
' // Purpose:    Template for creating new MDT 2013 based scripts
' //
' // Usage:      cscript MDT_Script_Template.wsf [/debug:true]
```

```
' //
' //
' // Customer History:
' //
' //
' // ***** End Header *****
' //**************************************************************

Option Explicit
RunNewInstance


' //**************************************************************
' // Global constants
' //**************************************************************



' //**************************************************************
' // End declarations
' //**************************************************************



' //**************************************************************
' // Main Class
' //**************************************************************

Class MDT_Script_Template

    ' //********************************************************
    ' // Class instance variable declarations
    ' //********************************************************

    Dim iRetVal

    ' //********************************************************
    ' // Constructor to initialize needed global objects
    ' //********************************************************

    Private Sub Class_Initialize

        ' Put your initialization code here

    End Sub


    ' //********************************************************
    ' // Main routine
```

```
    ' //**********************************************************

    Function Main

        ' Insert your code here

    End Function

End Class

    </script>
</job>
```

Comparing this template with the Pre-MDT 2010 template, there are a few differences:

- All code to be executed is encapsulated in a class that has the same name as the file. Make sure that the class name always matches the file name exactly.

- The class is not instantiated explicitly in the script itself. During runtime MDT creates a new instance of this class and calls the Class_Initialize function to initialize the class; it then calls the Main function to execute your custom code. Again, MDT does some default logging and error handling during this process.

> **Real World Note:** A common error when dealing with custom scripts based on this updated template is having different names on the file and the class within the file. Also be aware that several characters aren't allowed within class names even if they are allowed characters for file names, like a hyphen (-), for example.

At first view, it seems that there are only some minor, more structural changes. And that's true for most cases. However, there has been one addition to MDT that requires the use of the new template format. And that's when you are running automated or manual tests of your custom scripts that require an additional script to be loaded in advance, such as to set different values or prepare the environment if it's not being called during the deployment process, without any modifications to the original script.

For such cases, MDT allows you to supply the name of the script, internally called TestHook, that contains all the logic that needs to be executed first or might supply additional functions that simulate the deployment environment. We will take a closer look at this in the "Testing Custom Scripts" and "Debugging Custom Scripts" sections later in this chapter.

There is otherwise no general rule about which template to use. Both deliver more or less the same functionality in most use cases. The updated version is bit more structured and brings the mentioned testing capabilities, but at the same time has some limitations like limited characters to use for class names.

Existing Classes and Objects

There are a couple built-in classes and objects that can be used with custom scripts. If your custom scripts are based on the templates shown in the preceding section, the objects detailed in the following sections are available.

From ZTIUtility.vbs

The ZTIUtility.vbs VBScript file is used to initialize the MDT environment and set up classes that can then be used by scripts that reference it. After it has been initialized, the following objects can be used:

- **oFSO**. Standard FileSystemObject used for most folder- and file-related operations, like writing to files, copying folders, and so forth.

- **oShell**. Standard WScript shell object used for running a program locally, modifying the registry, creating shortcuts, or accessing system folders.

- **oEnv**. Process Environment object. We recommend using the MDT extended oEnvironment object.

- **oNetwork**. WScript Network object used to connect to network shares.

- **oEnvironment**. Configures environment variables gathered through WMI and MDT rule processing. Synchronizes the environment variables in the different environments like MDT, ConfigMgr OSD, Process Environment, and so forth. We recommend using this object in favor of oEnv.

- **oLogging**. Provides the logging functionality that all MDT scripts use, creating a single log file for each script, and also consolidates each script log file into a larger main log file, the BDD.LOG file. Custom scripts should reuse these capabilities instead of creating an additional custom logging mechanism.

- **oStrings**. Provides some string-related operations like encoding/decoding base64 strings, working with hex values, handling of lists and arrays that are based on a single string, and so forth.

- **oUtility**. Provides some commonly used utilities that any custom deployment script can use.

From ZTIDataAccess.vbs

The ZTIDataAccess.vbs VBScript file contains the Utility classes that handle additional data access to databases or web services and handling the results.

- **Database**. Provides access to databases. No default object available, so custom instances have to be created in the scripts that define how to access the database. The ZTIGather.wsf script uses this class by default when processing database rules from the CustomSettings.ini or Bootstrap.ini files.

- **WebService**. Provides access to web services. No default object is available, so custom instances have to be created in the custom scripts, defining how to contact the web service. The ZTIGather.wsf script uses this class by default when processing web service rules from the CustomSettings.ini or Bootstrap.ini files.

UserExit Scripts

MDT 2013 supports calling external VBScripts as part of the Gather process; these scripts are referred to as UserExit scripts. This capability allows you to integrate more complex logic into the Gather process without the need of changing the MDT scripts themselves.

Let's imagine you need to generate a computer name based on the MAC address, but have to strip off the colons and add a prefix. As you have seen in Chapter 8, the Gather process is already pretty powerful and handles easy and even slightly more complex scenarios by default. However, a requirement like the one in this scenario is too complex to be covered. Instead of writing an additional custom script based on the MDT template and calling it in a separate step in the task sequence to assign the computer name, we can put the logic in a script using a simpler template, reference it in the CustomSettings.ini, and then simply execute a function from this custom script that does the evaluation and hands the evaluated result back to the Gather process.

Configure the Rules to Call a UserExit Script

You can call a UserExit script by simply referencing the script in your rules. Then you can configure a property to be set to the result of a function of the VBScript. In this example, we have a VBScript named Setname.vbs (provided in the book sample files, in the Userexit folder).

```
[Settings]
Priority=Default

[Default]
OSINSTALL=YES
UserExit=Setname.vbs
OSDComputerName=#SetName("%MACADDRESS%")#
```

The UserExit=Setname.vbs calls the script and then assigns the computer name to what the SetName function in the script returns. As you can see, in this sample, the %MACADDRESS% variable is passed to the script.

The Setname.vbs UserExit Script

The Setname.vbs script takes the MAC address passed from the rules. The script then does some string manipulation to add a prefix (PC) and remove the semicolons from the MAC address.

```
Function UserExit(sType, sWhen, sDetail, bSkip)

  UserExit = Success

End Function
```

```
Function SetName(sMac)

  Dim re

  Set re = new RegExp
  re.IgnoreCase = true
  re.Global = true
  re.Pattern = ":"
  SetName = "PC" & re.Replace(sMac, "")

End Function
```

The first three lines of the script just make up a header that all UserExit scripts have. The interesting part is the lines between Function and End Function. Those lines do the magic of adding a prefix (PC), removing the colons from the MAC address, and returning the value to the rules by setting the SetName value.

Note: The purpose of this sample is not to recommend that you use the MAC address as a base for computer naming, but rather to show you how to take a variable from MDT, pass it to an external script, make some changes to it, and then return the new value to the deployment process.

Using the Logging Engine

While you can test and debug all the scripts pretty easily and well before they are deployed and used during a deployment. A lot of issues often arise if a script is used in production. As this typically happens on a remote machine that you might not have access to, identifying the reason for those issues might become pretty tough and make it even more difficult to solve.

This means that implementing a robust logging mechanism in your scripts is a key component of successful deployment into a production environment. MDT comes with a built-in, reasonably effective, and robust logging engine that you can and should leverage throughout all your scripts.

By default, MDT writes log entries to an individual log file per script and also writes these entries to an additional consolidated log file of all scripts. MDT takes care that those log files are always available throughout the deployment process, as the location of the log files might change depending on the current step in the deployment process.

The log files are created in a log format used by System Center Configuration Manager (ConfigMgr), so each entry contains some additional meta-information like timestamp or severity. ConfigMgr 2012 R2 comes with a tool named CMTrace.exe that makes reading those log files a lot easier than using Notepad. If you don't have ConfigMgr 2012 R2, you also can download CMTrace.exe as part of the ConfigMgr 2012 R2 Toolkit available from the Microsoft Download Center: http://www.microsoft.com/en-us/download/default.aspx.

Log Types

MDT differentiates between four different log types:

- **Informational**. Used to log information about the progress of the current action. Make sure to add enough information to be able to follow the process and identify potential pitfalls. But don't include very detailed information that won't be used in day-to-day operations.

- **Warning**. Used to log warnings that you would like to raise during the progress of the current action. Warnings should be used when something isn't as expected or 100 percent accurate, but won't have any negative effect on the deployment process. Trace32 and CMTrace highlight all warnings in yellow.

- **Error**. Used to log errors that you need to raise during the progress of the current action. An error is something that will cause your current action to fail. Errors don't necessarily force your whole deployment to fail, but they can have a huge negative impact on your current action at least. Trace32 and CMTrace highlight all errors in red, so you can easily spot them in the log.

- **Debug**. Used to log additional debug messages when troubleshooting. By default, MDT does not log any message that is marked as a debug message. However, each script and the whole deployment process can be started to log these additional debug messages. They should then include all necessary information to properly troubleshoot any issue. We recommend making intensive use of debug messages, even if rarely used, because when required, those messages are extremely important.

Create Log Entries

Creating log entries isn't difficult at all. MDT delivers the oLogging object, which you can use in any custom script. This enables you to use the same logging mechanisms in all your custom scripts and let MDT take care of the job for you. To create a log entry, you can use the following syntax:

```
oLogging.CreateEntry "Stealing with Pride is great!", LogTypeInfo

oLogging.CreateEntry "But be careful", LogTypeWarning

oLogging.CreateEntry "In case of an error", LogTypeError

oLogging.CreateEntry "You need some more details.", LogTypeDebug
```

Testing Custom Scripts

Another key element in successfully creating custom scripts is proper testing. As described already in Chapter 8, it's easy to set up an environment to test parts of your deployment process.

You primarily create a new folder that contains all your script files, including the referenced files, and then call the script to verify that it actually does what it's expected to do. But there is one problem: the script is typically written to run during a deployment process, on a completely different system. So, for example, the script might be written to do something while still running on WinPE, or run only under specific circumstances, or act differently depending on what values are gathered at runtime.

To test a custom script properly, you need to be able to simulate the environment in which the script will be executed later. Very often it's enough just to set MDT properties to the specific values that should be the source for most decisions taken in a custom script.

One way to achieve that is to have a specified CustomSettings.ini that sets all required MDT properties to their appropriate values and then run the ZTIGather.wsf script to evaluate it. That can work for some very simple scripts, but will become difficult if you need to have, for example, some hardware-specific settings like the current IP address set.

Another option is to hardcode the properties for testing in your custom script. This isn't a good option, however, because you then have two different versions of your custom scripts, one with and one without the test-code in it that you need to keep in synch.

The preferred option is to have a separate script that actually prepares your environment every time you want to test your custom script. This way you are able to set even hardware-dependent settings like IP address, MAC address, serial number, or other specific values. If your custom script is expected to run differently in different environments, you might even have several scripts so you can test all variations, including the ones that are supposed to fail. All you need to do then is to run the test preparation script just before your custom script.

The TestHook

And MDT has built-in support for environment preparation scenario, if your script is based on the updated MDT2010+ template. Using this template, you can supply a property called TestHook that should contain the path and name of a script that does all the preparation for your custom script to be tested. MDT then makes sure that it's evaluated and executed just before your custom script is executed.

The TestHook capability is typically used only on rather complex scripts that require a lot of conditions or cover several scenarios and each of these scenarios need to be tested using a different set of conditions. However, to understand the process, you use a rather simple script in this section's example.

To be able to use the TestHook features, you need to have three things in place: the custom script, the TextHook script, and the call to execute the script.

The Custom Script

The custom script you are going to test in this example simply creates a computer name based on the current MAC address and adds a prefix based on the type of computer, either a laptop or a desktop. In this guide we assume you have downloaded Notepad++ to C:\Setup on PC0001.

1. On **PC0001**, install **Notepad++** using the default settings.

2. Create a new folder **TestHookTesting** at **C:\Working**.

3. Copy the **MDT2010+ template** (Scripts\MDT_Script_Template.wsf) from the book sample files to **C:\Working\TestHookTesting** and rename it to **ZTIGenerateComputerName.wsf**.

4. Copy the following files from **\\MDT01\MDTProduction$\Scripts** to **C:\Working\TestHookTesting**.

   o **ZTIUtility.vbs**

   o **ZTIDataAccess.vbs**

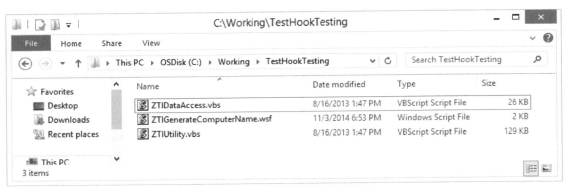

The C:\Working\TestHookTesting folder after copying the files.

5. Using **Notepad++**, edit the **ZTIGenerateComputerName.wsf** file:

   a. Change the **Class** name from **MDT_Script_Template** to **ZTIGenerateComputerName**.

Real World Note: If you don't change the class name, the script fails with a "Class not defined" error. MDT by default tries to create a class that has the same name as the script (minus the file extension).

---

b. Add the following VBScript snippet (copy from Scripts/Snippet.txt) to the **Main** function.

```
' Generate Computer name based on MacAddress
Dim sCN
sCN = oEnvironment.Item("MACAddress")
sCN = Replace(sCN,":","")

' Append Laptop/Desktop specific Prefix
If oEnvironment.Item("IsLaptop") = "TRUE" Then
  sCN = "L" & sCN
Else
  sCN = "D" & sCN
End If

' Update OSDComputerName property
oEnvironment.Item("OSDComputerName") = sCN
```

The TestHook Script

Because the TestHook script is being called from within an existing MDT script that already references at least the ZTIUtility.vbs script file, you have access to all its functionality out of the box.

1. On **PC0001**, using **Notepad++**, create a new file called **TestHook1.vbs** in the **C:\Working\TestHookTesting** folder, and add the following snippet:

```
oFileHandling.RemoveFolder "C:\MININT"

oEnvironment.Item("MacAddress") = "00:11:22:33:44:55"

oEnvironment.Item("IsLaptop") = "TRUE"
```

2. Save your changes.

3. Using **Notepad++**, create another file called **TestHook2.vbs** at **C:\Working\TestHookTesting** and add the following snippet:

```
oEnvironment.Item("MacAddress") = "55:44:33:22:11:00"

oEnvironment.Item("IsLaptop") = "FALSE"
```

4. Save your changes.

Execute the Script

To call an MDT script using the TestHook option, you need to set the TestHook property to the name of the TestHook script. If the script isn't located at the same location, you have to supply the path, as well.

1. On **PC0001**, open a **Command prompt** and change the current directory by executing the following command:

```
cd C:\Working\TestHookTesting
```

2. Execute the script using the first TestHook file by running the following command:

    `cscript ZTIGenerateComputerName.wsf /TestHook:TestHook1.vbs`

3. In the command prompt output, verify that the property **OSDComputerName** has been set to **L001122334455**.

4. Execute the script using the second TestHook file by running the following command:

    `cscript ZTIGenerateComputerName.wsf /TestHook:TestHook2.vbs`

5. In the command prompt output, verify that the property **OSDComputerName** has been changed to **D554433221100**.

Running the TestHook in a command prompt.

Debugging Custom Scripts

You greatly reduce the number of errors that can be introduced into your custom scripts by using already existing and tested functions from MDT, adding extensive logging, and thoroughly testing your custom scripts using methods like the aforementioned TestHook capabilities.

However, as your scripts become more complex and more references are included, it can become quite difficult to figure out why a script doesn't behave as expected. For example, with things like TestHook capabilities that even inject external code/scripts during runtime, one can imagine how difficult it could be to find an error. In addition, a specific error or behavior might show up only under certain conditions that aren't easily reproducible or even known.

That's when being able to debug a custom script really can help you find the issue.

One of the very few, but definitely one of the best products for this task is Microsoft Visual Studio. Debugging custom code written in VB.NET or C#, and even webpages and web applications, is supported even in the Visual Studio Express editions. However, although the exact type of code that can be debugged differs between the various editions of Visual Studio Express, there is one significant limitation. Debugging scripts (VBScript/JavaScript) that are not running within a webpage is not supported!

So, whereas all samples and guides in this book can be followed using Visual Studio Express, you need to use one of the "real" Visual Studio editions to debug a custom script or debug scripts running within a custom HTA page. However, they are all available as a 90-day trials from http://www.visualstudio.com/en-us/downloads. This should give you enough time to properly evaluate the additional functionality.

To follow the rest of this chapter, you need to have a "full" edition of Visual Studio 2013 (Standard, Professional, Premium or Ultimate) installed using the default settings.

Real World Note: If you happen to find an old copy of Visual Studio Express 2005 somewhere in your archives, you also can install and use this version because it is capable of all debugging.

Starting a Debugger

There are typically two ways that the debugger can be started, either directly when starting the script, or on the fly when running specific code in the script.

Start a Script Directly in the Debugger

The benefit of starting a script directly in the debugger is that you can go through the script step by step from the very beginning. In this guide, we assume you have a "full" edition of Visual Studio 2013 (Standard, Professional, Premium or Ultimate) installed on PC0002 using the default settings, and that you have downloaded the book sample files to C:\Setup on PC0002.

1. On **PC0002**, create the **C:\TestDebugging** folder, and then copy the **C:\Setup\Scripts\ZTIGenerateComputerName.wsf** script to it.

2. Copy the following files from **C:\MDT** to **C:\TestDebugging**.

    o   **ZTIUtility.vbs**

    o   **ZTIDataAccess.vbs**

3. Open an elevated **Command prompt** (run as administrator), and set current directory to **C:\TestDebugging**.

4. Start the debugging process by running the following command:

    ```
    cscript.exe //X ZTIGenerateComputerName.wsf
    ```

Note: The //X parameter forces the script to be executed using the debugger.

---

5. Click **Yes** in the **Visual Studio Just-In-Time Debugger**, and then click **Yes** two times more.

The Visual Studio Just-In-Time Debugger dialog box.

6. Press **F10** to continue the execution of the next step in the script.

7. Continue to press **F10** until you reach line **54** showing

    `oUtility.PrepareEnvironment`

8. Press **F11** to continue execution on the next step within the **oUtility.PrepareEnvironment** procedure.

> **Note:** F10 continues execution of the script by stepping over each line/command. F11 steps into a command and enables you to follow the execution even deeper into the script.

9. Press **F10** again to get to line **1516**.

10. Move the cursor over the **oLogging** variable in the line above (1515).

11. In the tooltip that appears, move the cursor over the left arrow to see the contents of the variables, which is very useful for debugging.

12. Stop the debugging by pressing **Shift-F5**.

```
1509        ' *** Public methods ***
1510
1511        Public Sub PrepareEnvironment
1512
1513            Dim sArg
1514
1515            Set oLogging = New Logging
1516   ⇨        Set oEnviron ◢ ⊘ oLogging [...] ⊞ ent
1517            Set oStrings =  ▷ ⊙ [Methods]
1518            Set oFileHandli         ⊘ Component      Q ▾ "ZTIGenerateComputerName"
1519                                    ⊘ Debug                 False
1520            set Arguments =         ⊘ LogFile        Q ▾ "ZTIGenerateComputerName.log"
1521                                    ⊘ LogPath               Object required
1522                                    ⊘ MasterLogFile  Q ▾ "BDD.log"
1523            ' Loop through         ⊘ NetworkLogging Q ▾ ""              t variables.  Enforce debug values.
1524
1525            On Error Resume Next
1526
1527            For each sArg in Arguments
1528                If UCase(sArg) = "DEBUG" then
1529                    If UCase(Arguments(sArg)) = "TRUE" or UCase(Arguments(sArg)) = "FALSE" then
1530                        oLogging.CreateEntry "'debug' parameter was specified.", LogTypeInfo
```

The content of variables available at runtime.

Active Debugging

Instead of having the debugger throw an exception directly, it's also possible to have the debugger start when a specifc part of your code is reached. This is especially helpful when the raw "area" of the error is already known or when extending the script in very small steps, which require you to execute a script often. However, the downside is that it requires a change in the script itself.

1. On **PC0002**, using **Visual Studio 2013**, open the **ZTIGenerateComputerName.wsf** script.

2. At line **66**, add the word **STOP** in a separate line as show in this snippet and save the changes:

```
...
sCN = Replace(sCN,":","")

STOP

' Append Laptop/Desktop specific Prefix
If oEnvironment.Item("IsLaptop") = "TRUE" Then
...
```

3. Open a command prompt using **Run as Administrator**.

4. Change the current directory to **C:\TestDebugging**.

5. Run the script with active debugging by running the following command:

```
cscript.exe //D ZTIGenerateComputerName.wsf
```

> **Note:** Adding the word STOP at any place within a VBScript stops execution of the script and forces the debugger to start. If debugging JavaScript files, you need to use the word DEBUGGER instead.

Debugging HTA pages

If you want to debug scripts within HTA pages, you need to configure Internet Explorer to allow debugging since that is disabled by default.

> On **PC0002**, configure **Internet Explorer** to allow script debugging, by open **Internet Options** and clear the two **Disable script debugging** check boxes.

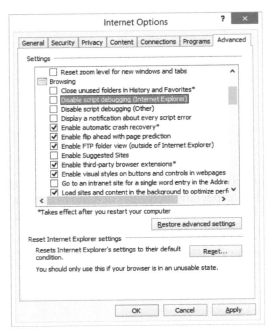

Enabling script debugging in Internet Explorer.

Real World Note: Don't forget to disable script debugging after testing/debugging has been completed. Otherwise scripts errors on any web page will raise a dialog asking if the error shall be debugged.

Debugging Task Sequence Actions

When troubleshooting task sequences in ConfigMgr, there is a trick you can use to run the action or script, over and over again, until you get your code right. The trick is to use the ServiceUI.exe file from MDT to start a command prompt that runs in the context of the task sequence.

This means that when you are developing custom scripts for ConfigMgr 2012, you can save a lot of time by having a test environment that allows you to interact with the task sequence while logged in to the full Windows operating system. As you probably know, the task sequence suppresses interaction by default, but this is where the trick of using ServiceUI.exe comes in handy.

Simply add this command where you want to debug scripts or other components in the task sequence:

```
"%deployroot%\tools\%architecture%\ServiceUI.exe"
-process:TSProgressUI.exe C:\Windows\System32\cmd.exe
```

In this example, we added the ServiceUI action directly after the Gather action in the Initialization phase. The ServiceUI action has to be run after the Use Toolkit Package and Gather actions because they contain the files and settings needed.

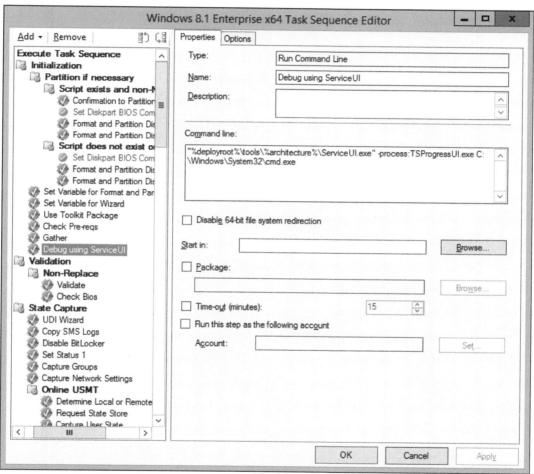

Adding the Debug using ServiceUI action.

191

Chapter 10

Using the MDT Database

The MDT database allows you to prestage information on your deployment in either the SQL Server 2012 SP1 Express database you installed on MDT01, or the full SQL Server 2012 SP1 standard database you installed on CM01, rather than have all the information in a text file (CustomSettings.ini). In this chapter, you learn about following configurations:

- Setting up and using the MDT database

- Configuring database permissions

- Extending the MDT database tables

- Adding stored procedures to the MDT database

Step-by-Step Guide Requirements

If you want to run the step-by-step guides exactly as they are written in this chapter, you need a lab environment configured as outlined in Chapter 3 and Appendix A. In this chapter, you use the following virtual machines:

DC01   CM01   PC0002

The VMs used in this chapter.

> **Note:** In this chapter, you use CM01 as the SQL Server for the MDT database, but all the information in this chapter is the same for both MDT 2013 Lite Touch (MDT01) and for ConfigMgr 2012 R2 (CM01). This means that if you didn't set up CM01 in Chapter 6, you can use MDT01 for all the guides in this chapter, as well. Just change CM01 to MDT01, and the database instance from CM01 to MDT01\SQLEXPRESS.

As an example of MDT database use, you can add all clients you want to deploy, specify their computer names, IP addresses, applications to be deployed, and all other sorts of settings for the machines.

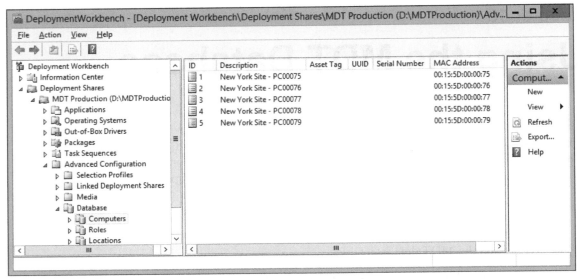

The Computers node in the MDT database, showing a few clients.

Setting Up the MDT Database

Even if you are new to SQL Server, getting the MDT database up and running is quite easy. There are basically three things you need to do:

- Verify that you meet the prerequisites
- Create the MDT deployment share
- Create the MDT database using the Deployment Workbench
- Configure permissions using SQL Server Management Studio

Database Prerequisites

No matter whether you use SQL Server Express or full SQL Server Standard, you need to have Named Pipes enabled. The hydration kit enabled Named Pipes as part of the deployment of MDT01 and CM01. You might wonder why we enable such a legacy protocol. The answer is that Named Pipes simply works best for connecting from WinPE to the SQL database.

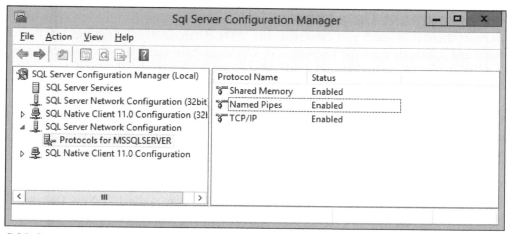

SQL Server Configuration Manager showing that Named Pipes is enabled.

Create the MDT Deployment Share

In these steps, you create a deployment share in the D:\MDTProduction folder on CM01. This deployment share is used to create the MDT database and manage the content.

1. On **CM01**, using the **Deployment Workbench**, right-click **Deployment Shares** and select **New Deployment Share**.

2. Use the following settings for the **New Deployment Share Wizard**:

    a. Path

        Deployment share path: **D:\MDTProduction**

    b. Share

        Share name: **MDTProduction$**

    c. Descriptive Name

        Deployment share description: **MDT Production**

    d. Options

        <default>

Create the Deployment Database

After the deployment share is created, you can create the MDT database. By default the MDT database is created and managed from the Deployment Workbench. In these steps, we assume you have installed CM01 as part of the hydration kit provided in the book sample files (and described in Appendix A).

Real World Note: If you want to use custom properties, you can extend the database, which is fully supported. Information on how to extend the MDT database is found in the "Extending the MDT Database" section later in this chapter.

1. On **CM01**, using **Deployment Workbench**, expand the **MDT Production** deployment share, expand **Advanced Configuration**, right-click **Database**, and select **New Database**.

2. In the **New DB Wizard**, on the **SQL Server Details** page, enter the following settings and click **Next**:
   - SQL Server Name: **CM01**
   - Instance: **<blank>**
   - Port: **<blank>**
   - Network Library: **Named Pipes**

3. On the **Database** page, select **Create a new database**; in the **Database** field, type **MDT** and click **Next**.

4. On the **SQL Share** page, in the **SQL Share** field, type **Logs$** and click **Next**. Click **Next** again and then click **Finish**.

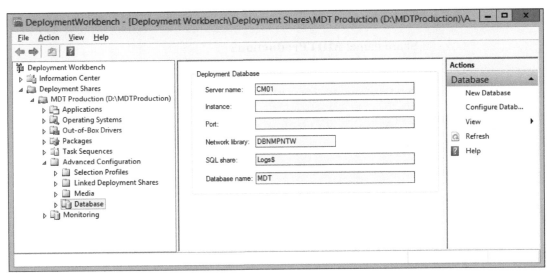

The MDT database created on CM01.

Configure Database Permissions

After creating the database, you need to assign permissions to it. In ConfigMgr, the network access account is used to access the database. In this environment, the network access account is VIAMONSTRA\CM-NAA.

1. On **CM01**, start **SQL Server Management Studio**.

2. In the **Connect to Server** dialog box, in the **Server name** list, select **CM01** and click **Connect**.

Connecting to the CM01 server in SQL Server Management Studio.

3. In the **Object Explorer** pane, expand the top-level **Security** node, right-click **Logins**, and select **New Login**.

4. On the **Login – New** page, in the **Login name** field, type **VIAMONSTRA\CM_NAA**. Then in the left pane, select **User Mapping**. Select the **MDT** database and assign the following roles:

   o **db_datareader**

   o **db_datawriter**

   o **public** (default)

5. Click **OK**, and close **SQL Server Management Studio**.

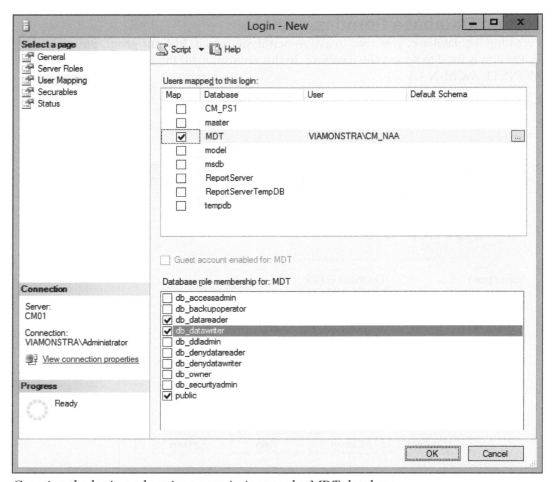

Creating the login and settings permissions to the MDT database.

Create Database Entries Manually

To start using the database, you add a computer entry and assign a description and computer name. In this section you use Deployment Workbench to add a computer to the database, in the next section you learn to do it in PowerShell.

Anyway, when adding a computer to the database you need to have an identifier. The MDT database supports for identifiers by default: Asset Tag, UUID, Serial Number, and MAC Address. The two most commonly used ones are Serial Number and MAC Address, and in this example, you use the computer's MAC Address.

1.   On **CM01**, using the **Deployment Workbench**, in the **MDT Production** deployment share, expand **Advanced Configuration**, and expand **Database**.

2. Right-click **Computers**, select **New**, and add a computer entry with the following settings:

    a. Identity tab

        ▪ Description: **New York Site - PC00075**

        ▪ MAC address: **00:15:5D:00:00:75**

    b. Details tab

        OSDComputerName: **PC00075**

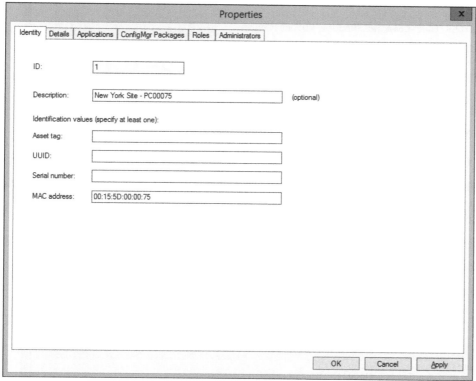

Adding the PC00075 computer to the database.

Create Database Entries Automatically

As fun as clicking through a UI is, automating the task via PowerShell is much more fun! In this section, you use a free PowerShell module developed by Michael Niehaus to create entries in the database. You learn to add individual entries and also to import entries from a comma-separated text file.

Real World Note: Michael Niehaus graciously allowed us to add his PowerShell module to the book sample files. For additional documentation, check Michael's blog: http://blogs.technet.com/b/mniehaus (search for "PowerShell" and you should find it).

The MDTDB PowerShell module contains 72 cmdlets to manage the MDT database.

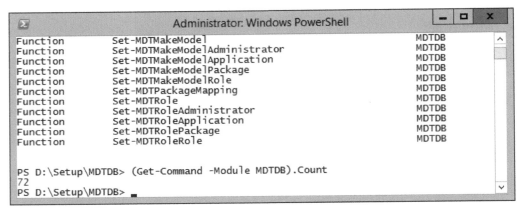

Finding out the number of cmdlets in a module.

Add a Single Computer to the MDT Database Using PowerShell

In this section, you use the New-MDTComputer cmdlet to create a new computer entry in the MDT database. In this example, we assume you downloaded and extracted the book sample files to D:\Setup on CM01.

1. On **CM01**, in an elevated (run as Administrator) **PowerShell** command prompt, run the following commands to import the MDT DB module (pressing **Enter** after each command):

   ```
   Set-Location 'D:\Setup\MDTDB'

   Import-Module .\MDTDB.psm1
   ```

2. Connect to the MDT database on CM01 using the following command:

   ```
   Connect-MDTDatabase -sqlServer CM01 -database MDT
   ```

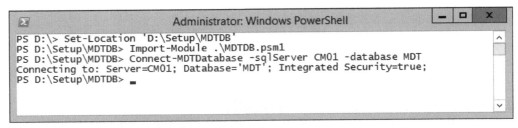

Connecting to the MDT database.

3. Create the computer entry by running the following command:

   ```
   New-MDTComputer -macAddress '00:15:5D:00:00:76'
   -description 'New York Site - PC00076'
   -settings @{OSDComputerName='PC00076'}
   ```

4. Using **Deployment Workbench**, review the new computer entries created by expanding the **Database** node and selecting **Computers**.

Real World Note: If you already had Deployment Workbench opened, you don't see entries created from outside of it until you click the Database node, press F5 to refresh, and go back to the node in which you were trying to find the entries.

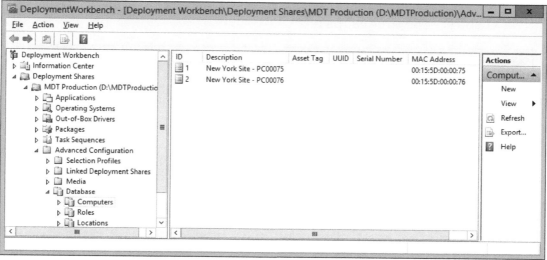

Deployment Workbench after adding the two computer entries.

Add Multiple Computers to the MDT Database Using PowerShell

In this section, you use the Import-Csv cmdlet and a comma-separated file to create a few new computer entries in the MDT database. The following figure shows a sample file holding the computers to import.

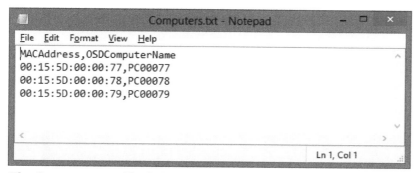

The Computers.txt file, holding the computers to import.

The script that drives the import is named Import-Computers.ps1. That script, as well as the Computers.txt file, is part of the book sample files.

1. On **CM01**, in an elevated (run as Administrator) **PowerShell** command prompt, run the following command:

```
Set-Location 'D:\Setup\Scripts'
```

2. Import the computers by running the following command:

```
.\Import-Computers.ps1
```

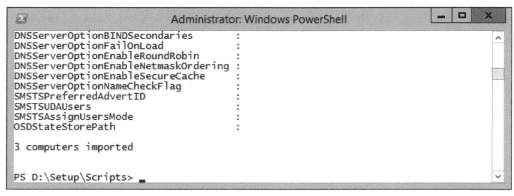

The computers imported.

3. Using **Deployment Workbench**, review the new computer entries created by expanding the **Database** node and selecting **Computers**.

Note: Again, since you updated records outside of the Deployment Workbench, you need to click the Database node, press F5 to refresh, and then go back to the Computers node.

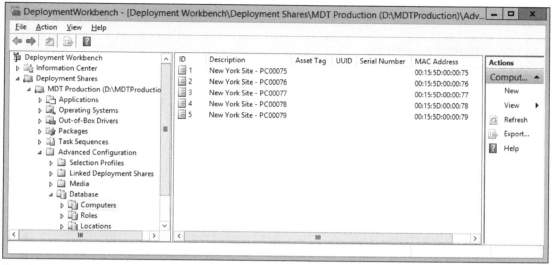

Deployment Workbench listing the imported computers.

Assigning Packages Using Roles

In addition to using computer-specific entries in the database, you can use roles to group settings together. In this section, you learn to add ConfigMgr packages to a role in the database and then assign the role to a computer.

Create and Assign a Role Entry in the Database

As when you reviewed the CustomSettings.ini samples in Chapter 8, you need to know the package ID and program name when adding packages for ConfigMgr. In the following sample, our packages had these settings:

- 7-Zip 9.20 - x64
    - PackageID = PS10000F
    - Program Name = Install
- Adobe Reader 11.0 - x86
    - PackageID = PS10000E
    - Program Name = Install

The preceding settings are used when you configure the role. In addition to these settings, you also need to find the MAC address on PC0002. An easy way to get the MAC address is to use PowerShell.

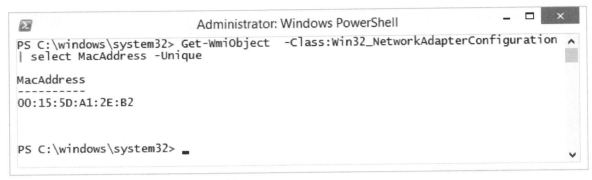

Using PowerShell to get the MAC address.

1. On **PC0002**, in an elevated **PowerShell** prompt, run the following command and make a note of the MAC address. (In our example, it was 00:15:5D:A1:2E:B2.)

   ```
   Get-WmiObject -Class:Win32_NetworkAdapterConfiguration |
   select MacAddress -Unique
   ```

2. On **CM01**, using **Deployment Workbench**, in the **MDT Production** deployment share, expand **Advanced Configuration** and then expand **Database**.

3. In the **Database** node, right-click **Computers**, select **New**, and add a computer entry with the following settings:

   a. Identity tab:

      - Description: **New York Site - PC0002**
      - MAC address: **00:15:5D:A1:2E:B2**

   b. Details tab:

      OSDComputerName: **PC0002**

Note: Use the real MAC address of your PC0002.

---

4. In the **Database** node, right-click **Roles**, select **New**, and create a role entry with the following settings:

5. Identity tab:

   a. Identity tab:

      - Role name: **Standard PC**

   b. ConfigMgr Packages tab: Add the following packages:

      - **PS10000F:Install**
      - **PS10000E:Install**

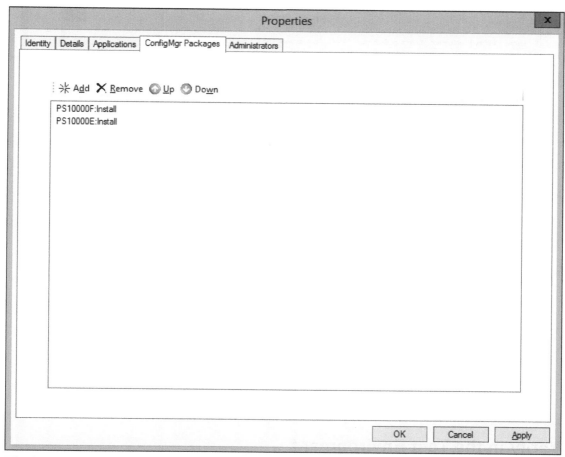

The Standard PC role with the ConfigMgr packages added.

Associate the Role with a Computer in the Database

After creating the role, you can associate it with one or more computer entries:

1. Using **Deployment Workbench**, expand **MDT Production**, expand **Advanced Configuration**, expand **Database**, and select **Computers**.

2. In the **Computers** node, double-click the **PC0002** entry, and add the following setting:

   Roles tab:

   Roles: **Standard PC**

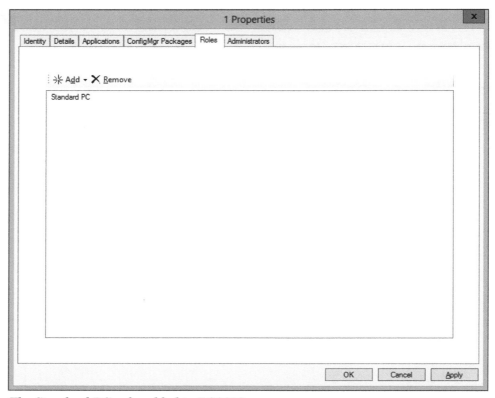

The Standard PC role added to PC0002.

Verify in the Test Environment

When the database is populated, you can use the test environment to simulate a deployment. The applications are not installed, but you can see which applications would be installed if you did a full deployment of the computer. In these steps, we assume you have copied the book sample files to C:\Setup on PC0002.

1. On **PC0002**, log on as **VIAMONSTRA\CM_NAA**.

2. Copy the **CustomSettings.ini** file from **C:\Setup\Database** to the **C:\MDT** folder (replacing the existing file).

3. Start an elevated **PowerShell prompt** (run as Administrator), navigate to the **C:\MDT** folder, and then execute the **Gather.ps1** script.

4. In the **C:\MININT\SMSOSD\OSDLOGS\ZTIGather.log** file, verify that the ConfigMgr packages are being assigned.

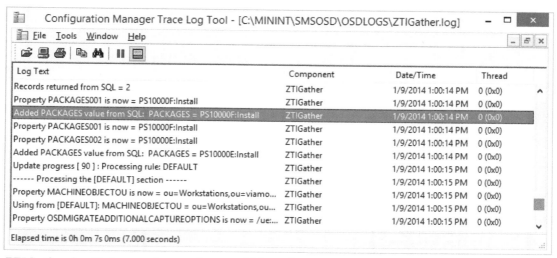

ZTIGather.log listing packages that would have been installed if you deployed this machine.

Generating Computer Names

When using the MDT database, you can create additional logic for settings in the database and then call this logic from the rules. In this section, you create a stored procedure and a table to generate computer names in MDT based on the prefix and a sequence number.

The procedure works like this: If the computer name is in the database (known computer), it will assign that name to the PC. If the computer is not in the database (unknown computer), it will generate a computer name based on the prefix and the next sequence number. A table (MachineNameSequence) in the database is used to keep track of computer names handed out already.

Create a Stored Procedure

In the book sample files, you find the stored procedure used for the automatic computer name generation. You also find two scripts that will create the stored procedure in the database, as well as the table used to track computer names. You also configure permissions in the database. In this example, we assume you have copied the book sample files to D:\Setup on CM01.

1. On **CM01**, using **SQL Server Management Studio**, open the **D:\Setup\ \Generate Computer Names\InsertComputerNames.sql** script and execute it by pressing **F5**.

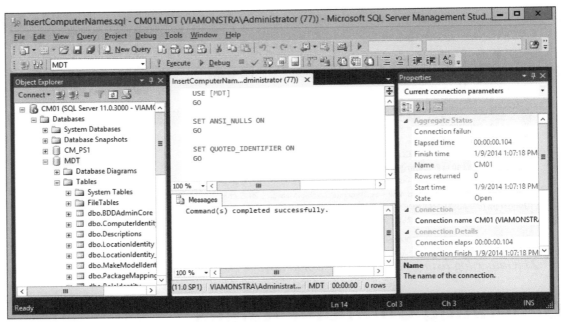

Running the InsertComputerNames.sql script.

2. In the left pane (Object Explorer), expand **Databases**, expand **MDT**, expand **Programmability**, and expand **Stored Procedures**.

Note: If you don't see the Object Explorer pane, you can enable it again by pressing F8, selecting Connect, selecting Database Engine, and then clicking OK.

3. Right-click the **dbo.InsertComputerName** stored procedure and select **Properties**.

4. In the **Stored Procedure Properties – InsertComputerName** window, in the left pane, select **Permissions**. In the right pane, click **Search**, click **Browse**, select **VIAMONSTRA\CM_NAA**, and click **OK** twice.

5. In the right pane, select the **Execute** check box in the **Grant** column, and click **OK**.

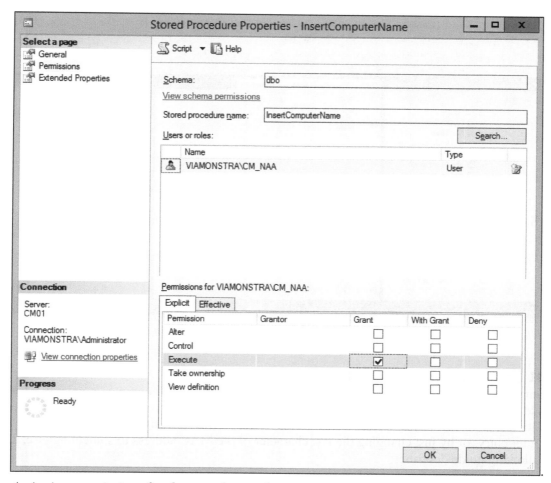

Assigning permissions for the stored procedure.

6. Using **SQL Server Management Studio**, open the **D:\Setup\Generate Computer Names\MachineName.sql** script and execute it (press F5).

7. In the left pane (Object Explorer), in the **MDT** database, expand **Tables**.

8. Right-click the **dbo.MachineNameSequence** table and select **Edit Top 200 Rows**.

9. In the **Prefix** field, type **PC**, and in the **Sequence** field, type **80**. Then press **Enter** to insert the record into the database. The number 80 is our starting point, so the first computer will have the name of 80, the next computer will then have a number of 81, and so forth.

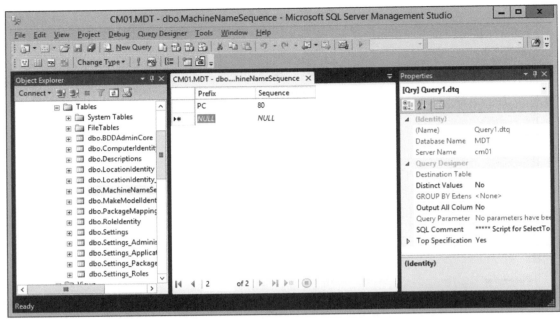

The MachineNameSequence table with the prefix and sequence added.

Test the Stored Procedure

Remember that the stored procedure generates a name only when the computer is unknown (i.e. not added to the database already), and earlier in the chapter, you did add the PC0002 machine to the database. This means that you first need to make PC0002 unknown, either by deleting the computer entry, or by just changing the last character of the MAC address to something else, as the following guide describes:

1. On **CM01**, in the **Deployment Workbench**, double-click the **PC0002** computer entry, and change the last character of the MAC address to something else. In our example, we changed the MAC address from 00:15:5D:A1:2E:B**2** to 00:15:5D:A1:2E:B**3**.

2. On **PC0002**, log on as **VIAMONSTRA\CM_NAA**.

3. Copy the **CustomSettings.ini** file from **C:\Setup\Generate Computer Names** to the **C:\MDT** folder (replacing the existing file).

4. Start an elevated **PowerShell prompt** (run as Administrator), navigate to the **C:\MDT** folder, and then execute the **Gather.ps1** script.

5. Review the **ZTIGather.log** in the **C:\MININT\SMSOSD\OSDLOGS** folder. Note the generated PC00081 computer name.

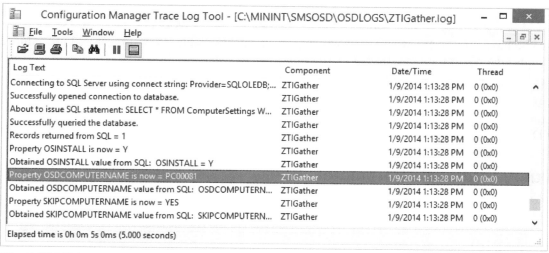

The PC00081 computer name generated by the stored procedure.

6. On **MDT01**, in the **Deployment Workbench**, select the **Database / Computers** node, and note that no new machines are listed. To refresh the view, you need to click the **Database** node, press **F5**, and then select the **Computers** node again.

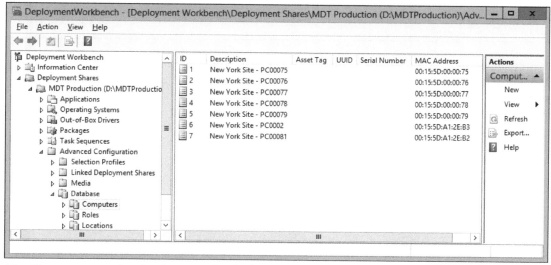

The Computers node after being refreshed, showing the inserted PC00081 computer.

Querying All Entries from a Table or View

As you have seen so far, it's pretty easy to query a database table, view, or a stored procedure and then use the result for some further processing.

This works fine as long as you use at least one parameter in the definition that limits the query. If you skip the parameters property in a database section or the property is empty, it normally would return all entries of the table or view. However, as this is typically not the expected behavior, MDT 2013 takes care of this and makes sure that no entry at all is returned instead of all entries.

Query Without a Parameter

To see the built-in behavior, use the following settings snippet and let it run in your Rules Simulation environment as described in Chapter 8:

```
[Settings]
Priority=Locations

[Locations]
SQLServer=CM01
Database=MDT
Netlib=DBNMPNTW
SQLShare=Logs$
Table=Locations
```

Now, evaluate the ZTIGather.log, and you can see that MDT automatically updated the query statement with a dummy clause of WHERE 0=1. Because 0=1 can never be true, no record is returned.

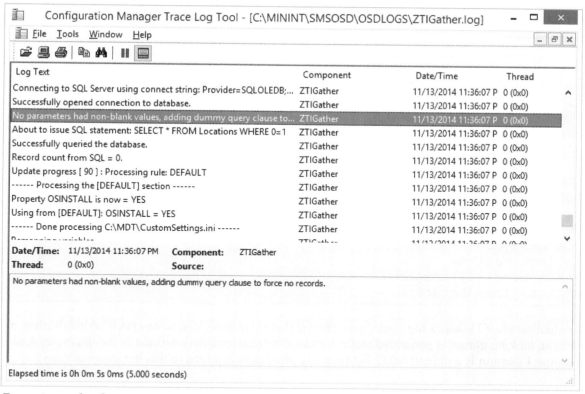

Executing a database query without a parameter.

By default, this behavior is helpful in most scenarios. However, imagine querying a database with tens of thousands of entries. Besides taking quite some time to fetch and process them, because MDT uses the first value for a certain property, it would always be set by the first record being returned, which most likely isn't the expected one.

However, in certain scenarios, it might be helpful to return a list of entries. One of those scenarios is covered later in this book in Chapter 12. There you will create a custom MDT 2013 Lite Touch Wizard pane that allows you to select from a list of locations. By default, this list is hardcoded in the CustomSettings.ini file. But being able to directly query the list of available locations from the MDT database would make this just a bit more useful.

Override the Default Behavior

To override this default behavior in certain cases, you can make use of a hacking technique called SQL injection. Don't worry. It won't cause any damage, and you are very likely to get out of jail in less than a year.

As before, use the following settings snippet and let it run again in your Rules Simulation environment:

```
[Settings]
Priority=Init,Locations
Properties=AllLocations

[Init]
AllLocations=' OR 1='1

[Locations]
SQLServer=CM01
Database=MDT
Netlib=DBNMPNTW
SQLShare=Logs$
Table=Locations
Parameters=AllLocations
AllLocations=Location
```

Evaluating the ZTIGather.log again, you can see that no dummy clause has been added. Rather, a strange looking clause is generated that returns a list of all locations defined in the database. And because Location is a default MDT list property, the result is added to this list automatically.

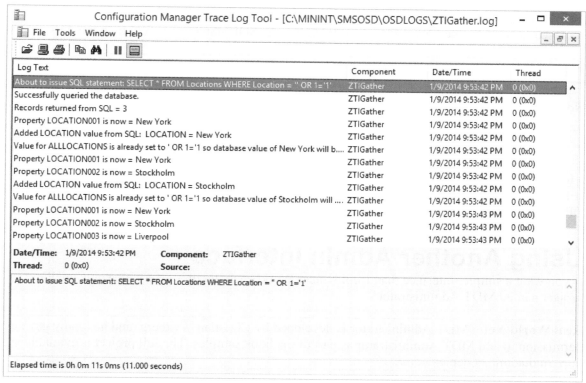

Executing database query using a modified parameter.

Reveal the Trick

The trick to change the behavior is actually quite simple.

You first define a custom property and set the value of this property to a specific string:

```
AllLocations=' OR 1='1
```

Then you configure the settings to use one of the columns in the table as a parameter, so it's used to create a clause for which to filter and lets it use the custom property as the value for which to filter. Because in MDT everything has to be configured Yoda style, the parameter definition looks like this:

```
Parameters=AllLocations
AllLocations=Location
```

The Gather process now uses this information to generate a SQL statement with the filter value enclosed in single quotes. So, without a filter value, the SQL statement would look like this:

```
SELECT * FROM Locations WHERE Location = ''
```

Now, by using this strange looking string, it turns into

```
SELECT * FROM Locations WHERE Location = '' OR 1='1
```

which translates into something like "Give me all locations, where the value of the Location column is empty or 1 equals 1," which will always be true as 1 is always 1, and using a Boolean OR, the expression is true as soon one element is true.

Using Another Admin Interface

If you want a simpler interface than Deployment Workbench, there is a very elegant CodePlex project named MDT Administrator.

Real World Note: MDT Administrator is developed by Christian Wistberg, and he kindly gave us permission to add MDT Administrator as part of the book samples. The full project is available at http://mdtadmin.codeplex.com/.

Set Up MDT Administrator

In these steps, you start the MDT Administrator and connect it to the MDT database:

1. On **CM01**, in the **D:\Setup\MDTAdmin** folder, start the **MDT Administrator.exe** file.
2. In the **One time nag** window, read the text and then click **OK**.
3. In **MDT Administrator**, in the left-hand corner, click **Connect**.
4. In the **Server configuration** window, type **CM01** and click **OK**.
5. In the **Database configuration** window, type **MDT** and click **OK**. You should now see the content of the MDT database.

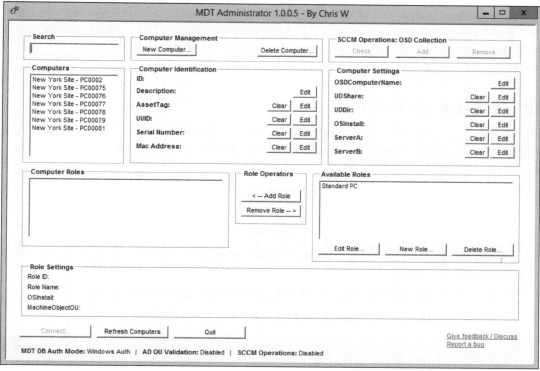

The MDT Administrator in action.

Use MDT Administrator

In these steps, you create a new computer and connect the Standard PC role to it:

1. On **CM01**, using **MDT Administrator**, in the **Computer Management** area, click **New Computer**.

2. In the **Enter Description** window, type in **New York Site – PC00054** and click **OK**.

    Note that the new PC is selected in the Computers list automatically.

3. In the **Available Roles** list, select the **Standard PC** role, and click **<- Add Role**.

Done, you have now you created a new computer and connected the Standard PC role to it.

Extending the MDT Database

Sometimes the existing fields in the database are just not enough. Luckily, the MDT database supports adding new fields to the tables. Please note, though, that if you do modify a table, you may have to update views that depend on that table.

Extending the MDT database is a straightforward process. Just make sure you have a good backup of the database before you begin.

> **Real World Note:** Configuring SQL backups are outside the scope of this book, but you can find a great post by Steve Thompson at this URL: http://tinyurl.com/ConfigMgrBackup. The post is actually for configuring a ConfigMgr backup, but you use the exact same process for the MDT database.

Edit the Settings Table

In this section, you add two new fields (ViaMonstraDepartment and ViaMonstraManager) to the Settings table. The Settings table holds all the computer settings that you added earlier in this chapter.

1. On **CM01**, using **SQL Server Management Studio**, in the left pane (Object Explorer), in the **MDT** database, expand **Tables**.

2. Right-click the **dbo.Settings** table and select **Design**.

3. In the middle pane, in the **Column Name** column, go all the way to the end, and add the following two fields:

    o   ViaMonstraDepartment, nvarchar(50), allow null values

    o   ViaMonstraManager, nvarchar(50), allow null values

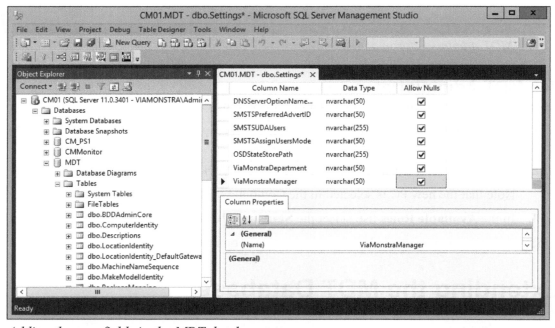

Adding the new fields in the MDT database.

4. On the ribbon, click **Save Settings** (Ctrl +S).

5. Using **Deployment Workbench**, in the **Database / Computers** node, double-click the **New York Site - PC00075** entry and click the **Details** tab.

6.   Scroll down to the bottom, and you should now see the fields.

The Details tab displaying the new fields that you added.

Update the ComputerSettings View

The ComputerSettings view, which you query from the CustomSettings.ini file to get settings for computers, does not yet "know" that you added those fields and needs to be updated.

1.   Using **SQL Server Management Studio**, click **New Query** on the ribbon.

2.   Switch to the **MDT database** by typing the following command and pressing **F5**:

```
Use MDT
```

3.   Confirm that the view is not yet updated by running the following command and pressing F5. (To run a single line in SQL Server Management Studio, simply select the line and press F5.)

```
Select ViaMonstraDepartment from ComputerSettings
```

4.   You should get an error back, saying "Invalid column name...."

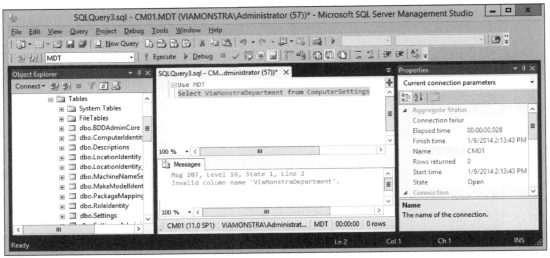

Trying to list a column that doesn't exist in the view (yet).

5. Update the ComputerSettings view by running the follow command and pressing F5:

```
Execute sp_refreshview ComputerSettings
```

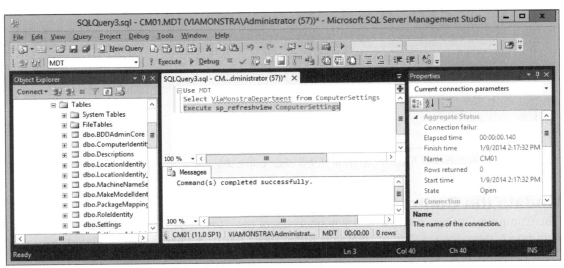

Updating the ComputerSettings view.

6. Confirm that the view is now updated by running the follow command and pressing F5:

```
Select ViaMonstraDepartment from ComputerSettings
```

7. The view should now have the ViaMonstraDepartment column.

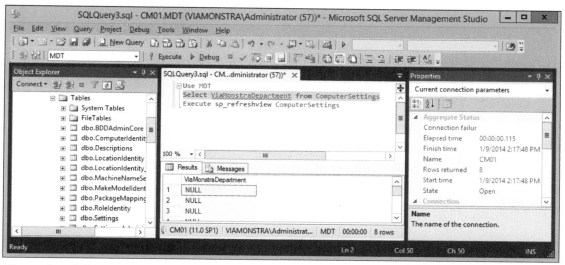

The updated ComputerSettings view.

Chapter 11

Using Web Services

Another powerful way to extend and further customize a deployment is to use web services. The best way to think about web services is to see them as similar to a webpage, meaning you can simply browse to its URL and perform its function. Some web services are just executed by loading the webpage, whereas others display a form allowing you to input parameters used by the web service. The difference is that a webpage is primarily targeted for humans, whereas a web service is primarily targeted for applications or any other piece of software.

Web services act a mediating instance between the computer being deployed and other systems that need to support this process with further information or action. For example, web services can be used to supply additional information about what specific settings to apply or what additional applications to install, or you can use them to execute an action in Active Directory, like moving a computer account.

Throughout this chapter, you learn how web services work in general, set up a free deployment-related web service that is used in several examples in the book, and, finally, create two custom web services using Visual Studio Express 2013 for Windows.

Step-by-Step Guide Requirements

If you want to run the step-by-step guides exactly as they are written in this chapter, you need a lab environment configured as outlined in Chapter 3 and Appendix A. In this chapter, you use the following virtual machines:

DC01   CM01   PC0001

The VMs used in this chapter.

You also need to have downloaded the following software:

- Visual Studio Express 2013 for Web

- The book sample files (http://stealingwithpride.com)

223

How Web Services Work

Web services are based on some common web standards. Communication typically happens via HTTP, the same protocol you use to browse the internet. This has the huge benefit of working fine even through firewalls and proxies, which is not the case with most other communication protocols.

Web services are platform-independent and (programming) language-independent. We don't need to care about what language has been used to create the web service or what platform it's running on. A web service can be used as kind of mediator between a system on the backend and the client that requires information or certain action to be executed by the system.

The information exchanged is typically based on XML or JSON (JavaScript Object Notation), depending on the web service's primary use. Both are text-based and at least human-readable, even if they are not supposed to be read by humans.

If comparing XML to JSON, XML is often seen as very bloated because the size of the same information in XML is considerably larger compared to JSON. But XML comes with a lot of accompanying information about the data transferred, which can be very useful. That information is more helpful the more unstructured or unknown the data are.

From the perspective of MDT, XML-based web services are typically easier to consume because VBScript comes with a lot of built-in functionality for XML support, but lacks any JSON support by default.

The Deployment Web Service

There are a couple deployment-related web services publicly available. One of the most popular ones is the "Deployment Web Service," and it's available for free on CodePlex. The version included in the book sample files is version 7.3.

Introducing the Deployment Web Service

The Deployment Web Service contains more than 150 functions, and they are divided into four main categories:

- Access to the MDT database
- Access to ConfigMgr 2007/2012
- Access to Active Directory information
- Access to the SCCM Client Center Automation library written by Roger Zander

In the following sections, you configure the MoveComputerToOU function, part of the Active Directory functions.

Installing and Configuring the Deployment Web Services

In this section, you install the Deployment Web Services and then set up ConfigMgr to use one of the included web services, the MoveComputerToOU web service. The steps are the following:

1. Create a service account and assign permissions in Active Directory.

2. Create an application pool and add the web application.

3. Testing the Active Directory web service.

4. Enable the MoveComputerToOU function for deployments.

Real World Note: The MoveComputerToOU function is also very useful for MDT 2013 Lite Touch deployments where you may have group policies that break the deployment. (ConfigMgr blocks group policies during deployment, but MDT 2013 Lite Touch does not.)

Create a Service Account and Assign Permissions

The service account used for the web service needs to have permissions in Active Directory to be able to move the computer objects. The account also needs NTFS permissions on CM01.

1. On **DC01**, using **Active Directory User and Computers**, in the **ViaMonstra / Service Accounts** OU, create a user account with the following settings:

   a. Name: **CM_WS**

   b. Password: **P@ssw0rd**

   c. Clear the **User must change password at next logon** check box.

   d. Select the **User cannot change password** check box.

   e. Select the **Password never expires** check box.

   f. Description: **Deployment WebService Account**

2. Grant permissions for the **CM_WS** account to the **ViaMonstra / Workstations** OU by running the following command:

   ```
   C:\Setup\Scripts\Set-OUPermissions.ps1 -Account CM_WS
   -TargetOU "OU=Workstations,OU=ViaMonstra"
   ```

3. Grant permissions for the **CM_WS** account to the **ViaMonstra / Servers** OU by running the following command:

   ```
   C:\Setup\Scripts\Set-OUPermissions.ps1 -Account CM_WS
   -TargetOU "OU=Servers,OU=ViaMonstra"
   ```

4. In the **ViaMonstra** OU, create an OU named **StagingOU**.

5. Grant permissions for the **CM_WS** account to the **ViaMonstra / StagingOU** OU by running the following command:

   ```
   C:\Setup\Scripts\Set-OUPermissions.ps1 -Account CM_WS
   -TargetOU "OU=StagingOU,OU=ViaMonstra"
   ```

6. On **CM01**, add the **CM_WS** account to the local **IIS_IUSRS** group.

Create an Application Pool for Deployment Web Services

When using a custom web service, it can be useful to have it running in its own application pool. The reasons for having a separate application pool are the following:

- To support running the web service with a different .NET Framework version

- To assign specific permissions to only that web service (Each application pool can be connected to only one security principal.)

- To be able to restart the web service without disrupting any other web applications

In these steps, you create the application pool for the Deployment Web Service and configure it to use the previously created service account:

1. On **CM01**, using **Internet Information Services (IIS) Manager**, expand the **CM01** node.

2. If you get prompted for **Web Platform Components**, select the **Do not show this message** check box and click **No**.

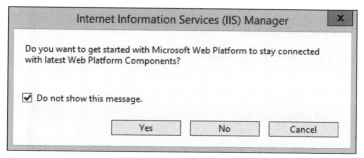

Saying no to the Microsoft Web Platform Installer (WebPI).

Real World Note: Even though the WebPI provides an easy way to download components of the Microsoft Web Platform, or popular web applications for blogging, content management, and so forth, we prefer to manage the components manually for better control. If you want to use the WebPI, you can still access it from the Get New Web Platform Components option in the menu on the right side.

3. Right-click **Application Pools**, select **Add Application Pool**, and configure the new application pool with the following settings:

    a. Name: **DeploymentWebService**

    b. .NET CLR version: **.NET CLR Version v4.0.30319**

    c. Managed pipeline mode: **Integrated**

    d. Select the **Start application pool immediately** check box, and click **OK**.

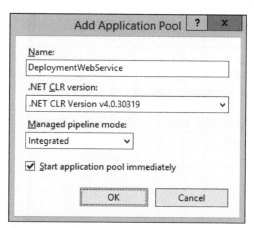

Creating the DeploymentWebService application pool.

4. Select the **Application Pools** node, right-click the new **DeploymentWebService** application pool, and select **Advanced Settings**.

5. Click on the **Identity** line and then click the browse "…" button.

6. Select **Custom account** and click **Set**. Use the following settings for the **Set Credentials** dialog box:

    a. Username: **VIAMONSTRA\CM_WS**

    b. Password and confirm password: **P@ssw0rd**

    c. Click **OK** twice.

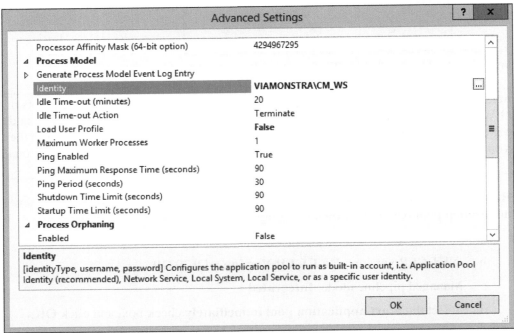

Identity configured for the application pool.

Real World Note: The samples in this book do not require this, but you also may need to enable the Load User Profile setting in the application pool when, for example, developing web services that create temporary files. This setting ensures that the temporary files are written into the service account profile under C:\Users instead of the default C:\Windows\Temp folder. This also can be required if security hardening on the web servers has restricted access to C:\Windows\Temp.

Install the Deployment Web Service

In this guide, we assume you have downloaded the book sample files to D:\Setup on CM01.

1. On **CM01**, create the **D:\ViaMonstraWebServices** folder, and then copy the **D:\Setup\DeploymentWebService** folder to **D:\ViaMonstraWebServices**.

2. Using **File Explorer**, assign the **VIAMONSTRA\CM_WS** account **Modify** permissions to **D:\ViaMonstraWebServices** (NTFS Permissions).

3. Using **Internet Information Services (IIS) Manager**, expand **Sites**, and expand **Default Web Site** to see the other web services installed by ConfigMgr.

4. Right-click **Default Web Site**, and select **Add Application**. Use the following settings for the application:

   a. Alias: **DeploymentWebServic**e

   b. Application pool: **DeploymentWebService**

   c. Physical Path: **D:\ViaMonstraWebServices\DeploymentWebService**

   d. Click **OK**.

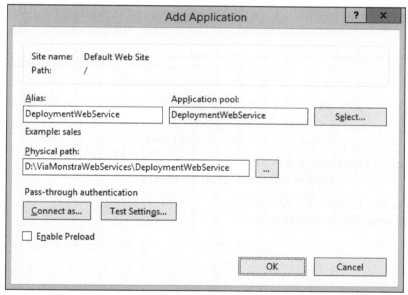

Adding the deployment web service (as a web application).

5. In the **Default Web Site**, select the **DeploymentWebService** web application, and in the right pane, double-click **Authentication**. Use the following settings for the Authentication dialog box:

   o   Anonymous Authentication: **Disabled**

   o   ASP .NET Impersonation: **Disabled**

      o   Forms Authentication: **Disabled**

      o   Windows Authentication: **Enabled**

Configuring the authentication settings.

Test the Web Service

A really nice thing about web services is that you can test them directly in a web browser.

1. On **DC01**, using **Active Directory Users and Computers**, in the **ViaMonstra /
   Workstations** OU, create a computer account named **PC00075**.

2. On **CM01**, using **Internet Explorer**, navigate to
   http://cm01/DeploymentWebService/ad.asmx.

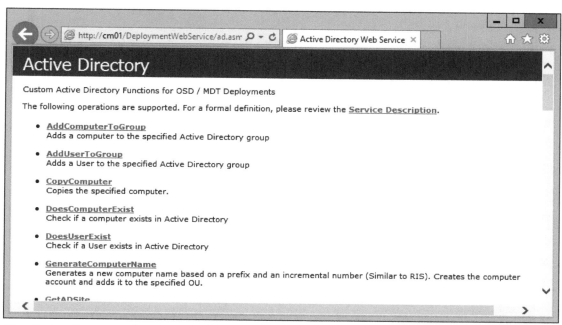

The Active Directory functions in the Deployment Web Service.

3. On the **Active Directory** page, scroll down, and select the **SetComputerDescription** function.

4. Complete the following:

    a.   ComputerName: **PC00075**

    b.   ComputerDescription: **Marketing Laptop**

    c.   Click **Invoke**.

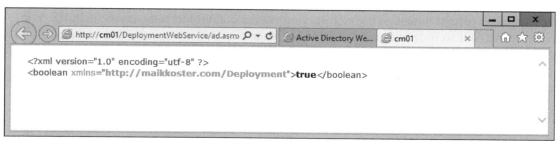

After invoking the SetComputerDescription function.

5. On **DC01**, using **Active Directory User and Computers**, select the **ViaMonstra / Workstations** OU and press **F5**. The PC00075 computer should now have a description.

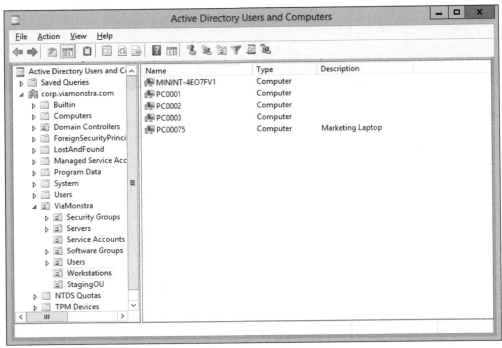

The PC00075 computer with computer description set.

Deployment Web Service Security Considerations

By now you probably realize the true power of web services. However, it's not only an advantage of having such a powerful toolset available. In its default implementation, the web service is configured to execute all actions under a certain user account. Although this makes it pretty easy to troubleshoot and verify the functions are working, all users with access to this web service now can execute actions that they may not be supposed to execute. So how do you secure web services?

First, you can restrict access to the web service via the default methods available in IIS. For example, make it so only authorized users are able to access the web service and execute all the actions. For any operation from this web service to any other server/service, the credentials of the application pool are used. So for testing, you just need to make sure that the application pool user has appropriate permission to execute the action. This means that if the application pool user has permission to delete a computer object within Active Directory and you have verified it is working, it most likely will work no matter who calls the web service.

If instead the user credentials are being passed through for authorization, each individual user needs to have appropriate permission for any of the requested operations. Some might have the permission to delete computer objects, some might not. So it might fail for certain users calling the web service due to security restrictions or (as before) due to other problems. So in this scenario, troubleshooting will be different for every user, as you have to ensure first that this particular user has appropriate permission to whatever he tried to do before doing any further troubleshooting on server or application level.

To create some kind of intermediate solution, you can implement another security layer in the Deployment Web Service. The basic idea is still to restrict access to the web service as you did before, but optionally you can choose the functions you would like to have available. There is no fancy role-based security whatsoever, but just a plain list of functions that are either excluded (supposing everything else is included) or included (supposing everything else is excluded by default). Or you can have a combination of both.

This can be configured either for all web services or individually for each part of the web service (AD, MDT, SCCM, SMSCliCtrV2). If a function is excluded, it neither shows up on the page that shows documentation of all available functions, nor is it be possible for anyone to call it, even if a user knows the name and correct properties.

Let's start with an example. By default, the web service excludes the following Active Directory functions that could be dangerous if they can be used by anyone:

- DeleteComputer

- DeleteComputerForced

- SetComputerAttribute

- DeleteUser

- DeleteUserForced

- SetUserAttribute

To store this information, a couple new application settings have been added to the web.config file. You can either edit them directly in the web.config file, or use IIS Manager.

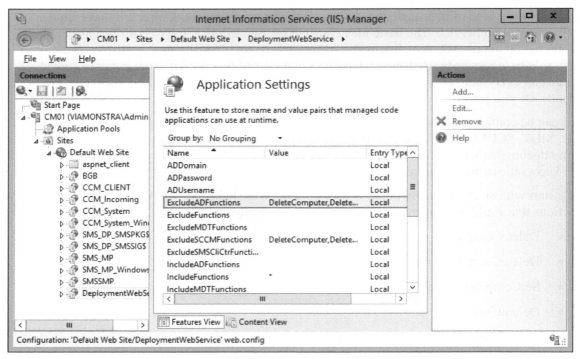

Configuring the Deployment Web Service settings.

As you can see, there are two generic include and exclude settings (IncludeFunctions and ExcludeFunctions) that will be used for all web service parts. By default, all functions are included (*). If all settings are empty, which will probably happen if you upgrade from a former version, everything will be available by default. This is to ensure backward compatibility. So if you upgrade from a former version to 7.3 without updating the web.config file, functions like DeleteComputer might be exposed to the public.

Excluding a function will always overrule an included function. So be sure to type in all the functions you do not want to be available within your environment. If you want to include only a few functions, excluding so many might not be the best option. In that case, just enter the ones you want to use in the appropriate "include" setting and be sure to remove the asterisk (*) from the "exclude" setting.

The combination of these settings should allow you to cover the most basic security demands between the former "all or nothing" and the very individual "pass-through authentication" approach.

Developing Web Services

Developing your own web services may seem a bit overwhelming at first, but after you learn the components involved, you realize it's not much harder than writing VBScripts or PowerShell scripts. A typical web service, when created in Visual Studio Express 2013 for Web, is composed of a few generic settings, a few references, and then one or more methods making up the web service. A method could be reading a list of OUs from Active Directory or the members of an Active Directory group, and is typically between 30 and 50 lines of code.

In this book, you see sample web services using both C# and VB.NET code. These are the most commonly used programming languages for developing web services. Even though they have different histories and syntaxes (C# syntax comes from the C programming language, and VB.NET comes from BASIC), you can achieve pretty much the same result no matter which language you prefer to use. Also, at least when it comes to web services, it's not that hard for a VB.NET developer to convert a C# sample to VB.NET and vice versa.

Web Service Components

In this section, you learn about the core code sections and files that make up a web service, as well as build a sample web service. A web service typically uses the following components:

- **Application Settings.** The web service stores generic application settings in a web.config file. This file can be edited directly with any text editor, but also from IIS Manager after you add the web service to IIS.

- **References.** In a web service, you can add references to components that you want to use. For example, if you want to query Active Directory, you add the Active Directory components as references to your web service.

- **Configurations.** The configurations are functions used to read settings from the web.config file to the web service. For example you can store the Active Directory domain name in the web.config file, and then read and use it in the web service code, avoiding any hardcoding of server and domain names in the code itself.

- **Methods.** Methods are the actual code, the programming logic.

Before starting to build your own web service, consider a few samples of the previously listed components.

Application Settings

The web.config file is an XML file that exists in the root of the web service folder and is used to set security settings, debugging (tracing) settings, and settings used for the web service code itself. Here are a few examples of application settings:

```
<appSettings>
 <add key="ConfigMgrSiteServer" value="CM01"/>
 <add key="ConfigMgrSiteCode" value="PS1"/>
 <add key="MDTDataBaseServer" value="CM01"/>
 <add key="MDTDatabase" value="MDT"/
 <add key="LDAPDomainName" value="dc=corp,dc=viamonstra,dc=com"/>
</appSettings>
```

References

In this example, you see a C# example on how to reference components (from .NET) to interact with Active Directory:

```
using System.DirectoryServices;
```

Configurations

In "Application Settings," you saw a few settings like MDTDataBaseServer and LDAPDomainName. Here is an example (again C#) that reads the LDAPDomainName from the web.config file:

```
LDAPDomainName =
WebConfigurationManager.AppSettings["LDAPDomainName"];
```

Methods

This is the C# or VB.NET code making up the web service. A web method can accept parameters if you want to send information to it and simply return something like a list of computers in an Active Directory group. Here is a C# code snippet for connecting to Active Directory and listing the members of a group:

```
[WebMethod]
public string GetADGroupMembers(String ADGroupName)
string LDAPPath = "";
LDAPPath = "LDAP://" + ADGroupName + "," + LDAPDomainName;
DirectoryEntry group = new DirectoryEntry(LDAPPath);

foreach(object dn in group.Properties["member"] )
{
    Console.WriteLine(dn);
}
```

Real World Note: The preceding code is just a short sample. If you have any groups with 1000 members, you need to add range retrieval to the code so you can obtain a portion of the members at a time.

Sample #1: List OUs from Active Directory

In the next chapter, you learn to use a custom frontend that displays a list of available OUs from Active Directory. This frontend uses a C#-based web service in the backend, and in this chapter, you create that web service using Visual Studio Express 2013 for Web.

Create a Sample Web Service

In these steps, we assume you have installed the free Visual Studio Express 2013 for Web on PC0001 (Windows 8.1 client) and extracted the book sample files to C:\Setup. Also, because the NLog engine needs to download its packages using the built-in NuGet Package Manager, make sure you have Internet access on PC0001.

1. On **PC0001**, verify that you have Internet access by opening a **PowerShell** prompt and running the following command:

    ```
    Test-NetConnection
    ```

2. Using **Visual Studio Express 2013 for Web**, open the **C:\Setup\SimpleFrontend\Webservice\Frontend.sln** solution file.

3. In the **Tools** menu, select **Library Package Manager / Manage NuGet Package for Solution**.

4. In the **Frontend.sln – NuGet Package Manager** window, in the upper right corner, click **Restore** to download the missing packages.

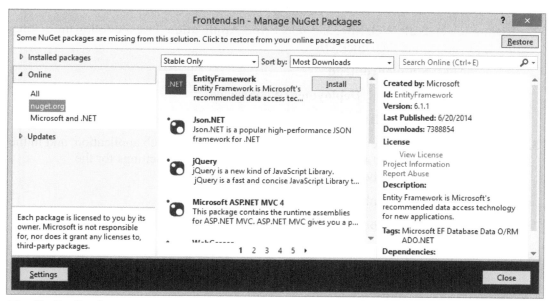

The NuGet Package Manager.

5. After the download is completed, close the **NuGet Package Manager** window.

237

6. On the ribbon, verify that **Release** is selected.

7. In the **Solution Explorer**, right-click the **Frontend** project, and select the **Build** action.

8. On **CM01**, create this folder structure:
   D:\ViaMonstraWebServices\SimpleFrontend\bin.

9. From **PC0001**, copy the following files from **C:\Setup\SimpleFrontend\Webservice\bin** to **D:\ViaMonstraWebServices\SimpleFrontend\bin** on **CM01**:

   o **Frontend.dll**

   o **NLog.dll**

10. From **PC0001**, copy the following files from **C:\Setup\SimpleFrontend\Webservice** to **D:\ViaMonstraWebServices\SimpleFrontend** on **CM01**:

   o **ConfigMgr.asmx**

   o **NLog.config**

   o **Web.config**

Install the Web Service

In these steps, we assume you created the DeploymentWebService application pool earlier in this chapter.

1. On **CM01**, using **Internet Information Services (IIS) Manager**, expand **Sites**.

2. Right-click **Default Web Site**, and select **Add Application**. Use the following settings for the application, and then click **OK**:

   a. Alias: **SimpleFrontend**

   b. Application pool: **DeploymentWebService**

   c. Physical Path: **D:\ViaMonstraWebServices\SimpleFrontend**

3. In the **Default Web Site** node, select the **SimpleFrontend** web application, and in the right pane, double-click **Authentication**. Use the following settings for the **Authentication** dialog box:

   a. Anonymous Authentication: **Disabled**

   b. ASP .NET Impersonation: **Disabled**

   c. Forms Authentication: **Disabled**

   d. Windows Authentication: **Enabled**

Test the Web Service

1. On **CM01**, using **Internet Explorer**, navigate to:
    http://CM01/SimpleFrontend/ConfigMgr.asmx.

2. Click the **GetOUList** link, and then click the **Invoke** button.

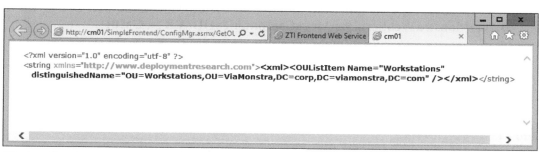

Listing the Active Directory OUs.

Sample #2: Move Computer to OU

In this sample, you create a VB.NET-based web service that moves a computer from one OU to another, something very useful when keeping existing computer names in a deployment. Like the first sample, this one uses the NLog logging engine (which we like).

Create a Sample Web Service

In these steps, we assume you have installed the free Visual Studio Express 2013 for Web on PC0001 (the Windows 8.1 client) and extracted the book sample files to C:\Setup. Like Sample #1, because the NLog engine needs to download its packages using the built-in NuGet Package Manager, make sure you have Internet access on PC0001.

1. On **PC0001**, using **Visual Studio Express 2013 for Web**, open the **C:\Setup\ MoveComputerToOU_VB \MoveComputerToOU_VB.sln** solution file.

2. In the **Tools** menu, select **Library Package Manager / Manage NuGet Package for Solution**.

3. In the **MoveComputerToOU_VB.sln – NuGet Package Manager** window, in the upper right corner, click **Restore** to download the missing packages.

4. After downloading is complete, close the **NuGet Package Manager** window.

5. On the ribbon, verify that **Release** is selected.

6. In the **Solution Explorer**, right-click the **MoveComputerToOU_VB** project, and select the **Build** action.

7. On **CM01**, in the **D:\ViaMonstraWebServices** folder, create the **MoveComputerToOU_VB\bin** folder structure.

8. From **PC0001**, copy the following files from **C:\Setup\MoveComputerToOU_VB\bin** files to **D:\ViaMonstraWebServices\MoveComputerToOU_VB\bin** on **CM01**:

    o **MoveComputerToOU_VB.dll**

    o **NLog.dll**

9. From **PC0001**, copy the following files from **C:\Setup\MoveComputerToOU_VB** file to **D:\ViaMonstraWebServices\MoveComputerToOU_VB** on **CM01**:

    o **AD.asmx**

    o **NLog.config**

    o **Web.config**

Install the Web Service

In these steps, we assume you created the DeploymentWebService application pool earlier in this chapter.

1. On **CM01**, using **Internet Information Services (IIS) Manager**, expand **Sites**.

2. Right-click **Default Web Site**, and select **Add Application**. Use the following settings for the application, and then click **OK**:

    a. Alias: **MoveComputerToOU_VB**

    b. Application pool: **DeploymentWebService**

    c. Physical path: **D:\ViaMonstraWebServices\MoveComputerToOU_VB**

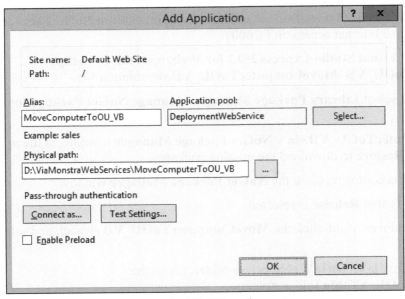

Adding the MoveComputerToOU_VB web service.

3. In the **Default Web Site** node, select the **MoveComputerToOU_VB** web application, and in the right pane, double-click **Authentication**. Use the following settings for the **Authentication** dialog box:

    a. Anonymous Authentication: **Disabled**

    b. ASP .NET Impersonation: **Disabled**

    c. Forms Authentication: **Disabled**

    d. Windows Authentication: **Enabled**

Test the Web Service

Again, you use Internet Explorer to test your web service.

1. On **DC01**, user **Active Directory Users and Computers**, in the **ViaMonstra / Workstations** OU, create a computer account named **PC00076**.

2. On **CM01**, using **Internet Explorer**, navigate to **http://cm01/MoveComputerToOU_VB/ad.asmx**.

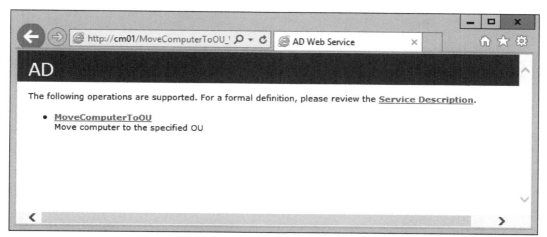

The sample Active Directory web service.

3. On the **AD** page, select the **MoveComputerToOU** function.

4. Complete the following:

    a. ComputerName: **PC00076**

    b. OUPath:
        OU=StagingOU,OU=ViaMonstra,DC=corp,DC=viamonstra,DC=com

    c. Click **Invoke**.

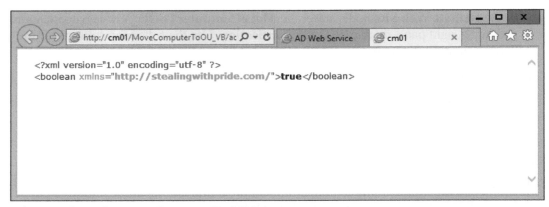

After invoking the MoveComputerToOU function.

5. On **DC01**, using **Active Directory User and Computers**, select the **ViaMonstra / StagingOU** and press **F5**. The PC00076 computer should now be in this OU.

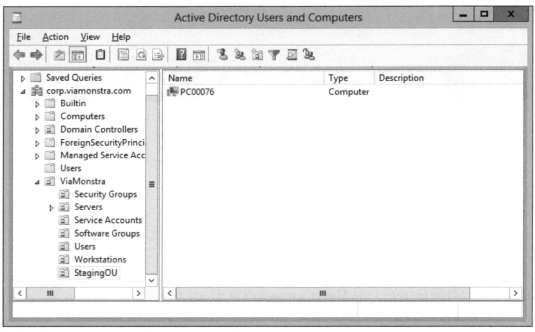

The PC00076 computer object after being moved by the web service.

Optional - Enable the MoveComputerToOU Function for Deployments

To enable the MoveComputerToOU function for your task sequence, you need to add a custom property named StagingOU to the rules and then add a few actions to the task sequence that actually move the computer to another OU. To make sure these actions are only used in computer refresh scenarios (the computer need to exist to be moved) you also set conditions on the actions.

1. On **CM01**, using **Notepad**, edit the **CustomSettings.ini** file in the **D:\Sources\OSD\Settings\Windows 8.1 x64 Settings** folder:

   a. Add **StagingOU** to the **Properties** line so the top section looks like this:

```
[Settings]
Priority=Default
Properties=OSDMigrateConfigFiles,OSDMigrateMode,StagingOU
```

   b. Add the **StagingOU** value in the **Default** section so it look like this:

```
[Default]
...
MachineObjectOU=ou=Workstations,ou=viamonstra,dc=corp,
dc=viamonstra,dc=com
StagingOU=OU=StagingOU,OU=ViaMonstra,DC=corp,DC=viamonstra,DC=com
...
```

2. Save the **CustomSettings.ini** file, and update the distribution points for the **Windows 8.1 x64 Settings** package.

3. Copy the following files from **D:\Setup\MoveComputer** to **D:\Sources\OSD\MDT\MDT 2013\Scripts**:

   o **CustomSettings.ini**

   o **Z_MoveComputer_StagingOU.wsf**

   o **Z_MoveComputer_SwapOUValues.wsf**

   o **Z_MoveComputer_TargetOU.wsf**

4. Update the distribution points for the **MDT 2013** package.

5. Using the **ConfigMgr console**, select **Task Sequences**, right-click the **Windows 8.1 Enterprise x64** task sequence, and then select **Edit**. Use the following settings:

   a. In the **PostInstall** group, after the **Apply Network Settings** action, add a **Run Command Line action** with the following settings:

      ▪ Name: **Move Computer to Staging OU**

      ▪ Command line: **cscript.exe "%DeployRoot%\scripts\ Z_MoveComputer_StagingOU.wsf"**

- Options / Condition: Add a **Task Sequence Variable** condition with the following settings:

DeploymentType equals **REFRESH**

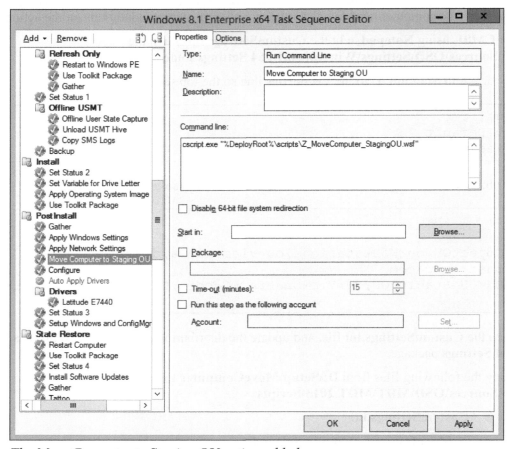

The Move Computer to Staging OU action added.

b. In the **State Restore** group, after the **Move State Store** action, add a new group with the following settings:

- Name: **Finalize**.

- Options / Condition: Add a **Task Sequence Variable** condition with the following settings:

DeploymentType equals **REFRESH**

c. In the **Finalize** group, add a **Run Command Line** action with the following settings:

- Name: **Swap Staging OU**

- Command line: **cscript.exe "%DeployRoot%\scripts\ Z_MoveComputer_SwapOUValues.wsf"**

d. In the **Finalize** group, after the **Swap Staging OU** action, add a **Run Command Line action** with the following settings:

- Name: **Move Computer to Target OU**

- Command line: **cscript.exe "%DeployRoot%\scripts\ Z_MoveComputer_TargetOU.wsf"**

e. Click **OK**.

Troubleshooting Web Services

Troubleshooting has always been one of the most critical and difficult parts of working with web services. Because the result of the web service is predefined, there is no easy way to respond with an error message in case of a problem. Most problems relate to security issues or to wrong or missing settings of the web service. So, the first thing to check should be whether the account that is executing the request has the appropriate permission to do so. In most cases, this is the account that has been configured for the web service, or rather for the application pool this web service is using.

Because our samples use the NLog engine, you can easily configure this logging provider to your own needs by specifying the detail level, the information to be logged, and also the target to which to log (XML file, database, event, and so forth.). By default only informational logging is written to a text log file located in the Logs folder of your web service. You should find a file per day so you also can archive or delete older logs easily. For your convenience, additional default logging options have been added to the nlog.config file and have been commented out. To enable Debug or even Tracing level logging, just uncomment the appropriate lines in the nlog.config file as shown in the following figure.

```
                                    NLog.config - Notepad                         _ □  ×

File  Edit  Format  View  Help
<?xml version="1.0" encoding="utf-8" ?>
<!--
  This file needs to be put in the application directory. Make sure to set
  'Copy to Output Directory' option in Visual Studio.
  -->
<nlog xmlns="http://www.nlog-project.org/schemas/NLog.xsd"
      xmlns:xsi="http://www.w3.org/2001/XMLSchema-instance" autoReload="true">

    <targets async="true">
        <target name="InfoAndAbove" xsi:type="File" fileName="${basedir}/Logs/${shortdate}_Info.log" />
        <target name="DebugAndAbove" xsi:type="File" fileName="${basedir}/Logs/${shortdate}_Debug.log" />
        <target name="TraceAndAbove" xsi:type="File" fileName="${basedir}/Logs/${shortdate}_Trace.log"/>
        <target name="debugger" xsi:type="Debugger" layout="${stacktrace} :: ${message}"/>
    </targets>

    <rules>
        <logger name="*" minlevel="Info" writeTo="InfoAndAbove" />
        <logger name="*" minlevel="Debug" writeTo="DebugAndAbove" />
        <logger name="*" minlevel="Trace" writeTo="TraceAndAbove" />
        <logger name="*" minlevel="Debug" writeTo="debugger" />
    </rules>
</nlog>
```

Sample Nlog.config file with all logging options enabled (uncommented).

Be aware that logging will use some resources on your server. So use the logging that's appropriate to your individual needs. For more information about configuring NLog, see Appendix D, "Adding Logging to Your Applications – NLog for Beginners." You also can find very good information in the NLog documentation at http://nlog-project.org/documentation.

Chapter 12

Customizing Frontends

This chapter gives you an in-depth view on customizing frontends (wizards) for both MDT 2013 Lite Touch and ConfigMgr 2012 R2. You learn to customize the built-in in wizards, add third-party wizards, and create your own. You also learn about some general tips and tricks for when using and customizing frontends. In this chapter, you learn about:

- The structure of the MDT 2013 Lite Touch Wizard

- How to use the MDT Wizard Studio

- Creating, changing, and testing a wizard pane

- Creating custom scripts

- Handling initialization and validation

- Copying existing wizard panes

- Setting up and using a custom HTA frontend

- Using and customizing UDI for ConfigMgr 2012

Step-by-Step Guide Requirements

If you want to run the step-by-step guide in this chapter, you need a lab environment configured as outlined in Chapter 3 and Appendix A. In this chapter, you use the following virtual machines:

DC01

CM01

MDT01

PC0001

The VMs used in this chapter.

You also need to have downloaded the following software:

- MDT 2013

- The book sample files (http://stealingwithpride.com)

MDT 2013 Lite Touch Wizard

The MDT Lite Touch Wizard is implemented as an HTML application (HTA). As described in Chapter 1, an HTA consists of HTML, mainly used to generate the user interface, and a scripting language used for the program logic. As the main scripting language for MDT is VBScript, the scripting language used for the Lite Touch wizard is VBScript, as well. However, it's not restricted to it, and any scripting language supported by Internet Explorer can be used. You learn how to use JavaScript to customize the wizard later in this chapter.

Implementing the wizard as an HTA makes it very flexible and easy to customize.

MDT Wizard Studio

The MDT Wizard Studio is one of the most useful tools when it comes to customizing the MDT Lite Touch Wizard. MDT Wizard Studio allows you to open and easily edit the configuration files that drive the MDT Lite Touch Wizard. It gives you a preview of how each pane will look when called from the wizard. Additionally, it allows you to call the wizard with the defined panes and manually override the MDT properties to test different scenarios as they would happen during deployment.

While not being a part of the original MDT installation itself, it can be downloaded for free from CodePlex (http://mdtwizardstudio.codeplex.com/). Throughout this book, we use the MDT Wizard Studio for all manipulation of the MDT 2013 Lite Touch Wizard, although it's still possible to implement all the mentioned changes manually in the corresponding XML files.

The original MDT Wizard Editor was written by Michael Niehaus, one of the former main developers and driving force behind MDT since the very beginning. It was targeted for MDT 2008 first and then updated for MDT 2010. However, with various changes in the following versions of MDT that weren't covered in the MDT Wizard Editor, and with the spirit of this book in mind, we created MDT Wizard Studio as the successor of the MDT Wizard Editor and to support all features and also add some capabilities that were missing in the original version.

The Structure of the MDT 2013 Lite Touch Wizard

To be able to customize the Lite Touch wizard, you first need to understand the individual components of the wizard and how they interact with each other.

Pane

The MDT Lite Touch Wizard consists of a series of panes, which can be seen as individual pages of the wizard. The user can typically navigate to the next or previous pane using default or custom buttons, or navigate directly to any previous pane using the navigation bar. However, the navigation can be limited to certain conditions and also be customized to specific requirements like hiding the navigation bar or continuing to the next pane by code, such as after a timeout.

In contrast to versions prior to MDT 2012, MDT now stores each pane in an individual file, making it a lot easier to create, test, and share individual panes.

The basic definition of a pane:

```
<Wizard>
  <Global>
    ...
  </Global>

  <Pane id="SelectTaskSequence" title="Task Sequence">
    ...
  </Pane>
</Wizard>
```

CustomScript

The CustomScript element allows you to reference external VBScript files. All referenced script files are imported when the wizard starts so that all functions within those scripts are available throughout the wizard.

Custom scripts can be defined either globally for a wizard definition file, or for each individual pane. They need to be available in the same folder as the definition file.

```
<Wizard>
  <Global>
    <CustomScript>DeployWiz_SelectTS.vbs</CustomScript>
  </Global>

  ...

</Wizard>
```

Condition

Conditions allow you to hide or better skip individual panes in the wizard. Giving you the option to present only those panes to the user that are required for your customized deployment. If no condition is defined for a pane, it will always be shown. If you define one or several conditions, all of them need to equal true, otherwise the pane will be skipped.

The conditions can either be defined as a VBScript command that is evaluated at runtime, or if the condition is more complex, be a function called from a separate script that returns true or false depending on the evaluation.

Most of the built-in panes are tied to one or several default MDT properties that are evaluated and set during the gather step (see Chapter 8). If, for example, you want to skip the pane that gives the user the option to select a task sequence, you only need to set the property SkipTaskSequence to YES. Here is a snippet from the corresponding wizard definition file that uses this condition:

```
<Pane id="SelectTaskSequence" reference="DeployWiz_SelectTS.xml">

  <Condition>
    <![CDATA[UCASE(Property("SkipTaskSequence"))<>"YES"]]>
  </Condition>

</Pane>
```

And the same condition again in the MDT Wizard Studio:

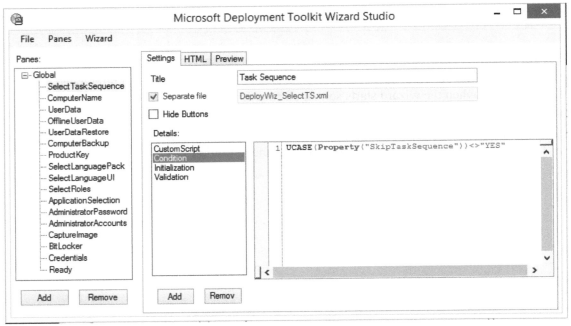

A condition in MDT Wizard Studio.

Real World Note: MDT has default properties to skip each of the original Lite Touch Wizard panes. We recommend creating a custom MDT property for each custom pane you are using, according to the schema SKIP{YourPaneName}.

Initialization

When a pane is about to be shown, you can define additional steps to be executed for the initialization of the pane. It can be used, for example, to set some default values or hide/unhide some elements on the pane based on some dynamic criteria.

The MDT Lite Touch Wizard comes with some predefined initialization routines, as well. The most important one for you to know is that the wizard automatically fills all the HTML elements having the same name as an MDT property with the value of the corresponding MDT property.

Assuming you want to show a text box that allows the user to enter a computer name, you can use the following HTML snippet:

```
<td>
   ComputerName
</td>
<td>
   <input type=text id="OSDComputerName" name="OSDComputerName" />
</td>
```

MDT will make sure that the current computer name is populated to this text box when the pane is shown. Additionally, MDT will read the entered value and write it back into the appropriate MDT property during the validation of the pane.

Real World Note: This default behavior is based on the name of an HTML element, not the id! Make sure that the id attribute of each element is unique throughout all your panes.

```
<Wizard>
  <Global>
    ...
  </Global>
  <Pane id="ComputerName" title="Computer Name">
    <Initialization>
      <![CDATA[InitializeComputerName]]>
    </Initialization>
  </Pane>
</Wizard>
```

> **Real World Note:** We recommend separating all your initialization code into a separate VBScript file for each pane. Then reference the script in your pane and call the function that handles all your initialization logic. This makes it easier to update the logic and also to reuse the pane and all corresponding code.

InitializationCloseout

The InitializationCloseout element is almost identical to the Initialization element. The only difference is that the code is executed after all built-in MDT logic has finished. That allows you to overwrite the built-in default behavior of MDT if necessary.

Please see the preceding "Initialization" section for more details.

Validation

When you are about to leave a pane either by clicking on the Next or Finish button, selecting a previous pane directly, or initiated by some code, you can add some logic to be evaluated to validate the data entered on the current pane.

The validation logic of a pane is typically encapsulated into a single function that is then called. If the result of the validation doesn't equal true, then the wizard will not move to the next pane, and the current one will remain open.

> **Real World Note:** If you have some validation logic in place, make sure you give the user visual feedback on what isn't sufficient and needs to be done to properly leave this pane. Otherwise the user will assume your wizard is broken.

As with initialization, the MDT Lite Touch Wizard comes with some predefined validation routines.

First, to ensure that an element like a text box has a value, you can add a label to your pane, where the "for" attribute points to the "id" of the element. During the initialization of the pane, MDT hides all those labels. Then, during the default validation, MDT checks whether the element is empty, and if it is, unhides the label and sets the current validation to false.

So, referring back to the sample in the "Initialization" section, let's assume you need to make sure that a computer name has been entered. The corresponding HTML could look like this:

```
<td>
  ComputerName
</td>
<td>
  <input type=text id="OSDComputerName" name="OSDComputerName" />
  <label class=ErrMsg for=OSDComputerName>* Required</label>
</td>
```

Second, after the validation has succeeded, MDT makes sure that all the values entered or chosen on the pane are stored in the corresponding MDT properties again. If there is no default MDT

252

property with this name, a custom one is created automatically. For this to work, each HTML element must have a valid name defined. If several controls have the same name, the values are stored in the corresponding MDT list property.

```
<Wizard>
  <Global>
    ...
  </Global>
  <Pane id="ComputerName" title="Computer Name">
    <Validation>
      <![CDATA[ValidateComputerName]]>
    </Validation >
  </Pane>
</Wizard>
```

Real World Note: As noted previously, we recommend separating all your validation code into a separate VBScript file for each pane. Then reference the script in your pane and call the function that handles all your validation logic. This makes it easier to update the logic and also to reuse the pane and all corresponding code.

Customizing the MDT 2013 Lite Touch Wizard

The MDT 2013 Lite Touch wizard comes with a lot of predefined panes. However, often there is a need to customize those panes. For example, you may need to localize them to a different language or adjust the wording, or you may need to exclude or add some information or combine several panes into one. You may even need to add a completely new pane that is required for your specific business needs.

Whenever you want or need to make changes to the wizard, we highly recommend that you follow these best practices:

- Keep your changes separate from your working wizard files:
    o Create a new folder for each new or changed pane
    o Copy an existing pane or create a new pane
    o Create new script files for all your custom code
    o Add this folder to your version control system
- Stick to a standardized naming convention for naming panes, script files, HTML elements, and so on.
- Thoroughly test your changes before putting them into production.

To see at least some of the capabilities of the MDT 2013 Lite Touch wizard, you create a new pane for the wizard in this section that covers a pretty typical requirement.

MDT offers us the possibility to define settings, applications, roles, and so forth, depending on the location of the computer. To use this feature, you create locations, preferably in the database, and configure them with all the required settings, such as keyboard layout, time zone, and others. Then you assign one or several gateways that are used at each individual location and thus can be used to identify a location by a given gateway.

When the computer boots up and runs the Gather step, it can now use the current gateway and check whether there are any settings available for the current location. A typical scenario is that computers are prepared at one or a few central locations and then shipped to different locations.

What you need is a new pane that allows you to optionally select a different location from the one where you are currently located.

So, in the following sections, you learn how to use the MDT Wizard Editor to create a new pane, modify it based on your requirements, test this new pane, and then import it into the existing MDT 2013 Lite Touch Wizard so that the new pane can be used together with all the required other panes.

Create a New Pane

When creating a new custom pane, we recommend creating it separate from your current wizard definitions. See each custom pane as a separate project.

> **Real World Note:** Following the best practice, make sure that you upload your new pane into your version control system and regularly commit all changes. This way you can keep track of all your changes. Just follow the steps in Chapter 7, which uses this sample to demonstrate how to use VisualSVN Server and TortoiseSVN as version control systems.

In these steps we assume you have downloaded the book sample files to C:\Setup on PC0001.

1. On **PC0001**, create the **C:\LocationSelection** folder in which to store the new wizard pane and all corresponding files.

   Optionally, but highly recommended, check this new folder into your repository to keep it under version control.

2. Using the **MDT Wizard Studio** (MDTWizardStudio.exe), select **File / New**.

3. Select the **C:\LocationSelection** folder you created in the first step and give it the name **DeployWizard_LocactionSelectionDef.xml**.

4. To rename the new default pane **Pane1**, select the pane and press **F2**, or right-click the pane and select **Rename**.

5. In the **Rename** dialog box, configure the following settings and click **OK**:

   o   Specify the pane ID: **LocationSelection**

   o   Specify the filename: **DeployWiz_LocationSelection.xml**

6. To save your changes, select **File / Save**.

Add a Condition

As with the default MDT 2013 Lite Touch Wizard panes, you want to be able to skip this new pane if, for example, the information has been prestaged already.

1. Select the pane **LocationSelection**.

2. Right-click in the **Details** area of the **Settings** tab and select **Add / Condition** from the context menu, or click the **Add** button and select **Condition**

3. In the **Details** text area, type

   ```
   Property("SkipLocationSelection")<>"YES"
   ```

4. Save your changes.

Update the HTML

The HTML is the visible part of the pane. For now, keep it simple and just add a short description and a drop-down box that will be filled with all available locations later.

1. Select the pane **LocationSelection**.

2. Select the **HTML** tab.

3. In the text area, remove the default text, and type the following HTML code snippet:

   ```
   <h1>Please select the location for this computer.</h1>
   <table>
     <tr>
       <td>
         Location
       </td>
       <td>
         <select size="1" id="cloc"
           name="CurrentLocation"></select>
       </td>
     </tr>
   </table>
   ```

Preview the Pane

When making changes to the HTML of the pane, it's often useful to have a quick look to see what the pane looks like as you make the changes.

To see a preview of the pane,

1. Select the pane **LocationSelection**.

2. Select the **Preview** tab of the selected pane.

Real World Note: Be aware that the preview of the pane does not include anything that is part of the initialization scripts. Especially content that is dynamically added, like the list of locations in this sample, is not shown. To see this content, you need to run a test of the wizard.

Add a Custom Script

As mentioned previously, the default initialization of the MDT Lite Touch Wizard takes care of the most typical scenarios and, for example, fills simple text boxes with the values of the correspondingly named MDT properties. However, because you used a drop-down box (HTML select element), you need to write a couple lines of VBScript code that create an entry for each location in your list. Following the best practice, you add a new custom script for this initialization task.

1. Select the pane **LocationSelection**.

2. In the **Settings** tab, right-click in the **Details** area and select **Add / CustomScript** from the context menu, or click the **Add** button and select **CustomScript**. Type in the following and click **Save**.

   File name: DeployWiz_LocationSelection.vbs

3. In the text area, type the following VBScript code snippet:

```vbscript
Sub InitializeLocation (DropDownID, MDTListProperty)
   ' Get drop-down list
   Dim oDropDown
   Set oDropDown = document.getElementByID(DropDownID)

   ' Get MDT Property
   Dim sMDTProp
   sMDTProp = oEnvironment.Item(DropDownID)

   ' Iterate through MDT list property
   For Each sItem In oEnvironment.ListItem(MDTListProperty)
      ' Create new option element
      Dim oOption
      Set oOption = document.createElement("OPTION")
      oOption.text = sItem
      oOption.value = sItem

      ' If item equals MDT property
      ' mark the current option as selected
      If sMDTProp = sItem Then
        oOption.selected = True
      End If

      ' Add option to DropDown
      oDropDown.Add(oOption)
   Next
End Sub
```

Have a quick view on this VBScript so you understand what it does. First, you get the drop-down list that you just added to your HTML content of the pane. The document is more or less the content of the current pane, and the DropDownID is handed over to the procedure, which makes it more flexible.

```
Dim oDropDown
Set oDropDown = document.getElementByID(DropDownID)
```

Then you try to find a MDT property with the same name as the drop-down list:

```
Dim sMDTProp
sMDTProp = oEnvironment.Item(DropDownID)
```

Finally, you loop through the list of locations and add an entry to the drop-down list for each location. Additionally, you check whether a location is already know and will mark this drop-down list entry as selected.

```
For Each sItem In oEnvironment.ListItem(MDTListProperty)
    Dim oOption
    Set oOption = document.createElement("OPTION")
    oOption.text = sItem
    oOption.value = sItem

    If sMDTProp = sItem Then
      oOption.selected = True
    End If

    oDropDown.Add(oOption)
  Next
```

When the wizard starts, it also reads all referenced script files and makes the containing code globally available so procedures and functions can be called from the panes.

Add the Initialization
As you have added the code that is required to fill the drop-down list, you now need to call this during the initialization of this pane.

To add a new initialization entry,

1. Select the pane **LocationSelection**.

2. Right-click in the **Details** area of the **Settings** tab and select **Add / Initialization** from the context menu, or click the **Add** button and select **Initialization**.

3. In the **Details** text field, type the following:

```
InitializeLocation "CurrentLocation", "Location"
```

This command will be executed when the pane is shown to the user. In this case, it calls the InitializeLocation procedure, which you defined before and added to the initialization scripts.

Add the Validation

As a best practice, you should always include some validation that ensures that all the data you want to collect on this pane has been properly entered. This is necessary for when you later rely on that data.

In your case, you need to make sure that a location has been selected. In theory, this should always be the case, assuming all locations have been properly defined. However, in practice, that is not always the case. To keep it simple, just check whether the value of the selected option has a value. To do this, you add another small function to the custom script of this pane that does the heavy lifting.

To add a validation,

1. Select the pane **LocationSelection**.

2. In the **Details** area, select the **CustomScript** entry and add the following function to the end of the script, which basically just loops through the drop-down list and returns true if at least one option has been selected:

```
Function ValidateLocation (DropDownID)

  Dim oDropDown
  Set oDropDown = document.getElementByID(DropDownID)

  bFound = False
  For Each oOption In oDropDown
    If oOption.Selected Then
      bFound = True
      Exit For
    End If
  Next

  ValidateLocation = bFound

End Function
```

3. Right-click in the **Details** area of the **Settings** tab and select **Add / Validation** from the context menu, or click the **Add** button and select **Validation**.

4. Type the following in the text area:

```
ValidateLocation("CurrentLocation")
```

5. Save the changes.

Test the Pane

Before putting anything into production, everything needs to be thoroughly tested.

Note: The MDT Wizard Studio supports an easy way to test a definition file for the MDT LiteTouch Wizard. As the testing requires several files from MDT itself, this feature requires MDT 2013 installed locally on the computer on which the MDT Wizard Studio is being executed. However, a plain installation is enough. There is no need to create a deployment share or do any of the other configurations described in Chapter 5.

In these steps we assume you have downloaded MDT 2013 to C:\Setup on PC0001.

1. Install **MDT 2013** on **PC0001** using the default settings.

2. Close, and re-open the **MDT Wizard Studio**. Then open the **C:\ LocationSelection\DeployWizard_LocationSelectionDef.xml** file again.

3. In **MDT Wizard Studio**, in the **Wizard** menu, select **Test**. It take a couple seconds for the necessary wizard files to be copied to the local folder of the pane(s) to be tested and the ZTIGather.wsf script to be executed to gather some local settings.

4. In the **Variables** window that opens, add the following variables and values to the end of the list and then click **Run**.

    o   **LOCATION001 = New York**

    o   **LOCATION002 = Stockholm**

    o   **LOCATION003 = Liverpool**

    o   **CURRENTLOCATION = Stockholm**

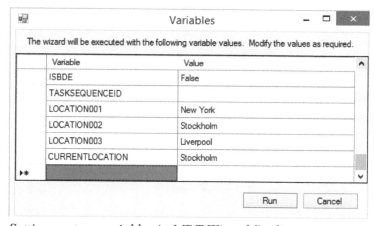

Setting custom variables in MDT Wizard Studio.

If there are no errors in the pane's scripts or HTML, you should see the MDT Lite Touch Wizard showing one pane called Select Location. On this pane, there should be a drop-down list filled with three different locations (New York, Stockholm, and Liverpool), and Stockholm should be selected.

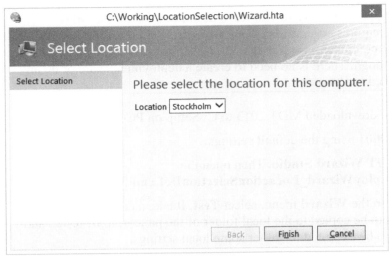

The Select Location pane in the MDT LiteTouch Wizard.

To finish the testing,

1. Select **Liverpool** as the location and click **Finish**.

2. Wait a few seconds and verify that the variable **CURRENTLOCATION** now has a value of **Liverpool**.

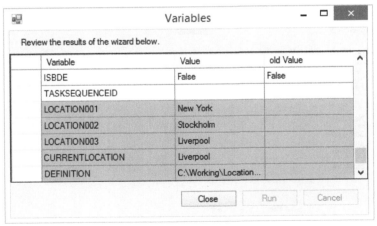

Reviewing variables in MDT Wizard Studio.

Import a Pane

After a pane has been created or modified and successfully tested, it can be imported into the series of panes that is currently being used for deployment. The import functionality from MDT Wizard Studio also makes sure that all files that are referenced by the pane are copied, as well.

Real World Note: For production environments, we recommend having a separate project that contains the definition of all the panes that are being used and also have it under version control. This way individual panes can be updated and tested separately from the whole series of wizard panes used in the production environment. And as soon as they are ready for production, they are simply imported into the main definition.

You are now going to create an additional project folder that contains a copy of the original MDT LiteTouch Wizard and import the new LocationSelection pane into this original wizard definition.

To do this, you have to complete these steps:

1. On **PC0001**, create a new folder named **MDTLiteTouchWizard** in **C:\Working**.

2. Copy the content of the folder **\\MDT01\MDTProduction$\Scripts** to the folder **C:\Working\MDTLiteTouchWizard**.

3. Using the **MDT Wizard Studio** on PC0001, select **File / Open** and open the wizard definition file **C:\Working\MDTLiteTouchWizard\DeployWiz_Definition_ENU.xml**.

4. In the **List of Panes**, select the pane **ComputerName**.

5. Select **Import** from the **Panes** menu, or right-click the **ComputerName** pane and select **Import**.

6. Select the file **C:\LocationSelection\DeployWiz_LocationSelection.xml**.

7. Verify that the **LocationSelection** pane has been added to the list of panes.

Real World Note: If a pane is in the wrong order, it can easily be dragged and dropped to the correct location.

8. Save the changes.

You should now test the updated wizard definition file as described in the "Test the Pane" section to verify that everything is still working as expected.

Finalize the LocationSelection Sample

You have created a new pane called LocationSelection that allows a specific location to be selected from a list of locations and verified that it is working as expected.

However, there are still two things missing to make this new pane usable: You need to add the updated files to the deployment share, and you need to update the rules (CustomSettings.ini).

1. On **PC0001**, copy all the **DeployWiz*** files from **C:\Working\MDTLiteTouchWizard** to **\\MDT01\MDTProduction$\Scripts** (replace existing files):

> **Note:** Most of these changes are directly related to what you have learned already in Chapter 8 about the Gather process. If you haven't worked through Chapter 8 yet and don't have a solid understanding of how the Gather process and the related components work, you might want to read through Chapter 8 first and then come back to this part.

2. On **MDT01**, using the **Deployment Workbench**, right-click the **MDT Production** deployment share and select **Properties**.

3. On the **Rules** tab, merge the following information (keep the existing [Default] section):

```
[Settings]
Priority=Init,Default
Properties=CurrentLocation

[Init]
Location001=New York
Location002=Stockholm
Location003=Liverpool
```

4. Apply the changes.

As you learned in Chapter 8, this defines a new custom property called CurrentLocation and fills the already existing list property Location with the three entries of New York, Stockholm, and Liverpool. If you now start a deployment, the newly created wizard pane should look exactly the way like it did during testing.

Instead of hard-coding the locations in the rules, you also can get this list on the fly, that is by querying a web service to return a list of locations in Active Directory or querying the deployment database for a list of locations, as demonstrated in Chapter 8.

The only thing missing now is to make use of the CurrentLocation property in your task sequences, for example as the condition for an application to be installed.

> **Real World Note:** Be aware that the full Gather process is evaluated before the wizard is executed. So if there are additional sections in the rules that define location-specific settings based on a property that is evaluated during the execution of the wizard, like demonstrated in this sample with the CurrentLocation property, the first Gather step in the task sequence has to be changed from gathering local data only to also processing the rules.

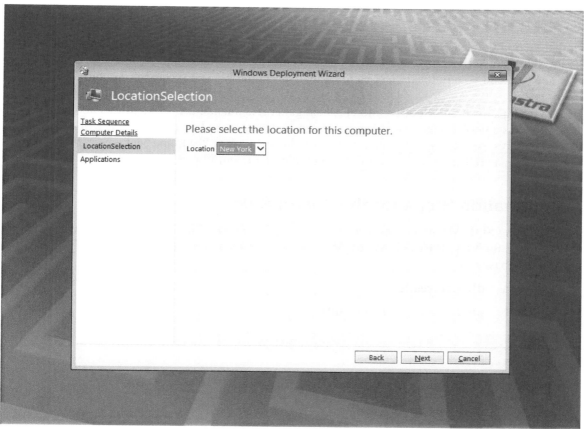

Deploying a machine with the new wizard pane.

Custom HTAs – Adding the Simple Frontend

In this section you learn to implement a custom HTA which allows you to easily set a computer name, select an Active Directory OU, and select a deployment task sequence in ConfigMgr 2012 R2. The backend communication is handled by the Sample #1 web service you created earlier.

> **Note:** Giving a deep introduction into HTAs in general is outside the scope of this book. It literally takes a book on its own. Also, a very good introduction has already been written by the Scripting Guys, so we highly recommend you to have a look at "Extreme Makeover: Wrap Your Scripts Up in a GUI Interface" at http://technet.microsoft.com/library/ee692768.aspx.

Configuration Steps for the Server Side

1. Using **SQL Management Studio**, in the top **Security** node, create a new security login in SQL for **VIAMONSTRA\CM_WS** and add the account to the following **CM_PS1** database roles:

    a. **db_datareader**

    b. **public** (selected by default)

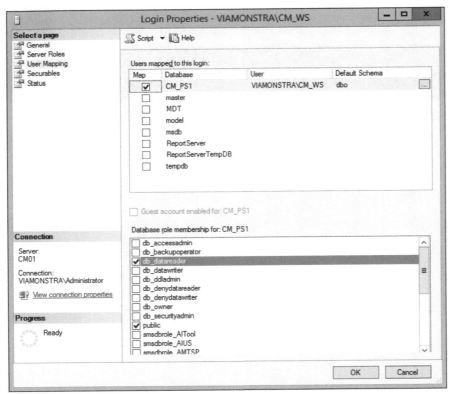

Configuring SQL permissions for the CM_WS account.

2. Verify that the web service works by starting **Internet Explorer**, navigating to **http://cm01/SimpleFrontend/ConfigMgr.asmx**, and testing the following methods:

    o   **GetOUList**

    o   **GetTaskSequenceList**

    o   **MoveComputerToOU**

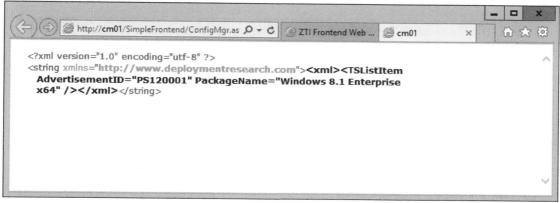

Testing the GetTaskSequenceList method.

Create the Boot Image

1. On **CM01**, using **Notepad**, review the **D:\Setup\SimpleFrontend\WinPE\Deploy\Scripts\Customsettings.ini** file.

2. Using the **ConfigMgr console**, in the **Software Library** workspace, expand **Operating Systems**, right-click **Boot Images**, select **Create Boot Image using MDT**, and create a new boot image package using the following settings:

    o   Package source folder to be created (UNC Path): **\\CM01\Sources\OSD\Boot\Zero Touch Simple Frontend x64**

Note: This folder does not exist (yet). You have to type in the name.

    o   Name: **Zero Touch Simple Frontend x64**

    o   Platform: **x64**

    o   Scratch Space: **<default>**

    o   Optional Components: **<default>**

    o   Select the **Enable command support (F8)** check box.

3. After the boot image is finished, in an elevated **Deployment and Imaging Tools** command prompt (run as Administrator), mount the boot image using the following commands (pressing **Enter** after each line):

```
md D:\Mount

cd /d "D:\Sources\OSD\Boot\Zero Touch Simple Frontend x64"

ImageX /mountrw WinPE.wim 1 D:\Mount
```

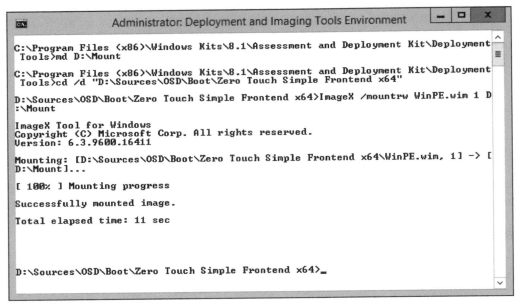

Mounting the boot image.

4. Using **File Explorer**, navigate to **D:\Setup\SimpleFrontend\WinPE** and copy the following folder and file to **D:\Mount** (replace and merge with existing files and folders):

   o **Deploy**

   o **TSConfig.ini**

5. Using **File Explorer**, navigate to **D:\Sources\OSD\MDT\MDT 2013\Scripts** and copy the following files to **D:\Mount\Deploy\Scripts**:

   o **ZTIDataAccess.vbs**

   o **ZTIGather.wsf**

   o **ZTIGather.xml**

   o **ZTIUtility.vbs**

6. Using **File Explorer**, copy the **D:\Sources\OSD\MDT\MDT 2013\Tools\x86\ Microsoft.BDD.Utility.dll** file to **D:\Mount\Deploy\Scripts\x86**.

7. Using **File Explorer**, copy the **D:\Sources\OSD\MDT\MDT 2013\Tools\x64\ Microsoft.BDD.Utility.dll** file to **D:\Mount\Deploy\Scripts\x64**.

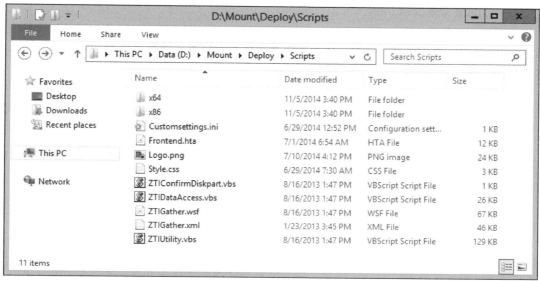

The D:\Mount\Deploy\Scripts folder after copying the files.

8. Close all **File Explorer** windows.

9. In the **Deployment and Imaging Tools** command prompt, unmount the boot image using the following command:

```
ImageX /unmount /commit D:\Mount
```

10. Using the **ConfigMgr console**, select the **Zero Touch Simple Frontend x64** boot image and select **Update Distribution Points** to update the boot image.

11. After updating the distribution points, distribute the **Zero Touch Simple Frontend x64** boot image to the **CM01** distribution point.

Configure the task sequence

1. Select **Task Sequences**, right-click the **Windows 8.1 Enterprise x64** task sequence and select **Properties**.

2. In the **Advanced** tab, configure the task sequence to use the **Zero Touch Simple Frontend x64** boot image.

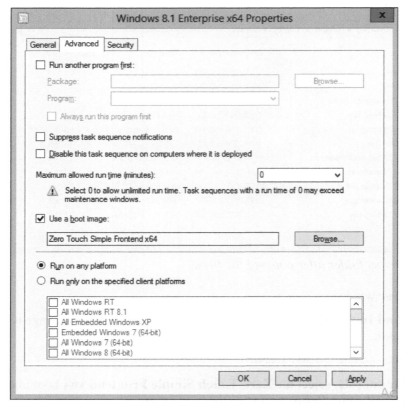

Changing the task sequence boot image.

Create the Boot Image Media

1. Right-click **Task Sequences**, and select **Create Task Sequence Media**.

2. On the **Select the type of media** page, select the **Bootable media option**, and select the **Allow unattended operating system deployment** check box. Then click **Next**.

3. On the **Select how media finds a management point** page, select the **Site-based media** option, and then click **Next**.

4. On the **Specify the media type** page, select the **CD/DVD set** option, and in the **Media File:** text box, type in **D:\Setup\CM2012 ZTI Simple Frontend.iso** and then click **Next**.

5. On the **Select security settings for the media** page, configure the following:

    a. Select the **Enable unknown computer support** check box.

    b. Clear the **Protect media with a password** check box.

    c. **Create self-signed media certificate**

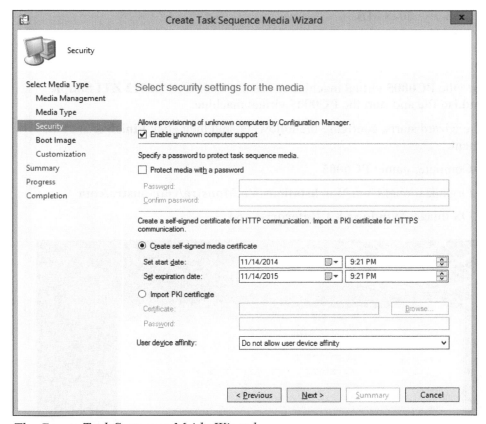

The Create Task Sequence Meida Wizard.

6. On the **Select the boot image for the media** page, configure the following:

    a. Boot image: **Zero Touch Simple Frontend x64**

    b. Distribution Point: **CM01.CORP.VIAMONSTRA.COM**

    c. Management Point: **CM01.corp.viamonstra.com**

7. On the **Customize the task sequence media** page, accept the default settings and click **Next** twice. Once the wizard completes, click **Close**.

8. Using **File Explorer**, copy the **D:\Setup\CM2012 ZTI Simple Frontend.iso** to **C:\ISO** on your host PC.

Deploy Windows 8.1 Using the Custom HTA

1. On the **Host PC**, create a virtual machine with the following settings:

   o   Name: **PC0005**

   o   Location: **C:\VMs**

   o   Memory: **2048 MB**

   o   Network: The virtual network for the New York site

   o   Hard disk: **60 GB**

2. Configure the **PC0005** virtual machine to use the **C:\ISO\CM2012 ZTI Simple Frontend.iso** file and start the **PC0005** virtual machine.

3. When the wizard starts, configure the following, and then click **Finish** to start the deployment:

   a.   Computer name: **PC0005**

   b.   Organizational Unit: **Workstations/ViaMonstra/viamonstra/com**

   c.   OS Image: **Windows 8.1 Enterprise x64**

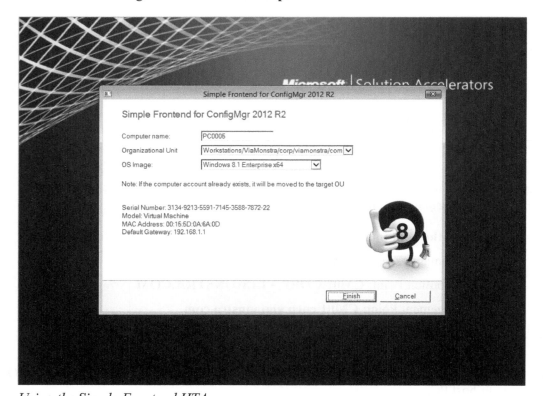

Using the Simple Frontend HTA.

Customizing and Using UDI

As you learned in Chapter 5, MDT 2013 adds user-driven installations, an optional deployment wizard, to ConfigMgr 2012 R2. In this section, you configure UDI for the ConfigMgr 2012 R2 bare metal deployment scenario.

The UDI wizard stores its configuration in two XML files. One core settings file, and one file for application installation (when using that feature).

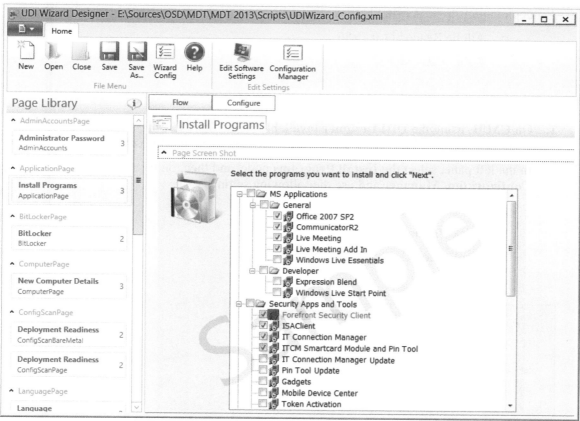

One of the default panes in the optional deployment wizard.

Prepare Application Deployments for UDI

In order for UDI to find applications to add to the wizard, they need to deployed to a collection. We recommend using an empty collection for this.

1.   On **CM01**, using the **ConfigMgr console**, in the **Assets and Compliance** workspace, create a device collection named **UDI Applications**. Limit it to **All Systems**, and use the default settings for remaining settings (add no members).

2.   Deploy the following packages to the **UDI Applications** collection. Configure the deployments to be **Available** (not required).

      o   Adobe Reader 11.0 - x86

      o   7-Zip 9.20 - x64

Configuring the UDI Settings File

1.   On **CM01**, using the **UDI Designer** (available on the Start screen), open the **D:\Sources\OSD\MDT\MDT 2013\Scripts\UDIWizard_config.xml** file.

2.   In the left pane, select the **Install Programs** node, and then, on the ribbon, click **Configuration Manager** and use the following settings:

      a.   Site Server Name: **CM01**

      b.   Click **Validate Site**.

      c.   Application Collection: **UDI Applications**

      d.   Click **OK**.

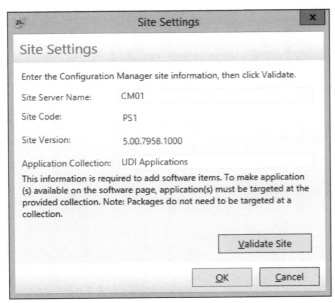

Configuring the site settings.

3. On the main page, expand the **StageGroup: New Computer** node.

4. Double-click the **Volume** page, and in the **Image Combo Box** section, expand the **Image Combo Behavior** node.

5. In the **Image Combo Box Values** section, right-click **Windows 7 RTM Images**, and click **Remove Item**.

6. In the **Image Combo Box Values** section, click **Add Item**. Use the following settings:

   o   Image Name: **Windows 8.1 Enterprise x64**

   o   Display Name: **Windows 8.1 Enterprise x64**

   o   Index: **1**

   o   Architecture: **amd64**

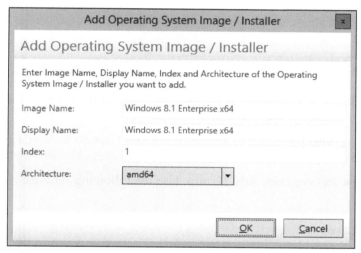

Adding an operating system image to the UDI wizard.

Real World Note: The name assigned here is only a label and has no relationship with the operating system image package your task sequence is configured to use. It's the index number that tells UDI which image to pick (a WIM file can have multiple indexes).

---

7. On the main page, click the **Flow** tab to return to the page overview.

8. Double-click the **New Computer Details** page, and scroll down to the **Network Details** section.

9. Expand the **Network Details** node, and in the **Domain or Workgroup Radio Buttons** area, select the **Domain** option.

10. Expand the **Domains and OUs** section (last option in the Network Details area), and select **Add Domain**. Use the following settings:

   o   Domain Name: **corp.viamonstra.com**

   o   Friendly Name: **ViaMonstra**

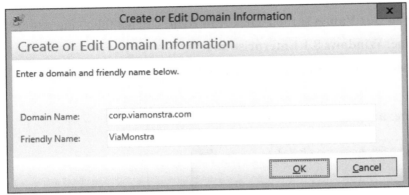

Configuring the domain settings.

11. Right-click the added **ViaMonstra** domain and select **Search Domain for OUs**. In the list, select the **ViaMonstra / Workstations** OU and click **OK**.

12. Double-click the **Install Programs** page, and in the **Software and Groups** section, right-click the **General Software** group and select **Remove Item**.

13. In the **Software and Groups** section, click **Add Group**. Use the following settings:

   o   Name: **Adobe**

   o   Nest Under: **Root Level**

Adding the Adobe software group.

14. Right-click the **Adobe** software group and select **Add Software to Group**. Use the following settings:

    a. **I want to add a Package/Program**

    b. In the **Search for 32 Bit Program** area, click **Select**, and then click **Search**.

    c. Select the **Adobe Reader 11.0 - x86** package, and click **OK**.

    d. In the **Program:** drop-down list, select **Install**.

    e. Select the **Use the same Package/Program for the 64-bit option** check box, and then click **Finish**.

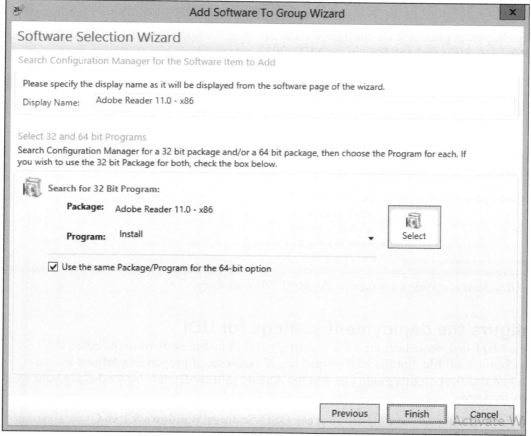

Adding an application to the UDI wizard.

15. Right-click the **Adobe** software group and select **Add Software Group**. Use the following settings:

    o Name: **Utilities**

    o Nest Under: **Root Level**

275

16. Right-click the **Utilities** software group and select **Add Software to Group**. Use the following settings:

    a. **I want to add a Package/Program**

    b. In the **Search for 64 Bit Program** area, click **Select**, and then click **Search**.

    c. Select the **7-Zip 9.20 - x64** package, and click **OK**.

    d. In the **Program:** drop-down list, select **Install**, and then click **Finish**.

17. Save the configuration via the **Save** button on the ribbon.

18. Using the **ConfigMgr console**, in the **Software Library** workspace, update the distribution point for the **MDT 2013** package.

> **Note:** In this example, the UDI configuration is stored in the UDIWizard_Config.xml and UDIWizard_Config.xml.app files in the MDT 2013 package.

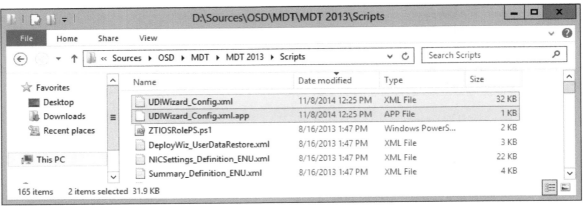

The UDI wizard configuration files in the MDT 2013 package.

Configure the deployment settings for UDI

Like the MDT task sequence, the UDI wizard also takes instructions from the rules, the CustomSettings.ini file, but the UDI wizard has it's own set of properties (defined by the ZTIGather.xml file). In this guide you add the domain join credentials by modifying your existing settings package.

1. Using **Notepad**, edit the **D:\Sources\OSD\Settings\Windows 8.1 x64 Settings\CustomSettings.ini** file.

2. Change line 2 to the following

```
Priority=UDI, Default
```

3. Then, before the [Default] section add the following lines:

    ```
    [UDI]

    OSDJoinAccount=VIAMONSTRA\CM_JD

    OSDJoinPassword=P@ssw0rd
    ```

4. Save the file, and update the distribution points for the **Windows 8.1 x64 Settings** package by right-clicking the **Windows 8.1 x64 Settings** package and selecting **Update Distribution Points**.

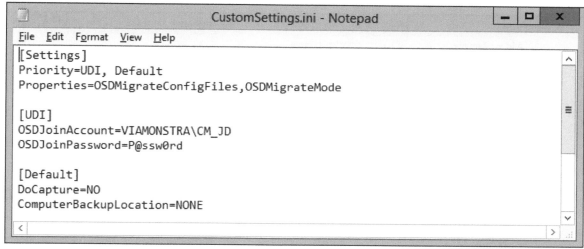

The updated CustomSettings.ini file.

Create the UDI Task Sequence

When creating a task sequence for UDI, you can either create a new task sequence from scratch and during the Create MDT Task Sequence wizard, select the Perform a "User-Driven Installation" option. However, if already have a task sequence that you are happy with, you can simple make a copy, and modify the copy to enable UDI.

1. Using **ConfigMgr Console**, in the **Software Library** workspace, **expand Operating Systems**, and select **Task Sequences**.

2. Right-click the **Windows 8.1 Enterprise x64** task sequence, and select **Copy**.

277

3. Right-click the new task sequence, and select **Properties**. Use the following settings:

   a. In the General tab, assign the name **Windows 8.1 Enterprise x64 – UDI**.

   b. In the Advanced tab, select the **Zero Touch WinPE 5.0 x64** boot image.

   c. Click **OK** twice.

4. Right-click the **Windows 8.1 Enterprise x64 – UDI** task sequence, and select **Edit**.

5. In the **Initialization** node, select **Set Variable for Wizard** action, and change the **SkipWizard** value to **NO**. Then click **OK**.

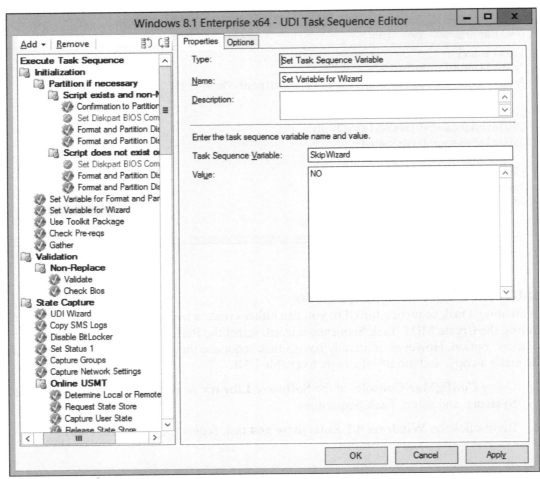

Enabling UDI in an existing task sequence.

Create a Deployment for the UDI Task Sequence

1. Using the **ConfigMgr console**, select **Task Sequences**.

2. Right-click the **Windows 8.1 Enterprise x64 – UDI** task sequence, and then select **Deploy**. Use the following settings:

   a. General

      Collection: **All unknown Computers**

   b. Deployment Settings

      ▪ Purpose: **Available**

      ▪ Make available to the following: **Configuration Manager clients, media and PXE**

   c. Scheduling

      <default>

   d. User Experience

      <default>

   e. Alerts

      <default>

   f. Distribution Points:

      <default>

Deploy Windows 8.1 Using UDI

1. On the **Host PC**, create a virtual machine with the following settings:

   a. Name: **PC0006**

   b. Location: **C:\VMs**

   c. Memory: **2048 MB**

   d. Network: The virtual network for the New York site

   e. Hard disk: **60 GB** (dynamic disk)

> **Note:** Again, if you are using Hyper-V in Windows Server 2012 R2, the new Generation 2 VMs can PXE boot without the need of using a legacy network adapter.

2.   Start the **PC0006** virtual machine, and press **Enter** to start the PXE boot (or press **F12** if you are using an earlier Hyper-V version). Then complete the **Task Sequence Wizard** using the following settings:

   a.   Password: **P@ssw0rd**

   b.   Select a task sequence to execute on this computer:
        Windows 8.1 Enterprise x64 - UDI

3.   Wait until the UDI wizard starts (after a minute or two). Use the following settings for the wizard:

   a.   On the **BitLocker** page, do not enable BitLocker.

   b.   On the **Volume** page, select the **Partition and form disk 0** check box.

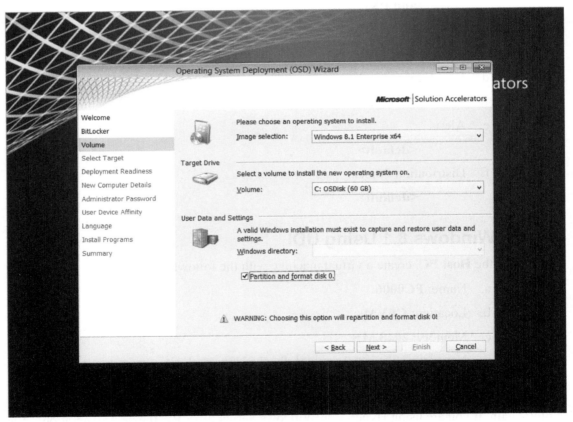

The Volume page of the UDI wizard.

   c.   On the **Select Target** page, accept the default settings.

   d.   On the **Deployment Readiness** page, accept the default settings.

e.   On the **New Computer Details** page, in the **Computer name** text box, type in **PC0006** (note that the other values are already set from CustomSettings.ini).

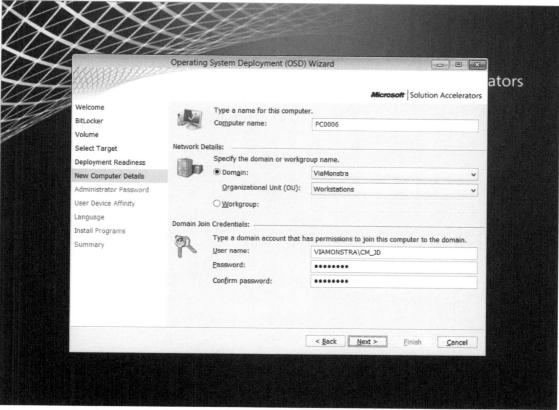

The domain join credentials automatically populated via the CustomSettings.ini file.

f.   On the **Administrator Password** page, type in a password of **P@ssw9rd**, and in the the **Account name(s):** text box, type in **VIAMONSTRA\Johan**.

g.   On the **User Device Affinity** page, accept the default settings.

h.   On the **Language** page, accept the default settings.

i.   On the **Install Programs** page, select both applications.

j.   On the **Summary** page, review the settings, and click **Finish** to start the deployment.

Chapter 13

Monitoring Deployments

With the increasing rate of automation within a deployment, there also is an increasing need to keep an eye on what is happening in the environment. Deployments can be initiated in various ways, and the larger and more distributed the environment is, the harder it is to actually get the deployment's current status.

In this chapter, you get an in-depth view of the monitoring capabilities of MDT 2013 and how to extend them. In this chapter, we provide guidance on:

- The monitoring components
- Viewing monitoring information
- Extending monitoring

Step-by-Step Guide Requirements

If you want to run the step-by-step guides in this chapter, you need a lab environment configured as outlined in Chapter 3 and Appendix A. In this chapter, youuse the following virtual machines:

DC01   CM01   MDT01   PC0001

The VMs used in this chapter.

You also need to have downloaded the following software:

- MDT 2013
- The book sample files (http://stealingwithpride.com)

Overview
The MDT monitoring option consists of three parts by default:

- The MDT Monitoring web service
- The client-side components
- The MDT Workbench

The MDT Monitoring Web Service
The MDT Monitoring web service is an optional component of MDT and acts as a central web service that is typically hosted on the MDT Server itself. But it can be installed on almost any other server, as well.

If this web service is enabled, all information from each client that is currently being deployed is sent to this central web service and stored in a local database. The same web service also is used to request this stored information for reporting purposes.

The Client-side Components
Whenever a new deployment is started on the client, MDT makes sure that it regularly sends status information to the MDT Monitoring web service. This typically happens when the deployment starts, when a step has finished, or when the whole deployment has finished. On long running steps, it also sends a heartbeat every five minutes.

The Deployment Workbench
The Deployment Workbench is the main tool used to see the current monitoring information of all deployments. It also allows you to get additional information for each individual deployment, including the option to create a remote connection to the client being deployed for troubleshooting purposes.

Enabling Deployment Monitoring
To enable the monitoring capabilities of MDT 2013, you complete the following steps:

1. On **MDT01**, using the **Deployment Workbench**, right-click the **MDT Production** deployment share and select **Properties**.

2. On the **Monitoring** tab, select the **Enable monitoring for this deployment share** check box and click **OK**.

> **Note:** It will take a while for the Deployment Workbench to create the monitoring database (SQL Server Compact Edition 3.5) and the Microsoft Deployment Toolkit Monitor Service. The workbench may appear to hang, but just give it a few more seconds and it will complete.

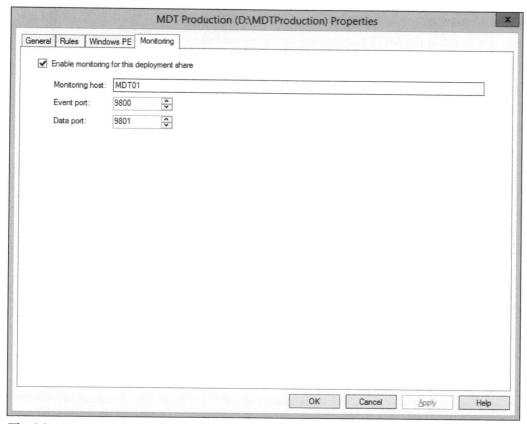

The Monitoring node in Deployment Workbench.

Verifying Monitoring

After you have enabled the monitoring capabilities using the MDT Deployment Workbench, you should verify that it has been enabled properly, that the monitoring web service is working, and that all required properties have been added.

Verify the Monitoring Service

First, you need to check whether the MDT Monitor Service has been installed on the MDT server and that it is running.

1. On **MDT01**, press **Windows logo key + X** and select **Computer Management**.

2. Expand the **Services and Applications** node and select **Services**.

3. Verify that the **Microsoft Deployment Toolkit Monitor Service** is available and running.

Verify the Web Service

After you have verified that the MDT Monitoring service is installed and running, you need to ensure that it also responds to requests.

1. On **PC0001**, open **Internet Explorer** and open the following URL:

   `http://mdt01:9801/MDTMonitorData/`

2. Verify that you get a valid response similar to the following screenshot.

```
<?xml version="1.0" encoding="utf-8" standalone="yes" ?>
- <service xml:base="http://mdt01:9801/MDTMonitorData/" xmlns:atom="http://www.w3.org/2005/Atom"
    xmlns:app="http://www.w3.org/2007/app" xmlns="http://www.w3.org/2007/app">
  - <workspace>
      <atom:title>Default</atom:title>
    - <collection href="Computers">
        <atom:title>Computers</atom:title>
      </collection>
    - <collection href="ComputerIdentities">
        <atom:title>ComputerIdentities</atom:title>
      </collection>
    - <collection href="NextIDs">
        <atom:title>NextIDs</atom:title>
      </collection>
    </workspace>
  </service>
```

MDT Monitoring web service.

Verify the MDT Deployment Share Properties

Finally, for MDT to be able to send out the monitoring events to the MDT Monitoring web service, the EventService property needs to be set and configured with the appropriate URL. This should have been done automatically when the service was enabled.

1. On **MDT01**, using the **Deployment Workbench**, right-click the **MDT Production** deployment share and select **Properties**.

2. On the **Rules** tab, verify that the following property is set in the **Default** section:

   `EventService=http://MDT01:9800`

Adding Monitoring Support for ConfigMgr 2012 R2

The MDT 2013 monitoring feature has been added primarily for MDT 2013 Lite Touch-based deployments. ZTI deployments are expected to use the built-in event system of ConfigMgr 2012 R2.

However, adding the MDT monitoring support for ZTI deployments, as well, gives you a couple benefits. It primarily allows you to monitor all current and recently finished deployments, using the MDT Deployment Workbench. And it gives you all the additional features, mainly the option to connect remotely to a running deployment in case local support is required.

> **Note:** This guide assumes that all guides from Chapter 6 have been done to configure the ConfigMgr 2012 R2 OSD environment.

1. On **CM01**, using the **Deployment Workbench**, right-click the **MDT Production** deployment share and select **Properties**.

2. On the **Monitoring** tab, select the **Enable monitoring for this deployment share** check box and click **OK**.

3. Using **Notepad**, edit the **D:\Sources\OSD\Settings\Windows 8.1 x64 Settings\CustomSettings.ini** file.

4. Add the following line to the **[Default]** section:

   ```
   EventService=http://CM01:9800
   ```

5. Save the **CustomSettings.ini** file.

6. Update the distribution points for the **Windows 8.1 x64 Settings** package by right-clicking the **Windows 8.1 x64 Settings** package and selecting **Update Distribution Points**.

Viewing Monitoring Information

The MDT Monitoring web service offers all current monitoring information as an OData stream, which can be accessed using various methods.

MDT Deployment Workbench

On default, the MDT Deployment Workbench is the typical tool being used to get access to the monitoring information.

1. On **MDT01**, using the **Deployment Workbench**, expand the node for the **MDT Production** deployment share.

2. Select the **Monitoring** node.

   This brings up a list of all current deployments.

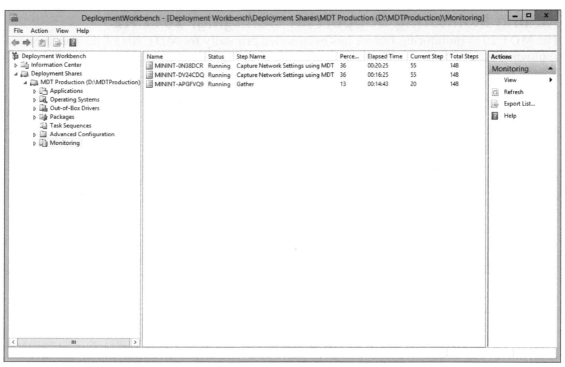

MDT 2013 Monitoring displaying a few machines being deployed.

To see more information about an individual deployment, you can right-click the appropriate entry and choose Properties. That displays all available details about this particular deployment, including:

- Computer name

- Deployment status

- Current step

- Progress

- Start/end time and current duration

- Nuumber of errors and warnings

Additionally, it offers the possibility of creating a remote connection to the computer being deployed using one of the following:

- **Remote desktop**: If the computer is presently running a full OS and remote desktop is enabled and accessible through the firewall

- **VM connection**: If the computer is presently in a full OS and is also a virtual machine hosted on a Hyper-V based server

- **DaRT Remote Control**: If the computer is currently running from WinPE and if the Diagnostics and Recovery Toolkit (DaRT) has been integrated into the MDT boot image

PowerShell

Another option is to get the monitoring information using PowerShell. And as the complete administration of MDT is built upon PowerShell, there are also a few commands available for the monitoring option. To get the monitoring details (assuming you have any), run the following PowerShell commands on MDT01:

```
Add-PSSnapin 'Microsoft.BDD.PSSNAPIN'

New-PSDrive -Name MDT -Root 'D:\MDTProduction' -PSProvider
MDTPROVIDER

Get-MDTMonitorData -Path MDT:
```

Microsoft Excel 2013

As the MDT Monitoring web service delivers an OData stream and Microsoft Excel 2013 natively supports OData as a data source, you also can use Microsoft Excel 2013 to get a list of all monitoring information. With some additional magic of auto-formatting, it's then pretty easy to create some nice reports.

1. Using **Microsoft Excel 2013**, create a blank workbook. Then on the **Data** tab, select **Get External Data / From Other Sources / From OData Data Feed**.

2. In the **Data Connection Wizard**, on the **Connect to a Data Feed** page, configure the following settings and then click **Next**:

    Link or File: **http://MDT01:9801/MDTMonitorData/Computers**

3. On the **Select Tables** page, select the **Computers** table and click **Next**.

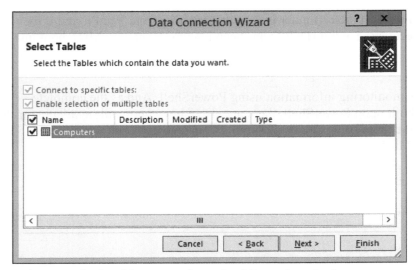

Selecting which tables to get from the OData data feed.

4. On the **Save Data Connection File and Finish** page, configuring the following settings, and then click **Finish**:

   o   File Name: **MDT01_Monitoring.odc**

   o   Description: **MDT01 Monitoring information**

   o   Friendly Name: **MDT01 Monitoring information**

5. In the **Import Data** dialox box, accept the default settings and click **OK**.

Using Excel 2013 to acquire an MDT Monitoring OData stream.

6. On the **Data** tab, click **Refresh All**, or press **Ctrl + Alt + F5** to update the data with the most recent monitoring information.

Extending Monitoring

The built-in MDT monitoring is pretty helpful itself for getting more information about your currently running deployments. However, it's also limited in some ways, as it is just a basic implementation.

Currently, one of main limitations is that it stores only the latest status per computer, which makes it impossible to get historical information, such as how often a computer has been deployed over its lifetime, common errors over time, or the increasing time of individual steps within the deployment process. Also, the information that is sent to the MDT Monitoring web service is pretty limited and not built to be extended easily.

To overcome these limitations, you can write a custom Monitoring Web Service that allows you to handle the monitoring data the way it need to be handled.

Process Overview

To be able to create a custom Monitoring web service, you first need to know some more technical details about how this process is implemented. When and how does it send the information? What information is being sent?

Events

The monitoring information is sent to the central MDT Monitoring web service at specific events throughout the progress of the deployment. Whereas some scripts used by MDT have their own specific events, the most common events throughout a deployment will happen

- When a deployment has started

- When a script/step has finished

- When an error occurred

- When a deployment has finished

There is a limitation, though, with ZTI deployments. As mentioned before, the primary target for MDT monitoring is LTI-based deployments. This means that even if possible, monitoring support in ZTI deployments is limited. One of the main limitations is because ZTI deployments aren't initiated by the MDT Lite Touch script, and due to this, the default events for the start and finish of a deployment are missing.

However, every time a MDT script is used to execute a certain step during the ZTI task sequence, which tends to happen quite often, events about the current status are sent. And the Task Sequence template of MDT 2013 for ConfigMgr 2012 R2 even includes an additional step at the end of the task sequence, that sends an explicit event, when the deployment has finished.

Event Information

On each event, the following information is sent to the MDT monitoring web service:

- LTI guid: A unique identifier identifying a single deployment that is created by the MDT Monitoring web service as soon as a new deployment has started

- Computer name

- Event ID (see Appendix C)

- EventType: Informational, Warning, or Error

- Current step name

- Current step number

- Total amount of steps

- MAC Address(es) and UUID

- IP address

- DaRT port and ticket

- VM host and VM name

Event Target

The final piece of information missing is the target to which the MDT monitoring events are sent. As you remember, MDT uses the EventService property to store the URL to the MDT Monitoring service. It then adds a hardcoded path to this URL so that the final target is

http://CM01:9800/MDTMonitorEvent/PostEvent

When creating a custom web service, you need to make sure that your custom function is available at /MDTMonitorEvent/PostEvent. Otherwise you would need to make changes to the original MDT scripts, which would break compatibility with the existing MDT monitoring and also cause problems with the next MDT update.

The Design

As the intention of this book isn't to create a full-blown monitoring solution, but rather to give you the necessary information to start your own solution if required, the design of your sample custom MDT Monitoring web service is pretty simple and straightforward:

- It offers a PostEvent function that behaves the same way as the one supplied by MDT.

- All events are written to a .csv file.

- All events are forwarded to the original MDT Monitoring web service to stay as compatible as possible.

The Project

The complete monitoring example project is available in the book sample files. The code snippets shown here are based on C#.

Requirements

In the other chapters of this book, we mainly use ASMX-based web services for most of the examples simply because they are very easy to set up and understand. As this project has some specific requirements, we chose a different platform to host the custom monitoring web service called ASP.NET Web.API. This is a free framework, already integrated with Microsoft Visual Studio 2013, that gives you an easy way to build RESTful web services.

One of the principal benefits of using ASP.NET Web.API is that it uses conventions to extract information from the URL to route to the appropriate controller and action. Think of a controller as your former ASMX-based web service class and the action as a method within this web service. In addition, it integrates nicely with another free framework ASP.Net MVC which can be used to create some webpages for reporting purposes. The monitoring example project from the book sample files already contains a simple webpage with some monitoring information that you can tweak for your own deployments. However, the following steps cover only the web service itself.

Open the Project

If you just want to view the example project, here follows the steps to open it. If you want to create the project from scratch, simply skip to the next section. In this example we assume you have downloaded the book samples files to C:\Setup on PC0001. Also, make sure you have Internet access on PC0001.

1. On **PC0001**, using **Visual Studio Express 2013 for Web**, open the **C:\Setup\ MDTMonitoring\MonitoringDemo.sln** solution file.

2. In the **Tools** menu, select **Library Package Manager / Manage NuGet Package for Solution**.

3. In the **MonitoringDemo.sln – NuGet Package Manager** window, in the upper right corner, click **Restore** to download the missing packages.

4. Then close the **NuGet Package Manager** window.

Create the Project

If you rather want to create the project from scratch to finish on your own, this is the guide you want to follow. However, to avoid having you type in everything by hand, you find a text file named MDTMonitor.txt in the MDTMonitoring folder in the sample files, that you can copy and paste code snippets from.

1. On **PC0001**, using **Microsoft Visual Studio 2013 (Express)** , click **New Project** on the **Start screen**, or select **File / New / Project**.

2. On the **New Project** page, search for **MVC** and select **ASP.NET MVC 4 Web Visual C#**. Use the following properties:

   o   Name: **MonitoringDemoCSharp**

   o   Location: **C:\Working**

   o   Solution name: **MonitoringDemo**

   o   Create directory for solution: **Selected**

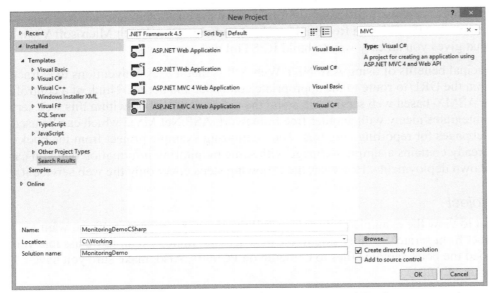

A new ASP.NET MVC 4 Web Application project in Visual Studio.

3. On the **Project Template** page, select **Web.API** and click **OK**.

> **Real World Note:** This creates a minimal ASP.NET Web.API project. We recommend reading through http://asp.net/webapi and http://asp.net/mvc, especially the tutorials that provide a great start into building web services and web applications.

4. In the **Solution Explorer**, right-click the **Controllers** folder and select **Add / Controller**, using the following properties:

   o   Controller name: **MDTMonitorEventController**

   o   Template: **Empty API controller**

   o   Click **Add**.

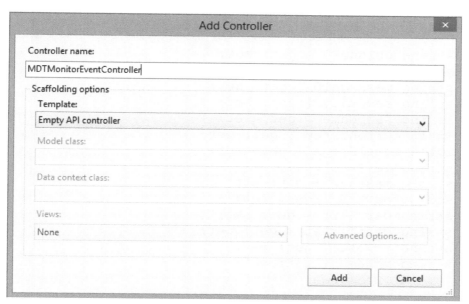

Adding an empty API controller in Visual Studio.

> **Note:** MDT uses a hardcoded value of MDTMonitorEvent as part of the web service URL. As you need to make sure that all requests to this particular URL will be processed properly, you use a default behavior of ASP.Net MVC, which is using this part of the URL to look for the appropriate controller and action.

Create the MonitorEvent Class

Instead of typing all individual properties that are to be posted on each monitor event at several places in the code, you make use of a feature from ASP.Net Web.API called model binding. You add a new model (class) that contains all those properties, so you can use it as a container for your MonitorEvent properties. ASP.Net Web.API will then try to match each property being sent via the MDT web service call to the corresponding property of this class.

> **Note:** Again, a friendly reminder about the MDTMonitor.txt file in the MDTMonitoring folder in the sample files, that you can copy and paste code snippets from.

1. Using **Visual Studio**, in the **Solution Explorer**, right-click the **Models** node and select **Add / Class**. Use the following settings:

   o   Name: **MonitorEvent**

   o   Template: **Class Visual C#**

2. Modify the **MonitorEvent** class to look like this:

```
public class MonitorEvent
```

```
{

    public string uniqueID { get; set; }
    public string computerName { get; set; }
    public string messageID { get; set; }
    public string severity { get; set; }
    public string stepName { get; set; }
    public Int16 currentstep { get; set; }
    public Int16 totalSteps { get; set; }
    public string id { get; set; }
    public string message { get; set; }
    public string dartIP { get; set; }
    public string dartPort { get; set; }
    public string dartTicket { get; set; }
    public string vmHost { get; set; }
    public string vmName { get; set; }

}
```

3. Save your changes.

Add the PostEvent Method

As mentioned previously, MDT sends the monitoring event information to a web service method called PostEvent. You now implement this method and mimic the same behavior as the original MDT Monitoring web service.

1. Using **Visual Studio**, in the **Solution Explorer**, expand the **Controllers** node, right-click **MDTMonitorEventController.cs**, and select **View Code**.

2. Add the following snippet to the line after the last **using** statement:

```
using MonitoringDemoCSharp.Models;
using System.Reflection;
using System.IO;
```

3. Add the following **PostEvent** method to the MDTMonitorEventController class.

```
[HttpGet]
public string PostEvent([FromUri]MonitorEvent monitorEvent)
{
  // Ensure there is a unique DeploymentID
  if (string.IsNullOrEmpty(monitorEvent.uniqueID))
  {
    monitorEvent.uniqueID = Guid.NewGuid().ToString();
  }
  // Read properties
  string param = "";
  string csv = "";
```

```
var props = typeof(MonitorEvent).GetProperties();
foreach (PropertyInfo prop in props)
{
  object value = prop.GetValue(monitorEvent) ?? "";
  string strValue = value.ToString();
  param += string.Format("{0}={1}&", prop.Name, strValue);
  csv += string.Format("{0};", value.ToString());
}

// Create URL
string MDTURL =
"http://CM01:9800/MDTMonitorEvent/PostEvent?";
Uri MDTURI = new Uri(MDTURL + param);

// Send data
WebClient client = new WebClient();
client.OpenRead(MDTURI);

// Write properties to file
csv += Environment.NewLine;
string path =
   System.Web.Hosting.HostingEnvironment.MapPath("~/");
File.AppendAllText(path + "MonitorEvents.csv", csv);


// Return DeploymentID
return monitorEvent.uniqueID;

}
```

4. Save the changes.

Now, take a quick look at what this actually does:

```
[HttpGet]
public string PostEvent([FromUri]MonitorEvent monitorEvent)
```

The [HttpGet] tells ASP.Net Web.API that this method can be reached using an HTTP GET request. You have to add this because the method is called PostEvent, and based on the default naming conventions, it would be restricted to HTTP POST requests only. The [FromUri] in the parameter definition tells ASP.Net Web.API to automatically map the properties from the HTTP request to the properties defined within the MonitorEvent object. As you named the properties of the MonitorEvent object exactly like they are called from MDT, they should match.

```
if (string.IsNullOrEmpty(monitorEvent.uniqueID))
   {
     monitorEvent.uniqueID = Guid.NewGuid().ToString();
   }
```

This ensures that you have a unique deployment ID per deployment. If a new deployment is started, this value will be empty. In that case, a new GUID is created and later returned to the client.

```
var props = typeof(MonitorEvent).GetProperties();
  foreach (PropertyInfo prop in props)
  {
    object value = prop.GetValue(monitorEvent) ?? "";
    string strValue = value.ToString();
    param += string.Format("{0}={1}&", prop.Name, strValue);
    csv += string.Format("{0};", value.ToString());
  }
```

Because you want to forward all supplied properties to the MDT server and also store them locally in a file, you need to write down all properties with their values. However, as you don't want to type them all, let the computer do the hard work.

At first, this might seem more complicated, but it just gets a list of properties from the MonitorEvent property and then iterates over each property and creates two different strings.

```
// Create URL
string MDTURL = "http://CM01:9800/MDTMonitorEvent/PostEvent?";
Uri MDTURI = new Uri(MDTURL + param);

// Send data
WebClient client = new WebClient();
client.OpenRead(MDTURI);
```

This creates the URL to the MDT server, including all parameters, and then opens this URL.

Real World Note: The best practice is to store information like the name of the MDT server in a settings file so it can be adjusted later. The monitoring demo project from the book sample files stores this value in the web.config file.

```
// Write properties to file
csv += Environment.NewLine;
string path =
  System.Web.Hosting.HostingEnvironment.MapPath("~/");
File.AppendAllText(path + "MonitorEvents.csv", csv);
```

This writes a new line to a MonitorEvents.csv file at the root of the web application.

```
// Return DeploymentID
  return monitorEvent.uniqueID;
```

And, finally, the unique deployment ID is returned back to the client.

The MonitorEvents.csv file created by the web service.

Change the Default Behavior

The PostEvent function itself is now ready to be used. However, you need to apply two small changes to the default behavior of ASP.Net Web.API.

Default Routing

By default, ASP.Net Web.API uses the HTTP verbs GET, POST, PUT, and DELETE to identify which controller action should be used, which is a huge help on plain REST-based web services. It uses the route template "api/{controller}/{id}" to parse the requested URL.

To be able to use individual actions in the controller, the route template needs to be changed to "api/{controller}/{action}/{id}".

1. Using **Visual Studio**, in the **Solution Explorer**, expand the **App_Start** folder, right-click **WebApiConfig.cs**, and select **View Code**.

2. Update the first **MapHttpRoute** call in the **Register** method to look like the following snippet (it's routeTemplate line that is different):

```
config.Routes.MapHttpRoute(
    name: "DefaultApi",
    routeTemplate: "api/{controller}/{action}/{id}",
    defaults: new { id = RouteParameter.Optional }
);
```

3. Save the changes.

Return XML

ASP.Net Web.API returns the result as either JSON or XML, based on the request from the client. If no specific output format is specified by the client, it defaults to JSON. That isn't the preferred way for this web service because MDT doesn't specify this return type and can't handle the JSON result. So, to avoid a change within MDT, it's easier to tell ASP.Net Web.API to answer those requests using XML.

1. Using **Visual Studio**, in the **Solution Explorer**, right-click **Global.asax** and select **View Code**.

2. Add the following code below the other "using" statements:

    ```
    using System.Net.Http.Formatting;
    ```

3. Add the following code snippet at the end of the **Application_Start** method:

    ```
    foreach (var item in
    GlobalConfiguration.Configuration.Formatters)
    {
      if (typeof(XmlMediaTypeFormatter) == item.GetType())
      {
        item.AddRequestHeaderMapping("Accept", "*/*",
            StringComparison.OrdinalIgnoreCase, false,
            "application/xml");
      }
    }
    ```

4. Save the changes.

> **Note:** This snippet iterates over all configured formatters. These are the ones used to automatically format the web service response into the appropriate format and add a specific mapping to the ones that format into XML. In this case, it adds "*/*", which is the accept header MDT uses by default.

Add the GetSettings Method

The monitoring itself is now working properly. However, if you would integrate this web service into the deployment and look closely to the logs on a client, you would recognize that there is an error being logged when the Gather step is executed.

This happens because the Gather step is calling another method called GetSettings. This method has been created to publish additional settings to a computer if monitoring is enabled. For this sample, the functionality isn't required. However, to get rid of the error message in the logs, you need to add at least a basic implementation of this function which returns an empty string.

1. Using **Visual Studio**, in the **Solution Explorer**, expand the **Controllers** node, right-click **MDTMonitorEventController.cs**, and select **View Code**.

2. Add the following code snippet after the **PostEvent** method:

```
[HttpGet]
public string GetSettings(string uniqueID)
{
  return "";
}
```

3. Save the file.

Publish the Project

There are several options for how to publish a web application to a web server. However, most of them require some additional software to be installed on the web server. Probably the simplest way is to publish to the local file system. This creates a folder that can then be copied to the web server.

1. Using **Visual Studio**, in the **Solution Explorer**, right-click the **MonitoringDemoCSharp.cs** project and select **Publish**.

2. In the **Publish Web** wizard, on the **Profile** page, select **<New Profile...>** , give it the name **FileSystem**, and click **Next**.

3. On the **Connection** page, use the following properties:

   o   Publish method: **File System**

   o   Target location: **C:\Working\MonitoringDemo\Deploy_CSharp**

4. On the **Settings** page, use the **Release** configuration.

5. Click **Publish**.

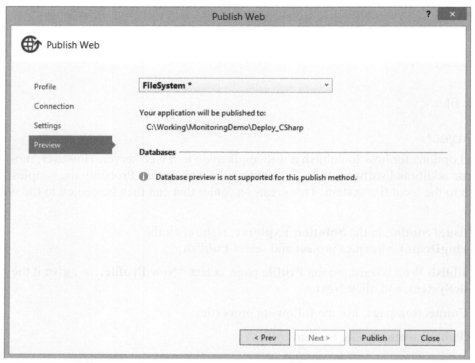

Publishing a web service project.

Add the Project to the Web Server

For this project, you use CM01 to host the web application, as this has already been configured to use IIS. In this guide, we assume you created the DeploymentWebService application pool in the preceding chapter.

1. On **CM01**, using **File Explorer**, create the **MonitoringWebService** subfolder in **D:\ViaMonstraWebServices**.

2. Copy the content of **\\PC0001\C$\Working\MonitoringDemo\Deploy_CSharp** to **D:\ViaMonstraWebServices\MonitoringWebService**.

3. Using **Internet Information Services (IIS) Manager**, expand the **CM01** node, expand **Sites**, and expand **Default Web Site** (to see the other web services installed by ConfigMgr).

4. Right-click **Default Web Site**, and select **Add Application**. Use the following settings for the application:

    a. Alias: **MonitoringWebService**

    b. Application pool: **DeploymentWebService**

    c. Physical path: **D:\ViaMonstraWebServices\MonitoringWebService**

    d. Click **OK**.

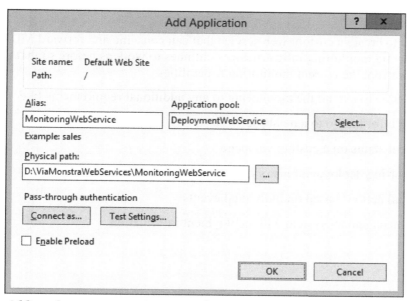

Adding the custom monitoring web service as a web application.

Integrate the Web Service into the Deployment

All it takes to use this monitoring web service now is to update the EventService property in MDT.

1. On **CM01**, using **Notepad**, open the file **D:\Sources\OSD\Settings\Windows 8.1 x64 Settings\CustomSettings.ini**.

2. In the **Default** section, add the following property at the end

    ```
    EventService=http://CM01/MonitoringWebService/api
    ```

3. Save the changes and close the **CustomSettings.ini** file.

4. Using the **ConfigMgr console**, in the **Software Library** workspace, expand **Application Management**, and then select **Packages**.

5. Update the distribution points for the **Windows 8.1 x64 Settings** package by right-clicking the **Windows 8.1 x64 Settings** package and selecting **Update Distribution Points**.

6. Start a deployment, and review the modified event information in the **D:\ViaMonstraWebServices\MonitoringWebService\MonitorEvents.csv** file.

Summary

You have now learned how to create a custom web service that can consume and forward MDT monitoring events. The existing monitoring infrastructure continues to work as before so that this custom handling doesn't interrupt the current monitoring capabilities.

Based on this, it's now possible to extend the monitoring to any additional requirements like

- Writing monitoring information to a database

- Showing deployment status on a custom webpage

- Evaluating and reporting deployment history, usage, duration, and so forth

- Triggering additional actions based on individual events

- Updating an asset management system with deployment information

- And many more…

Chapter 14

Integrating with Orchestrator

This chapter is a quick technical drilldown to System Center Orchestrator 2012 R2 (further referenced as Orchestrator). In this chapter, you learn about the components of Orchestrator and also about the following:

- Configuring access for managing and executing runbooks
- Installing and configuring integration packs
- Creating, modifying, and testing runbooks
- Executing runbooks from a MDT Lite Touch task sequence

Step-by-Step Guide Requirements

If you want to run the step-by-step guide in this chapter, you need a lab environment configured as outlined in Chapter 3 and Appendix A. In this chapter, you use the following virtual machines:

DC01   MDT01   CM01   OR01   PC0001

The VMs used in this chapter.

You also need to have downloaded the following software:

- Orchestrator 2012 R2 Integration Pack for System Center 2012 R2
- The book sample files (http://stealingwithpride.com)

Overview

Orchestrator is a workflow management solution mainly targeted for data centers and it provides tools to build, test, debug, deploy, and manage automation of your environment. It's supposed to support the IT administrator in performing many tasks and procedures to keep the health of their computer environment up-to-date and their business running.

The main use scenario for this product is the orchestration and automation between the different System Center and also other products. However, as it's a generic workflow solution, it can be used to automate other tasks, as well.

The Orchestrator workflows are called runbooks, and each runbook can contain several activities that are executed sequentially. From a generic point of view, a runbook can be compared with the various actions, or steps, that you have in MDT task sequence.

However, Orchestrator comes with a huge amount of available activities and can easily be extended using integration packs that add integrated support for other products. From a deployment perspective, you can use Orchestrator to overcome some limitations of task sequences or as an alternative for many custom scripts.

Orchestrator Components

To quickly master Orchestrator, it's valuable to first learn what the major components are and what they are used for.

Management Server

The management server is the communication layer between the Runbook Designer and the orchestration database. From a redundancy perspective, there can be only one management server per Orchestrator installation. However, runbooks can still be executed if the management server isn't available. They just can't be edited using the Runbook Designer.

Runbook Server

A runbook server is where an instance of a runbook runs. Runbook servers communicate directly with the orchestration database. You can deploy multiple runbook servers per Orchestrator installation to increase capacity and redundancy.

Orchestration Database

The database is a Microsoft SQL Server database that contains all of the deployed runbooks, the status of running runbooks, log files, and configuration data for Orchestrator.

Runbook Designer

The Runbook Designer is the tool used to build, edit, and manage Orchestrator runbooks.

Runbook Tester

The Runbook Tester is a run-time tool used to test runbooks developed in the Runbook Designer.

Orchestration Console

The Orchestration console is a Silverlight-based web application that lets you start or stop runbooks and view real-time status on a web browser.

Orchestrator Web Service

The Orchestrator web service is a Representational State Transfer (REST)-based service that enables custom applications to connect to Orchestrator to start and stop runbooks, and retrieve information about operations by using custom applications or scripts. The Orchestration console and MDT 2013 use this web service to interact with Orchestrator.

Deployment Manager

The Deployment Manager is a tool used to deploy integration packs (IPs), runbook servers, and Runbook Designers.

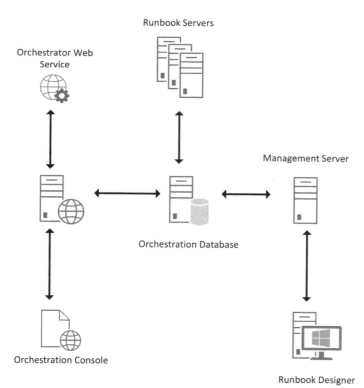

Orchestrator architecture.

Runbook

A runbook is the heart of Orchestrator. Think of it as similar to a task sequence in MDT 2013 or ConfigMgr 2012 R2. It typically contains a series of activities that are linked and executed in a certain order.

Integration Pack (IP)

An integration pack is a collection of custom activities specific to a product or technology. Microsoft and other companies provide integration packs with activities to interact with their product from an Orchestrator runbook.

Orchestrator Integration Toolkit

The Orchestrator Integration Toolkit lets you extend your library of activities beyond the collection of standard activities and integration packs. The Integration Toolkit has wizard-based tools to create new activities and integration packs for Orchestrator.

Configuring Orchestrator

Before you can actually start using Orchestrator for your deployments, a few things have to be in place.

Configure Permissions

You now learn how to configure administrative access to Orchestrator and how to set permissions to execute runbooks.

Real World Note: By default, administrative access to Orchestrator is given using a local security group on the Management Server called OrchestratorUsersGroup (the name of that group is a bit misleading) with the Domain Administrator as default member. We recommend that you always create a security group in the domain that contains all Orchestrator administrators and add this to the local security group.

---

1. On **OR01**, log on as **VIAMONSTRA\Administrator** using a password of **P@ssw0rd**.

2. Using **Computer Management**, add the **VIAMONSTRA\Orchestrator Administrators** group to the local **OrchestratorUsersGroup** group.

3. Using the **Runbook Designer** (available on the Start screen), right-click **Runbooks** and select **Permissions**.

4. Click **Advanced** and then on **Add**.

5. Click **Select a principal** and select the **VIAMONSTRA\Orchestrator Runbook Users** group that has already been created for you by the hydration kit.

6. Click the **Clear all** button, and then click **Show advanced permissions**.

7. Select the following permissions and apply the changes:

    o **Read Properties**

    o **List Contents**

    o **Publish**

8. Close the **Runbook Designer**.

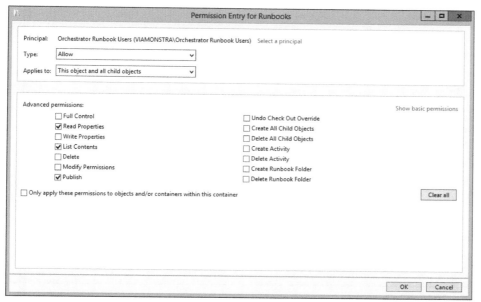

Permissions for the Orchestrator Runbook Users group.

Real World Note: To be able to execute a runbook, a user requires the Publish permission.

Import Integration Packs into Orchestrator

One of the core features of Orchestrator is its extensibility using integration packs. Although it comes with about 74 different activities already built in, they can cover only some typical basic tasks. You now learn how to import new integration packs into Orchestrator to extend the functionality.

1. On **OR01**, download the **System Center 2012 R2 Integration Packs** from http://www.microsoft.com/en-us/download/details.aspx?id=39622 to a temporary location.

2. Run the **System_Center_2012_R2_Integration_Packs.exe** file and expand the files to **C:\Setup\Integration Packs**.

3. Using the **Deployment Manager**, right-click **Integration Packs** and select **Register IP with Orchestrator Management Server**.

4. Add the following files from **C:\Setup\Integration Packs**:

    o **SC2012R2_Integration_Pack_for_Configuration_Manager.oip**

    o **System_Center_2012_R2_Integration_Pack_for_ActiveDirectory.oip**

5. Accept the Software License Terms.

6. Select **Integration Packs** and verify that both integration packs have been added successfully.

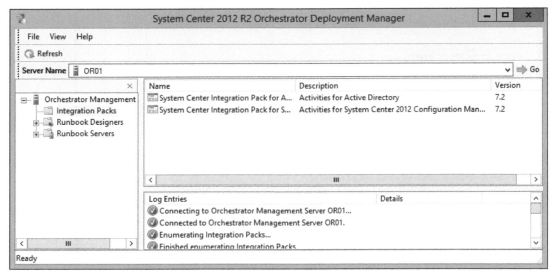

System Center 2012 R2 Orchestrator integration packs.

Deploy Integration Packs

Before an integration pack can actually be used in a runbook, it needs to be deployed to all Runbook Designers and runbook servers. You now learn how to deploy an integration pack.

Real World Note: We recommend deploying integration packs to all Runbook Designers and all runbook servers by default. However, if a certain integration pack can be deployed only to a specific Runbook Designer or runbook server (e.g. because of some additional software that needs to be installed that isn't available on all tunbook servers), make sure that the runbooks containing an activity from such an integration pack can be edited and executed only on the servers that have it deployed, and the execution needs to be limited to only those runbook servers.

1. On **OR01**, using the **Deployment Manager**, right-click **Integration Packs** and select **Deploy IP to Runbook Server or Runbook Designer**.

2. Select the following integration packs:

   o **System Center Integration Pack for Active Directory**

   o **System Center Integration Pack for System Center 2012 Configuration Manager**

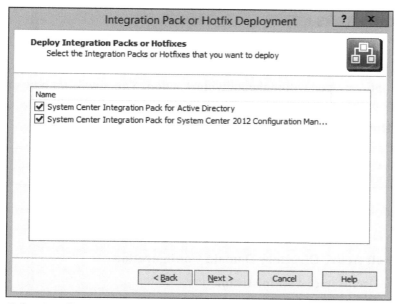

Selecting the integration packs.

3. On **Computer Selection**, add **OR01**.

4. Keep the default option **Stop all running Runbooks before installing the Integration Packs** and finish the wizard.

    Wait a few seconds while the integration packs are deployed.

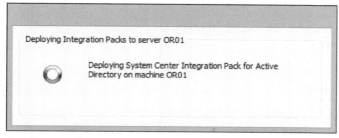

Deploying the integration packs.

5. Using **Deployment Manager**, expand the **Runbook Designer** node, select **OR01**, and verify that both integration packs have been added successfully.

6. Expand the **Runbook Servers** node, select **OR01**, and verify that both integration packs have been added there successfully, as well.

Configure Integration Packs

As most integration packs are used to connect to a different system or product, information on how to connect to those systems or products is required. Instead of adding this information on each individual action, most integration packs allow you to define one or several configurations and then select one of those configurations within the individual action. You now learn how to configure the Active Directory and ConfigMgr integration packs.

1.   On **OR01**, using the **Runbook Designer**, select **Options / Active Directory**.

> **Real World Note:** If the configuration for an integration pack isn't available after you've deployed it, just close and reopen the Runbook Designer.

2.   Add a new configuration using the following information:

    a.   Name: **corp.viamonstra.com**

    b.   Type: **Microsoft Active Directory Domain Configuration**

    c.   Configuration User Name: **Administrator**

    d.   Configuration Password: **P@ssw0rd**

    e.   Configuration Domain Controller Name (FQDN): **dc01.corp.viamonstra.com**

    f.   Configuration Default Parent Container: **DC=corp,DC=viamonstra,DC=com**

    g.   Click **OK**, and then click **Finish**.

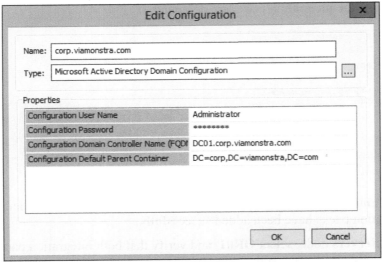

Microsoft Active Directory Domain Configuration.

> **Real World Note:** In a production environment, you should always use a separate service account that is used by Orchestrator to access Active Directory and has only the permissions that are required by the activities used in the runbooks.

3. Using the **Runbook Designer**, select **Options / SC 2012 Configuration Manager**.

4. Add a new configuration using the following information:

   a. Name: **corp.viamonstra.com**

   b. Server: **CM01.corp.viamonstra.com**

   c. User Name: **Administrator**

   d. Password: **P@ssw0rd**

   e. Click **Test Connection** to verify that it successfully connected.

   f. Click **OK**, and then click **Finish**.

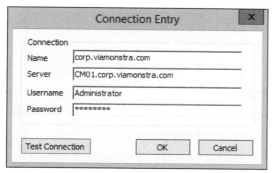

ConfigMgr 2012 R2 Configuration.

Using Orchestrator

To demonstrate the capabilities of Orchestrator, you now create two runbooks that each cover pretty typical but still easy to implement scenarios. For demonstration purposes, they have been simplified and, for example, contain no error handling and almost no validation.

However, the book sample files also contain several runbooks for similar scenarios with some additional validation and error handling that you can import into your environment. So. in the spirit of this book, feel free to steal from them.

Adding a Computer to a Group

A fairly common task during deployments is to add the newly deployed computer to one or several Active Directory groups, for example, to give it appropriate access. This task is typically solved using web services as shown in Chapter 12. However, you can achieve the same task using Orchestrator.

The benefit of using Orchestrator for such tasks really comes into play as soon as those tasks become a bit more complex and involve several actions to be executed based on certain conditions.

Create the Runbook

1. On **OR01**, using the **Runbook Designer**, right-click the **Runbooks** node, select **New /
    Folder**, and name it **Add Computer to Group**.

> **Real World Note:** We recommend creating a folder per runbook and also structuring several
> runbooks into logical groups. This makes it easier to handle them later.

2. Right-click the folder **Add Computer to Group** and select **New / Runbook**.

3. Right-click the runbook **New Runbook** and select **Rename**.

4. Confirm to check out the runbook.

> **Note:** Runbooks can be edited only if they are checked out. However, the latest version of the
> runbook before the checkout will still be available to be executed. This way, ongoing changes to a
> runbook won't interrupt any production process that is already using it.

5. Name the runbook **Add Computer to Group**.

6. From the **Runbook Control** activities, drag the **Initialize Data** activity onto the runbook.

7. Right-click the **Initialize Runbook** activity and select **Properties**.

8. Click **Add**. Then click the new **Parameter 1** parameter that was added and rename it
    Computer name. Then click **Finish**.

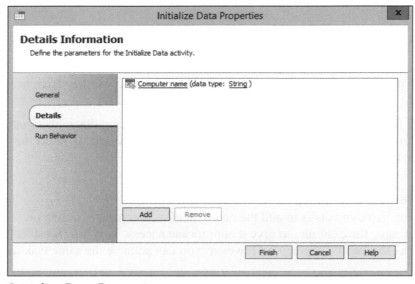

Initialize Data Properties.

9. From the **Active Directory** activities, drag the **Get Computer** activity next to the
    Initialize Runbook activity on the runbook.

10. Move the cursor onto the **Initialize Data** activity and then onto the small arrow that shows up until the cursor converts into a crosshair. Then click this arrow and keep the mouse button pressed. Move the cursor onto the **Get Computer** activity and release the mouse button. Both activities should now be connected by an arrow.

Connecting activities.

Real World Note: Connecting activities can be a bit tricky sometimes, especially when there are a lot of activities in the runbook. Make sure you wait a moment on each activity until the connecting points (arrows) pop up, and if dragging a link to a different activity, wait until the connecting points on the target activity show up, as well, before you release the mouse button.

---

11. Right-click the **Get Computer** activity on the runbook and select **Properties**.

12. Select the configuration **corp.viamonstra.com**.

13. Click **Optional Properties.** Then double-click **Return Distinguished Name only** and select **OK**.

14. In the value field for **Return Distinguished Name only**, type **True** (or select it from the Item Selection dialog box).

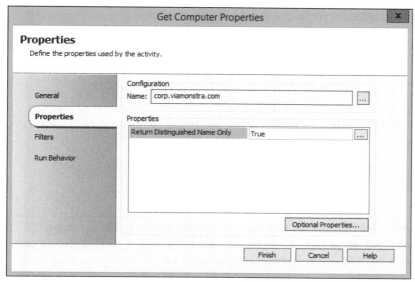

Get Computer Properties.

15. Select the **Filters** node and click **Add**.

16. Select **Common Name** from the list as the **Name**, and keep the **Relation** as **Equals**.

17. Right-click in the **Value** field and select **Subscribe / Published Data**.

18. Select **Computer Name** from the **Initialize Data** activity, and click **OK**.

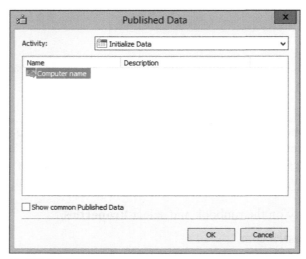

Published Data.

> **Real World Note:** Typically each activity publishes some data that can be consumed by later activities. Ensure that you have a link between the activities before you start using published data.

19. Click **OK** again to add the new filter.

Filter Settings.

> **Real World Note:** The entries for Published Data can sometimes be pretty hard to read, depending on the size of the field, especially when combining information from different data sources. Just right-click any field and select Expand to open up a larger dialog box that shows the same content and is easier to handle.

20. Click **Finish**.

21. From the **Active Directory** activities, drag the **Add Computer To Group** activity next to the **Get Computer** activity on the runbook.

22. Create a link from the **Get Computer** activity to the **Add Computer To Group** activity.

23. Right-click the link and select **Properties**.

24. On the **Include** tab, click the existing **Get Computer** filter.

25. Select **Count** and click **OK**.

26. Click **value**, type **1**, and click **OK** and **Finish**.

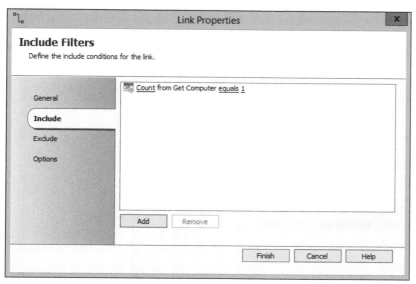

Link Properties.

Real World Note: We highly recommend that you always limit links to the expected result or condition. As in this sample, the Get Computer activity could also return a list of computers based on the filter. However, the runbook is expected to be executed for exactly one computer only. So a count of 0 or more than 1 is considered an error and shouldn't be executed. In a production environment, you should have additional activities that handle these conditions, as well, and log an error in the event log, for example, to be able to troubleshoot and fix them later.

When working with several conditions be aware that they will be evaluated using a logical OR. So if any condition matches, the link will be used. To be able to use several conditions together, a combination of Include and Exclude conditions have to be used, and Exclude conditions will always overrule Include conditions.

27. Right-click the **Add Computer To Group** activity and select **Properties**.

28. Select the configuration **corp.viamonstra.com**.

29. For **Group Distinguished Name**, type

> **CN=7-Zip 9.20 - x64,OU=Software**
> **Groups,OU=ViaMonstra,DC=corp,DC=viamonstra,DC=com**

Note: Type the text as one line. For simplicity reason we use an already existing security group that is used in Chapter 6 to deploy the application 7-Zip. Optionally, you could search for this group in an additional Get Group activity or have the user supply a group in the Initialize Data activity on the fly.

---

30. Right-click the value field for **Computer Distinguished Name** and select **Subscribe / Published Data**.

31. Select the **Distinguished Name** property from the **Get Computer** activity, click **OK** and **Finish**.

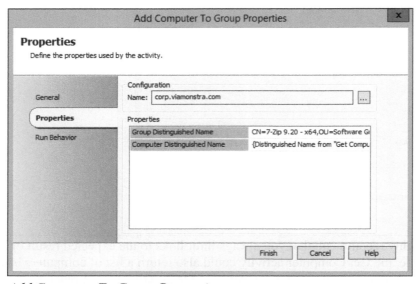

Add Computer To Group Properties.

32. On the toolbar, click **Check In**.

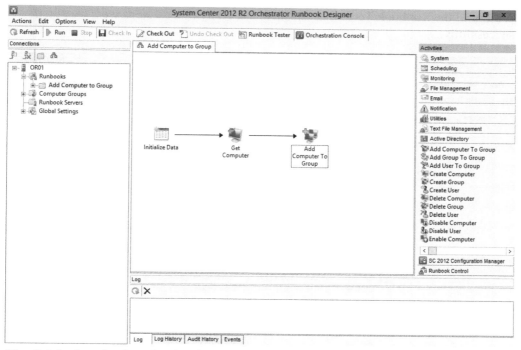

The finished runbook in Runbook Designer.

Test the Runbook

Before a runbook is used in production, it should always be tested. You now learn to use the Runbook Tester tool to test a runbook.

> **Real World Note:** The Runbook Tester executes a runbook using your current credentials, so results might differ as the runbook servers typically use a different service account for runbook execution. In the current sample, this doesn't matter as the Active Directory activities are using the credentials from the configuration.

1. On **OR01**, using the **Runbook Designer**, expand the **Runbooks** node and select the folder **Add Computer to Group**.

2. Select the **Add Computer to Group** runbook and click **Runbook Tester** in the toolbar.

3. Confirm that you want to check out the runbook.

> **Real World Note:** Runbooks can only be tested if they are checked out. Be sure either to check them back in again after the testing has been finished, or undo the checkout if no additional changes have been applied.

4. Click **Run** in the **Runbook Tester**.

5. Use the computer name **PC0001** and click **OK**.

6. Wait until the Runbook Tester has finished and verify that all steps were executed successfully.

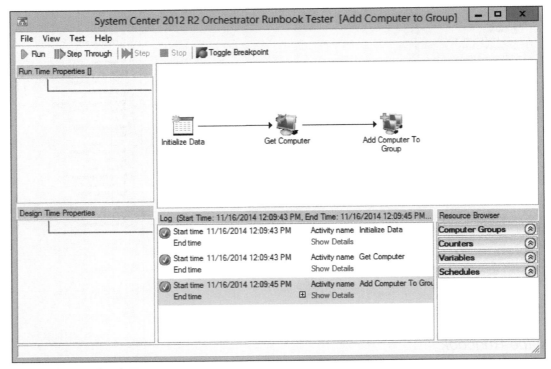

Using the Runbook Tester.

7. On **DC01**, using **Active Directory Users and Computers**, navigate to **ViaMonstra / Software Groups**, right-click the group **7-Zip 9.20 – x64** and select **Properties**.

8. On the **Members** tab, verify that **PC0001** has been added as a member to this group.

9. On **OR01**, using the **Runbook Tester**, run the runbook again using computer name **PC0001**.

10. Verify that the activity **Add Computer To Group** failed.

11. In the log entry for **Add Computer To Group**, click **Show Details** and note the Error summary text.

Real World Note: Don't expect or assume a certain behavior from an activity, and always test a runbook in different conditions. In this particular case, the activity will fail if the specified computer is already a member of that group. We highly recommend that you take care of such conditions, if possible, in the runbook itself instead of ignoring a possible error. In this particular case, it would be recommended to check first whether the computer is already a member of that group and only add it if it isn't. However, this is outside the scope of this sample, though it is supplied in the sample files for the book.

12. On **DC01**, using **Active Directory Users and Computers**, navigate to **ViaMonstra /
    Software Groups**, right-click the group **7-Zip 9.20 – x64**, and select **Properties**.

13. On the **Members** tab, select **PC0001**, click **Remove**, and then confirm that the computer
    is to be removed from this group.

14. On **OR01**, using the **Runbook Designer**, check in the **Add Computer to Group**
    runbook.

Waiting for Something – Looping

Another fairly common task comes from the need to pause the task sequence for a specific period
of time or have it wait for something. This might be some missing information, a required
component not being available at the moment, or some external process that has to finish before
the task sequence can continue or might fail otherwise.

Process Overview

As an abstract, and definitely not recommended, way of solving this task, you are now going to
create a runbook that will continuously check whether Notepad.exe is running on the Orchestrator
server and continue only when Notepad has been closed. Similar solutions could check whether a
specific file exists, some database entry has changed to a specific value, or a web service has
returned the expected result.

Create the Runbook

1. On **OR01**, using the **Runbook Designer**, right-click the **Runbooks** node, select **New /
   Folder**, and name it **Wait for Notepad**.

2. Right-click the folder **Wait for Notepad** and select **New / Runbook**.

3. Right-click the runbook **New Runbook** and select **Rename**.

4. Confirm to check out the runbook.

5. Name the runbook **Wait for Notepad**.

6. From the **Runbook Control** activities, drag the **Initialize Data** activity onto the runbook.

> **Note:** The Initialize Data activity acts as an entry point for the runbook. Only runbooks with an
> Initialize Data activity as their very first activity can be executed from MDT, for example. So even
> if there isn't any data that needs to be supplied to the runbook, it requires that the runbook have
> the Initialize Data activity. There can be another type of runbooks that starts with a Monitoring
> activity that can be started and then execute the following activities every time on certain events;
> however, that's outside the scope of this book.

7. From the **Monitoring** activities, drag the **Get Process Status** activity onto the runbook
   next to the **Initialize Data** activity.

8. Create a link from the **Initialize Data** activity to the **Get Process Status** activity.

9. Right-click the **Get Process Status** activity, select **Properties**, and configure the following properties:

    o   Computer: **localhost**

    o   Process: **Notepad.exe**

10. Right-click the **Get Process Status** activity, select **Looping**, select the **Enable** check box, and type **5** as value for **Delay between attempts**.

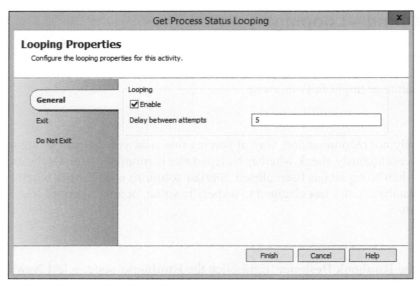

Activity Properties - Looping

11. Select the **Exit** node and click the word **success** in the condition.

12. Clear the **success** check box and select **failed** in the Results; then click **OK** and **Finish**.

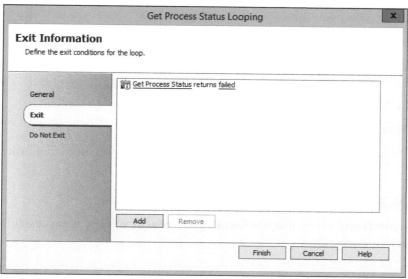

Activity Properties – Exit condition

Real World Note: Be careful when configuring looping on an activity, as you might end up with an infinite loop. Make sure that you always have an exit condition that will apply at some point in time. One recommendation is to add a condition for the number of iterations this loop has already gone through.

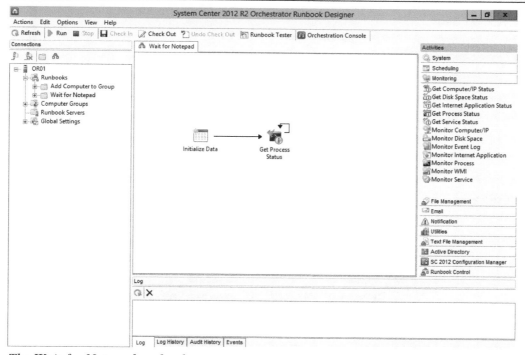

The Wait for Notepad runbook.

Test the Runbook

1. On **OR01**, make sure you don't have **Notepad** running.

2. Using the **Runbook Designer**, expand the **Runbooks** node and select the folder **Wait for Notepad**.

3. Select the **Wait for Notepad** runbook and click **Runbook Tester** in the toolbar.

4. Click **Run** in the **Runbook Tester**.

5. Verify in the **Log** that the **Get Process Status** activity is executed only once and **failed**.

6. Start **Notepad**.

7. Using the **Runbook Tester**, run the **Wait for Notepad** runbook again.

8. **Wait** at least **10 seconds** and verify that the **Get Process Status** activity is successfully executed once every five seconds.

9. Close **Notepad**.

10. Verify in the **Log** that the next execution of the **Get Process Status** activity fails and the runbook finishes.

11. Close the **Runbook Tester**, and in **Runbook Designer**, check in the **Wait for Notepad** runbook.

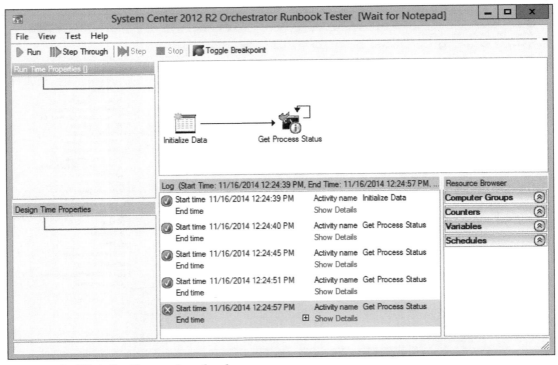

Testing the Wait for Notepad runbook.

Calling a Runbook from MDT 2013

MDT 2013, both as standalone and when integrated with ConfigMgr 2012 R2, has a built-in step you can use to execute an Orchestrator runbook. This makes it easy to integrate Orchestrator runbooks into the deployment process. You now learn how to add a step to an empty custom MDT 2013 Lite Touch task sequence that executes one of the runbooks that you just created.

1. On **MDT01**, using the **Deployment Workbench**, expand the **MDT Production** deployment share, right-click **Task Sequences**, and click **New Task Sequence**.

2. Using the **New Task Sequence Wizard**, create a new task sequence using the following information:

    a. Task sequence ID: **DEMO_OR1**

    b. Task sequence name: **Execute Orchestrator runbook**

    c. Task sequence template: **Custom Task Sequence**.

3. Right-click the new **Execute Orchestrator runbook** task sequence and select **Properties**.

4. In the **Task Sequence** tab, remove the default **Install Applications** action, and then click **Add / General / Execute Orchestrator Runbook**.

5. Select the **Execute Orchestrator Runbook** step and in **Properties**, use **OR01.corp.viamonstra.com** as the **Orchestrator Server** and click **Browse**.

6. Expand the **Add Computer to Group** folder, select the runbook **Add Computer to Group**, and click **OK**.

Selecting a runbook.

7. Name the **Execute Orchestrator Runbook** action **Add Computer to Group**.

8. Select the option to **Specify explicit runbook parameters** and use the following information:

     Computer name: **%ComputerName%**

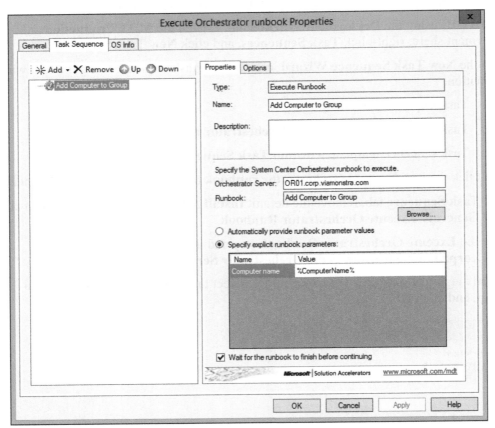

Execute Orchestrator runbook Properties.

9. Click **OK**.

Test the Task Sequence

1. On **DC01**, using **Active Directory Users and Computers**, navigate to **ViaMonstra /
   Software Groups**, right-click the **7-Zip 9.20 – x64** group, and select **Properties**.

2. On the **Members** tab, verify that **PC0001** has not been added as a member to this group.
   Remove it from the group if necessary.

3. On **PC0001**, open a new command prompt using **Run as Administrator**, and run the
   following command:

   ```
   cscript.exe \\MDT01\MDTProduction$\Scripts\LiteTouch.vbs
   ```

4. In the **Windows Deployment Wizard**, on the **Task Sequence** page, select the **Execute
   Orchestrator runbook** task sequence and click **Next**.

5. On the custom **LocationSelection** page (if you created it in Chapter 12), select **New
   York**, and click **Next**.

6. On the **Credentials** page, use the user name **Maik** with a password of **P@ssw0rd**.

7. Wait until the task sequence has completed, then on the **Deployment Summary** page,
   click **Finish**.

8. Using **CMTrace.exe**, open the **C:\Windows\Temp\DeploymentLogs\BDD.log** and
   verify that the runbook executed successfully.

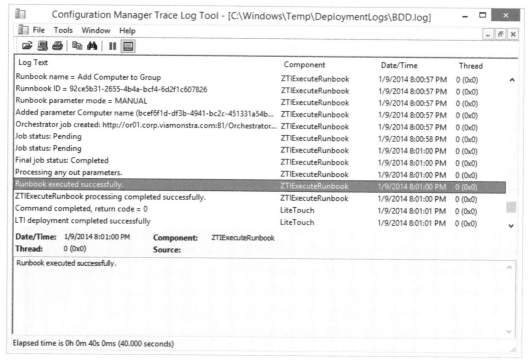

The BDD.log showing execution of an Orchestrator runbook.

9. On **DC01**, using **Active Directory Users and Computers**, navigate to **ViaMonstra /
    Software Groups**, right-click the group **7-Zip 9.20 – x64**, and select **Properties**.

10. On the **Members** tab, verify that **PC0001** has been added successfully as a member to this
    group.

11. On **OR01**, using the **Runbook Designer**, expand the **Runbooks** node and select the **Add
    Computer to Group** folder.

12. Select the **Add Computer to Group** runbook and verify in the **Log History** that the
    runbook has executed successfully (Click the green refresh button to update the view).

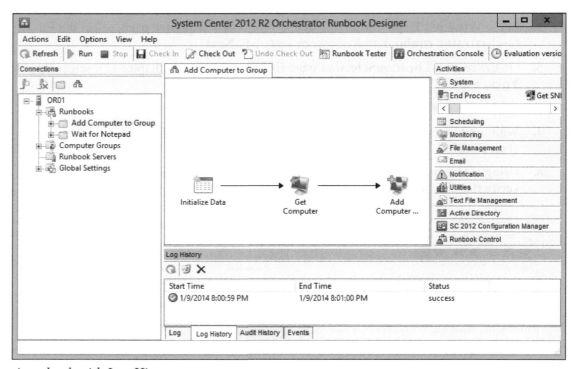

A runbook with Log History.

Note: Double-click a Log History entry in the Runbook Designer to see more information about
each individual activity that has been executed.

Appendix A

Using the Hydration Kit to Build the PoC Environment

As you learned in Chapter 1, hydration is the concept of using a deployment solution, like MDT 2013, to do a fully automated build of an entire lab, or proof-of-concept environment. If you want to see for yourself how we set up this environment, check out the http://stealingwithpride.com website for a video that shows you the hydration process.

Note: This appendix is here to help you quickly spin up a lab environment that matches up with all the guides we use in this book. The virtual machines you deploy are in no way configured for production deployment, but will work great in your lab. If you are interested in how to build a ConfigMgr 2012 R2 server for production use, we recommend getting the book *System Center 2012 R2 Configuration Manager - Mastering the Fundamentals*, 3rd Edition, by Kent Agerlund. Check this link: http://www.deploymentartist.com/Books.aspx.

Here are the detailed steps for installing and configuring the hydration kit provided in the book sample files. This hydration kit allows you to build the same environment that is used for this book in a virtual environment. We recommend using Hyper-V in Windows Server 2012 R2 as your virtual platform, but we have tested the hydration kit on the following virtual platforms:

- Hyper-V in Windows 8.1 and Windows Server 2012 R2

- VMware Workstation 10.0

- VMware ESXi 5.1 and 5.5

As you learned in Chapter 3, to set up a virtual environment with all the servers and clients, you need a host with at least 16 GB of RAM, even though 32 GB RAM is recommended. Either way, make sure you are using SSD drives for your storage. A single 480 GB SSD is enough to run all the scenarios in this book.

Real World Note: Don't go cheap on the disk drive. If using a normal laptop or desktop when doing the step-by-step guides in this book, please, please, please use a SSD drive for your virtual machines. Using normal spindle-based disks are just too slow for a decent lab and test environment. Also, please note that most laptops support at least 16 GB RAM these days, even if many vendors does not update their specifications with this information.

The Base Servers

Using the hydration kit, you build the following list of servers.

New York Site Servers (192.168.1.0/24)

- **DC01.** Domain Controller, DNS, and DHCP
- **MDT01.** File Server, WDS, and SQL Server 2012 SP1 Express
- **CM01.** SQL Server 2012 SP1 and ConfigMgr 2012 R2
- **VC01.** File Server and SQL Server 2012 SP1 Express
- **OR01.** Optional Server. SQL Server 2012 SP1 and Orchestrator 2012 R2

The Base Clients

In addition to the servers, you also use a few clients throughout the book guides. Two clients are created in this appendix, and the others are installed as part of the book guides.

New York Site Clients (192.168.1.0/24)

- **PC0001.** Windows 8.1 Enterprise x64
- **PC0002.** Windows 8.1 Enterprise x64

Internet Access

As you learned in Chapter 3, the guides in this book do not require you to have Internet access on the virtual machines, but we do recommend configuring them for it. We commonly use a virtual router (running in a VM) to provide Internet access to our lab and to test VMs. Our favorite router is the Vyatta router, but you can use a server running Windows Server 2012 R2 with routing configured, as well.

> **Real World Note:** For detailed guidance on setting up a virtual router for your lab environment, see this article: http://tinyurl.com/usingvirtualrouter.

Setting Up the Hydration Environment

To enable you to quickly set up the servers and clients used for the step-by-step guides in this book, we provide you with a hydration kit (part of the book sample files) that will build all the servers and clients. The sample files are available for download at http://stealingwithpride.com.

How Does the Hydration Kit Work?

The hydration kit that you download is just a folder structure and some scripts. The scripts help you create the MDT 2013 Lite Touch offline media (big ISO), and the folder structure is there for you to add your own software and licenses when applicable. You can use trial versions for the lab software, as well. The overview steps are the following:

1. Download the needed software.

2. Install MDT 2013 Lite Touch and Windows ADK 8.1.

3. Create a MDT 2013 deployment share.

4. Populate the folder structure with your media and any license information.

5. Generate the MDT 2013 media item (big ISO).

6. Create a few virtual machines, boot them on the media item, select what servers they should become, and about two hours later you have the lab environment ready to go.

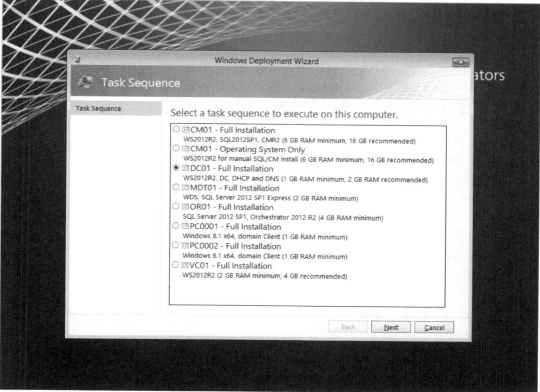

The end result: You boot a VM from the ISO and simply select which server to build.

Preparing the Downloads Folder

These steps should be performed on the Windows machine that you use to manage Hyper-V or VMware. If you are using Hyper-V or VMware Workstation, this machine also can be the host machine.

Download the Mandatory Software

1. On the Windows machine that you use to manage Hyper-V or VMware, create the **C:\Downloads** folder.

2. Download the following mandatory software to the **C:\Downloads** folder:

    o   The book sample files (http://stealingwithpride.com)

    o   ADK 8.1 (To download the full ADK, you run adksetup.exe once and select to download the files.)

    o   BGInfo

    o   ConfigMgr 2012 R2

    o   ConfigMgr 2012 R2 PreReqs

Note: To download the ConfigMgr 2012 R2 prerequisites, run the SMSSETUP\BIN\X64\Setupdl.exe application from the ConfigMgr 2012 R2 installation files, specify a temporary download folder, and click Download.

---

    o   MDT 2013

    o   SQL Server 2012 SP1 Express with Tools x64

    o   SQL Server 2012 with SP1 x64 Standard (trial or full version)

    o   Microsoft Visual C++ 2005 SP1 runtimes (both x86 and x64)

    o   Microsoft Visual C++ 2008 SP1 runtimes (both x86 and x64)

    o   Microsoft Visual C++ 2010 SP1 runtimes (both x86 and x64)

    o   Microsoft Visual C++ 2012 SP1 runtimes (both x86 and x64)

Note: All the Microsoft Visual C++ downloads can be found on the following page: http://support.microsoft.com/kb/2019667.

---

    o   Windows Server 2012 R2 (trial or full version)

    o   Windows 8.1 Enterprise x64 (trial or full version)

332

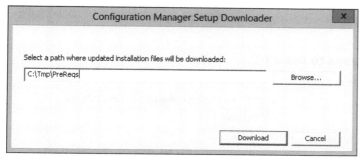

Running the Setupdl.exe to download the ConfigMgr 2012 R2 PreReqs.

Download the Optional Software

If you want to test the optional System Center 2012 R2 Orchestrator integration guide in Chapter 14, you also need to download the following setup files. If not, skip these steps and continue with the next section ("Prepare the Hydration Environment").

Download the following software to the **C:\Downloads** folder:

System Center 2012 Orchestrator R2 (trial or full version)

Preparing the Hydration Environment

The Windows machine that you use to manage Hyper-V or VMware needs to have PowerShell installed.

Note: MDT 2013 requires local administrator rights/permissions. You need to have at least 60 GB of free disk space on C:\ for the hydration kit and about 300 GB of free space for the volume hosting your virtual machines. Also make sure to run all commands from an elevated command prompt.

Create the Hydration Deployment Share

1.   On the Windows machine that you use to manage Hyper-V or VMware, install **ADK** (**adksetup.exe**) selecting only the following components:

      o   **Deployment Tools**

      o   **Windows Preinstallation Environment (Windows PE)**

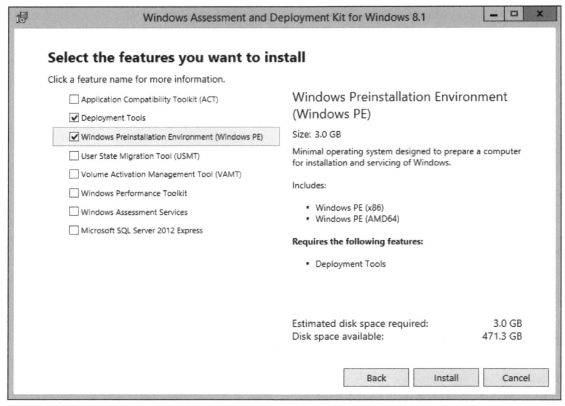

The Windows ADK 8.1 setup.

2. Install **MDT 2013 (MicrosoftDeploymentToolkit2013_x64.msi)** with the default settings.

3. Extract the book sample files and copy the **HydrationADVOSDV1** folder to **C:**.

4. You should now have the following folder containing a few subfolders and PowerShell scripts:

    C:\HydrationADVOSDV1\Source

5. In an elevated (run as Administrator) **PowerShell** command prompt, navigate to the hydration folder by running the following command:

    ```
    Set-Location C:\HydrationADVOSDV1\Source
    ```

6. Still at the **PowerShell** command prompt, with location (working directory) set to **C:\HydrationADVOSDV1\Source**, create the hydration deployment share by running the following command:

    ```
    .\CreateHydrationDeploymentShare.ps1
    ```

7.   After creating the hydration deployment share, review the added content using **Deployment Workbench** (available on the Start screen).

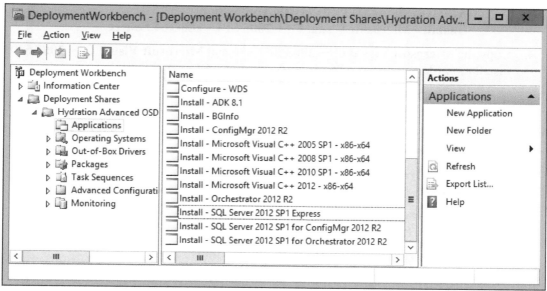

Deployment Workbench with the readymade applications listed.

Populate the Hydration Deployment Share with the Mandatory Setup Files

In these steps, you copy the installation files to the correct target folder in the hydration structure:

1.   Copy the ADK 8.1 installation files to the following folder:

C:\HydrationADVOSDV1\DS\Applications\Install - ADK\Source

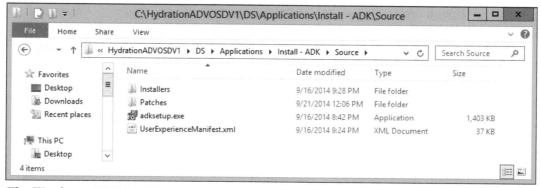

The Windows ADK 8.1 files copied.

2.   Copy the **BGInfo** file (**bginfo.exe**) to the following folder:

C:\HydrationADVOSDV1\DS\Applications\Install - BGInfo\Source

3. Copy the **Microsoft Visual C++ 2005 SP1 x86** and **Microsoft Visual C++ 2005 SP1 x64** installation files **(vcredist_x86.exe and vcredist_x64.exe)** to the following folder:

> **C:\HydrationADVOSDV1\DS\Applications**
> **Install - Microsoft Visual C++ 2005 SP1 - x86-x64\Source**

4. Copy the **Microsoft Visual C++ 2008 SP1 x86** and **Microsoft Visual C++ 2008 SP1 x64** installation files **(vcredist_x86.exe and vcredist_x64.exe)** to the following folder:

> **C:\HydrationADVOSDV1\DS\Applications**
> **Install - Microsoft Visual C++ 2008 SP1 - x86-x64\Source**

5. Copy the **Microsoft Visual C++ 2010 SP1 x86** and **Microsoft Visual C++ 2010 SP1 x64** installation files **(vcredist_x86.exe and vcredist_x64.exe)** to the following folder:

> **C:\HydrationADVOSDV1\DS\Applications**
> **Install - Microsoft Visual C++ 2010 SP1 - x86-x64\Source**

6. Copy the **Microsoft Visual C++ 2012 x86** and **Microsoft Visual C++ 2012 x64** installation files **(vcredist_x86.exe and vcredist_x64.exe)** to the following folder:

> **C:\HydrationADVOSDV1\DS\Applications**
> **Install - Microsoft Visual C++ 2012 - x86-x64\Source**

7. Copy the **SQL Server 2012 SP1 Express with Tools x64** installation file **(SQLEXPRWT_x64_ENU.exe)** to the following folder:

> **C:\HydrationADVOSDV1\DS\Applications**
> **Install - SQL Server 2012 SP1 Express\Source**

8. Copy the **SQL Server 2012 with SP1 x64** installation files (the content of the ISO, not the actual ISO) to the following folder:

> **C:\HydrationADVOSDV1\DS\Applications**
> **Install - SQL Server 2012 SP1\Source**

9. Copy the **ConfigMgr 2012 R2** installation files (extract the download) to the following folder:

> **C:\HydrationADVOSDV1\DS\Applications**
> **Install - ConfigMgr 2012 R2\Source**

10. Copy the **ConfigMgr 2012 R2 PreReqs** files to the following folder:

> **C:\HydrationADVOSDV1\DS\Applications**
> **Install - ConfigMgr 2012 R2\PreReqs**

11. From the **C:\HydrationADVOSDV1\DS\Applications\Install - ConfigMgr 2012 R2\Source\SMSSETUP\BIN\X64** folder, copy the **extadsch.exe** file to the following folder:

> **C:\HydrationADVOSDV1\DS\Applications**
> **Configure - Extend AD for ConfigMgr 2012\Source**

12. Copy the **Windows Server 2012 R2** installation files (the content of the ISO, not the actual ISO) to the following folder:

> **C:\HydrationADVOSDV1\DS\Operating Systems\WS2012R2**

13. Copy the **Windows 8.1 Enterprise x64** installation files (again, the content of the ISO, not the actual ISO) to the following folder:

> **C:\HydrationADVOSDV1\DS\Operating Systems\W81X64**

Populate the Hydration Deployment Share with the Optional Setup Files

If you want to run the optional System Center 2012 R2 Orchestrator integration guides in Chapter 14, you also need to add the following setup files. If not, skip these steps and continue with the next section ("Create the Hydration ISO").

1. Extract the **System Center 2012 R2 Orchestrator** installation files to a temporary location.

2. Copy the extracted files to the following folder. (You should have SetupOrchestrator.exe and a few other files.)

> **C:\HydrationADVOSDV1\DS\Applications**
> **Install - Orchestrator 2012 R2\Source**

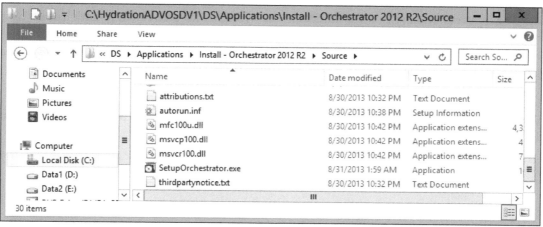

The optional, extracted Orchestrator 2012 R2 installation files.

Create the Hydration ISO (MDT 2013 Update Offline Media Item)

1. Using **Deployment Workbench** (available on the **Start screen**), expand **Deployment Shares**, and expand **Hydration Advanced OSD V1**.

2. Review the various nodes. The **Applications**, **Operating Systems**, and **Task Sequences** nodes should all have some content in them.

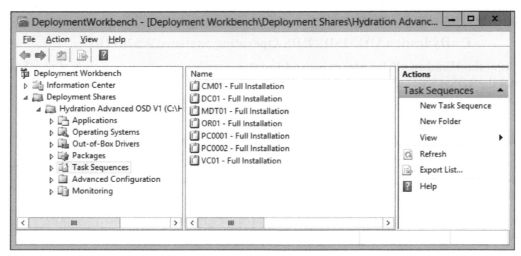

The Hydration deployment share, listing all task sequences.

3. Expand the **Advanced Configuration** node, and then select the **Media** node.

4. In the right pane, right-click the **MEDIA001** item, and select **Update Media Content**.

> **Note:** The most common reason for failures in the hydration kit are related to antivirus software preventing the ISO from being generated correctly. If you see any errors in the update media content process, disable (or uninstall) your antivirus software, and then try the update again. Anyway, the media update will take a while to run, a perfect time for a coffee break. ☺

After the media update, you will have a big ISO (**HydrationADVOSDV1.iso**) in the **C:\HydrationADVOSDV1\ISO** folder. If you included the optional software for Orchestrator 2012 R2, the ISO will be about 17 GB in size.

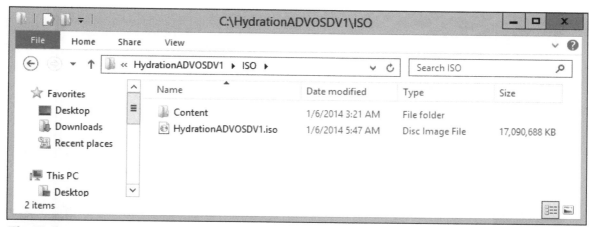

The Hydration ISO media item, including the optional software.

Real World Note: Everything you do in the Deployment Workbench (and more) can be done via PowerShell. This means that the media item also can be updated via PowerShell. We have added a sample script that runs the update media content action in the hydration kit. Check out the UpdateHydrationMediaItem.ps1 script in the C:\HydrationADVOSDV1\Source\Extra folder.

Deploying the New York Site VMs

In these steps, you deploy and configure the virtual machines for the New York Site.

Deploy DC01

This is the primary domain controller used in the environment, and it also runs DNS and DHCP.

1.   Using **Hyper-V Manager** or **VMware Sphere**, create a virtual machine with the following settings:

     a.   Name: **DC01**

     b.   Memory: **1 GB** (minimum, 2 GB recommended)

     c.   Hard drive: **100 GB** (dynamic disk)

     d.   Network: The virtual network for the New York site

     e.   Image file (ISO): **C:\HydrationADVOSDV1\ISO\HydrationADVOSDV1.iso**

2.   Start the **DC01** virtual machine. After booting from **HydrationADVOSDV1.iso**, and after WinPE has loaded, select the **DC01** task sequence.

Real World Note: Using a dynamic disk is really useful for a lab and test environment because the host PC uses only the actually consumed space on the virtual hard drive and not the size that you type in like a fixed disk would.

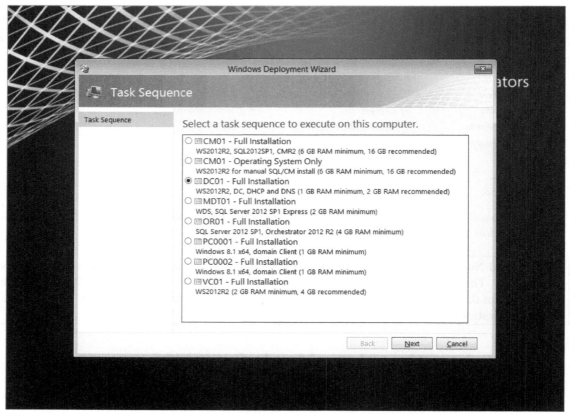

The Task Sequence list showing the hydration task sequences.

3. Wait until the setup is complete and you see the **Hydration completed** message in the final summary.

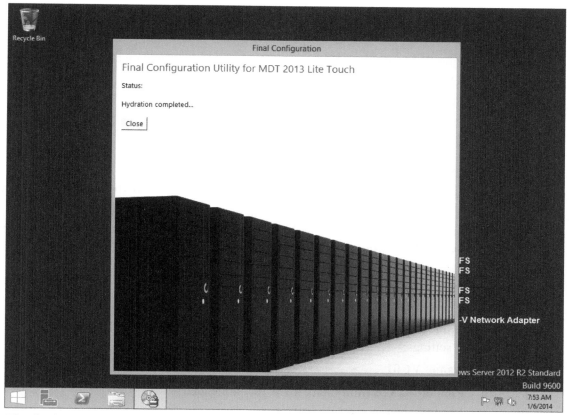

The deployment of DC01 completed, showing the custom final summary screen.

Deploy MDT01

MDT01 is the server used for MDT 2013 Lite Touch. MDT01 also runs SQL Server 2012 SP1 Express and WDS.

1. Using **Hyper-V Manager** or **VMware Sphere**, create a virtual machine with the following settings:

    a. Name: **MDT01**

    b. Memory: **2 GB** (minimum, 4 GB recommended)

    c. Hard drive: **300 GB** (dynamic disk)

    d. Network: The virtual network for the New York site

    e. Image file (ISO): **C:\HydrationADVOSDV1\ISO\HydrationADVOSDV1.iso**

2. Start the **MDT01** virtual machine. After booting from **HydrationADVOSDV1.iso**, and after WinPE has loaded, select the **MDT01** task sequence. Wait until the setup is complete and you see the **Hydration completed** message in the final summary.

Deploy CM01

CM01 is the server used for ConfigMgr 2012 R2.

1. Using **Hyper-V Manager** or **VMware Sphere**, create a virtual machine with the following settings:

    a.   Name: **CM01**

    b.   Memory: **6 GB** (minimum, 16 GB recommended)

    c.   Hard drive: **300 GB** (dynamic disk)

    d.   Network: The virtual network for the New York site

    e.   Image file (ISO): **C:\HydrationADVOSDV1\ISO\HydrationADVOSDV1.iso**

2. Start the **CM01** virtual machine. After booting from **HydrationADVOSDV1.iso**, and after WinPE has loaded, select the **CM01** task sequence. Wait until the setup is complete and you see the **Hydration completed** message in the final summary.

Deploy VC01

VC01 is the server used for Visual SVN Server.

1. Using **Hyper-V Manager** or **VMware Sphere**, create a virtual machine with the following settings:

    a.   Name: **VC01**

    b.   Memory: **2 GB** (minimum, 4 GB recommended)

    c.   Hard drive: **300 GB** (dynamic disk)

    d.   Network: The virtual network for the New York site

    e.   Image file (ISO): **C:\HydrationADVOSDV1\ISO\HydrationADVOSDV1.iso**

2. Start the **VC01** virtual machine. After booting from **HydrationADVOSDV1.iso**, and after WinPE has loaded, select the **VC01** task sequence. Wait until the setup is complete and you see the **Hydration completed** message in the final summary.

Deploy OR01

OR01 is the optional System Center 2012 R2 Orchestrator server. Only deploy this machine if you want learn about the Orchestrator integration with MDT 2013 and you have added the optional software (System Center 2012 R2 Orchestrator) to the hydration kit.

1. Using **Hyper-V Manager** or **VMware Sphere**, create a virtual machine with the following settings:

    a.   Name: **OR01**

    b.   Memory: **4 GB** (minimum, 8 GB recommended)

    c.   Hard drive: **300 GB** (dynamic disk)

      d.   Network: The virtual network for the New York site

      e.   Image file (ISO): **C:\HydrationADVOSDV1\ISO\HydrationADVOSDV1.iso**

2.   Start the **OR01** virtual machine. After booting from **HydrationADVOSDV1.iso**, and after WinPE has loaded, select the **OR01** task sequence. Wait until the setup is complete and you see the **Hydration completed** message in the final summary.

Deploy PC0001

This is a client running Windows 8.1 Enterprise x64 in the domain.

1.   Using **Hyper-V Manager** or **VMware Sphere**, create a virtual machine with the following settings:

      a.   Name: **PC0001**

      b.   Memory: **2 GB**

      c.   Hard drive: **100 GB** (dynamic disk)

      d.   Network: The virtual network for the New York site

      e.   Image file (ISO): **C:\HydrationADVOSDV1\ISO\HydrationADVOSDV1.iso**

2.   Start the **PC0001** virtual machine. After booting from **HydrationADVOSDV1.iso**, and after WinPE has loaded, select the **PC0001** task sequence. Wait until the setup is complete and you see the **Hydration completed** message in the final summary.

Deploy PC0002

This is an extra client running Windows 8.1 Enterprise x64 in the domain.

1.   Using **Hyper-V Manager** or **VMware Sphere**, create a virtual machine with the following settings:

      a.   Name: **PC0002**

      b.   Memory: **2 GB**

      c.   Hard drive: **100 GB** (dynamic disk)

      d.   Network: The virtual network for the New York site

      e.   Image file (ISO): **C:\HydrationADVOSDV1\ISO\HydrationADVOSDV1.iso**

2.   Start the **PC0002** virtual machine. After booting from **HydrationADVOSDV1.iso**, and after WinPE has loaded, select the **PC0002** task sequence. Wait until the setup is complete and you see the **Hydration completed** message in the final summary.

Appendix B

MDT Classes and Functions in ZTIUtility.vbs

The ZTIUtility.vbs script contains a large set of utility functions that most of the MDT scripts use. This appendix serves as a reference for its classes and functions.

Logging

The Logging class is used for trace logging within the MDT scripting environment. By default, log entries are written to a log file that has the same name as the script and to a master log file called BDD.log. When referencing ZTIUtility.vbs, it's globally available using the oLogging object and offers the following functions:

- **CreateEntry (Message, Type).** Writes the specified message of the specified type to the log file. The type has to be one of the following standard log types:

  - **LogTypeInfo**. For informational messages.

  - **LogTypeWarning**. For warning messages.

  - **LogTypeError**. For error messages.

  - **LogTypeVerbose**. For more detailed messages and debugging, use LogTypeVerbose. Those messages are logged only when debug has been set.

  - **LogTypeDeprecated**. Written as informational messages by default. This will show up as an error in the log if debug has been set.

- **CreateEvent (EventID, Type, Message, Parameters).** Standard MDT event messaging routine used to send event status messages to a networked log file and/or to the central monitoring web service if configured. For a list of standard EventIDs being used within MDT, please refer to Appendix C. It expects the same types as in the CreateEntry function, except LogTypeDeprecated isn't supported here. In addition to this, CreateEvent also logs the specified message using the default logging mechanism.

- **GetDiscoveryArray.** Returns an array of values that can be used to discover the current client. This is used primarily in the ZTIGather.wsf script. The values returned are:

  - **Phase**

  - **AssetTag**

  - **UUID**

345

- o **MacAddress** (up to the first four values if available)
- o **SLShare**
- o **UDShare**
- o **UDDir**

- **CopyLog.** Copies all deployment related logs to a central network share, which has to be defined before using the SLShare property.

- **ReportProgress (Message, PercentComplete).** Is used to update the progress indicator of the task sequence during long running transactions.

- **ReportFailure (Message, ErrorCode).** Used to report a failure. It uses CreateEvent to log the error.

- **TRACEEX (ReturnCode, ErrorCode, Message, Fatal).** Performs an inline check of the condition and writes out the message. ReturnCode can be either an integer or a Boolean value. As an integer, 0 and 3010 are interpreted as success, and everything else as failure. As a Boolean value, true is success, and false a failure. On success, the message is written as a verbose entry to the log file. On failure, a warning entry is written.

- **ProcessResults (ReturnCode).** Used to handle the result and identify any errors that have been raised but not handled properly. If error handling within the VBScript has been set to "On Error Resume Next," code execution continues even if an error occurs. If this is expected behavior, the error should be handled in the script itself and then cleared. However, if the error hasn't been cleared, ProcessResults logs the error number and description. It calls CreateEvent to log the information for success or failure.

- **FormatError (ErrorCode).** Returns a string with the supplied ErrorCode. ErrorCodes above 16777216 are returned as decimal and hexadecimal values.

Environment

The Environment class is used handle access to the properties used within the MDT scripting environment. It makes sure that the different "environments" like operating system variables, task sequence variables, MDT variables, and the persistence store (Variables.dat file) are properly aligned and changes are reflected in each. When referencing ZTIUtility.vbs, it's globally available using the oEnvironment object and offers the following functions:

- **GetOSDV4 (Variable).** Returns the variable from the SMS task sequence environment.

- **SetOSDV4 (Variable, Value).** Sets the variable from the SMS task sequence environment to the specified value.

- **GetDAT (Variable).** Returns the variable from the persistence store.

- **SetDAT (Variable, Value).** Sets the variable from the persistence store to the specified value.

- **ObfuscateEncode (Variable, Value)**. Encodes the value using Base64Encode if the variable is one of the default MDT variables containing sensitive information.

- **ObfuscateDecode (Variable, Value)**. Decodes the value using Base64Decode If the variable is one of the default MDT variables containing sensitive information.

- **Exists (Variable)**. Returns true if the variable exists and contains a value, and false if the variable doesn't exist or contain a value.

- **Item (Variable)**. A property rather than a function. It is the default way to read or set a variable within the MDT scripting environment. It returns the value of the variable, or if the variable isn't defined yet or doesn't have a value assigned, it returns an empty string. You also can use this to set the value of a variable.

Real World Note: The Item property is the preferred way of reading and writing variables within the MDT scripting environment. Using this property ensures that the other environments are updated, sensitive information is encoded or decoded, and the variables are persisted and still available after a reboot. Only use the other functions like GetOSDV4/SetOSDV4, GetDAT/SetDAT, et.al., if there is no other choice.

- **ListItem (Variable)**. As with Item, a property. It returns a list variable as a dictionary object or can be used to set the value for a list. If setting the value of a list, the supplied value needs to be an object that can be enumerated like a dictionary or an array, for examle. Be aware that you have to supply the whole list and not just an item to add.

Real World Note: Within the MDT scripting environment, lists are handled internally as individual variables with the base variable name and a trailing three-digit incrementing number. So if the ListItem MacAddress contains several MAC addresses of the local computer, they are returned as a dictionary when using the ListItem property. However, as each one is stored as an individual variable, they also are available as MacAdress001, MacAddress002, MacAdress003, and so forth.

- **Substitute (Value)**. A very handy function that takes a value as a string that can contain further variables (enclosed in %), or even custom VBScript functions (enclosed in #), and evaluate them into the real values. So, for example, callingoEnvironment.Substitute("#left(%SerialNumber%,6") will return a string that contains the first six characters from the computer's serial number.

- **Release**. Is used to release the object that contains the SMS task sequence environment.

Utility

The Utility class is used as a container class for many different useful functions that are used within the MDT scripting environment. It also does most of the heavy lifting when the ZTIUtility.vbs is referenced and initializes most of the other classes described here. When referencing ZTIUtility.vbs, the Utility class is available globally using the oUtility object and offers the following functions:

- **PrepareEnvironment**. Used to prepare the environment and is called automatically when the ZTIUtility.vbs is referenced and initialized. It initializes the oLogging, oEnvironment, oStrings, and oFileHandling objects as described in this appendix. It also ensures that arguments from the current command line are stored as variables and that the LogPath is set appropriately.

- **GetPA**. Returns the current processor architecture And ensures that the naming for 64-bit systems is consistently set to x64.

- **RunNewInstance**. The default function being called when a custom script is based on the MDT2010+ template. It tries to create a new instance of a class based on the current script name and execute the function named Main.

- **RunNewInstanceEx (ClassName, ClassInstance, MainMethod)**. Called mainly by RunNewInstance. This function tries to create a new instance of the supplied ClassName and store it in the ClassInstance object. It then executes the function named in Main, which is typically the function Main from the script itself.

- **ConvertBooleanToString (Value)**. Converts the supplied (Boolean) value into its string representation of true or false.

- **ResetLocalRootPath**. Resets the local root path.

- **ReadIni (File, Section, Item)**. Returns the value of the item of the specified section within the specified .ini file. It returns an empty string if the item isn't found.

- **WriteIni (File, Section, Item, Value)**. Sets the item in the specified section within the specified .ini file to the specified value. If the section or item doesn't already exist, it is created.

- **Sections (File)**. Returns a dictionary of sections within the specified .ini file.

- **SectionContents (File, Section)**. Returns a dictionary of all lines of the specified section in the specified .ini file.

- **RegRead (Key)**. Returns the value of the specified key or value name.

- **RegWrite (RegistryKey, Value)**. Writes the specified value to the specified key or value name.

- **SafeSleep (Time)**. Lets the current script pause for the specified amount of time (in milliseconds).

- **RunCommandLog (Exec, ExternalHook, Limit)**. Runs the command and logs a heartbeat every five minutes. Optionally, an external hook, such as a custom function, can be supplied that is called on every heartbeat and can be used to update the progress, for instance. Also an optional limit in minutes can be supplied. If the runtime then exceeds the limit, it is cancelled.

- **StandardConsoleProcessing (Exec, LastProgress)**. Used to process a command that is being executed using the console. It logs the output of the console and also logs the success or failure of the execution. It is used by RunCommandLog.

- **RunCommandStart (Command, Input)**. Executes the supplied command and returns the shell object with the current status. Optionally, additional input can be supplied as an array. This is typically individual lines of text that are passed to the shell object of the command using the RunCommandWrite function. This function is very helpful if you need to pipe additional commands into some executable. Within MDT, for example, it's used in the ZTIDiskpart.wsf script to automate the Diskpart commands.

- **RunCommandWrite (Exec, Command)**. Takes a shell object of a command that has been executed (e.g. by RunCommandStart) and executes the specified command within the supplied object. To illustrate how RunCommandStart and RunCommandWrite work together, it is useful to execute some diskpart commands. For example,

RunCommandStart could be called like the following:

```
Set oExec = oUtility.RunCommandStart("Diskpart.exe", empty)
```

oExec then contains a shell object of "Diskpart.exe". Then RunCommandWrite can be used to execute individual commands within this shell object like

```
oUtility.RunCommandWrite oExec, "LIST DISK"
```

RunCommandWrite also makes sure that the individual commands are logged and then piped through to the shell object.

- **RunCommandLog (Exec, ExternalHook, Limit)**. Takes a shell object of a command that has been executed and logs a heartbeat every five minutes. Optionally, an external hook, such as a custom function, can be supplied that is called on every heartbeat and can be used to update the progress, for instance. Also an optional limit in minutes can be supplied. If the runtime then exceeds the limit, it is cancelled.

- **RunCommandEx (Command, Input, ExternalHook, Limit)**. Executes the supplied command using RunCommandStart and RunCommandLog.

- **RunWithHeartbeat (Command)**. Executes the supplied command and logs a heartbeat every five minutes. It internally calls RunCommandEx with an infinite timeout.

- **RunWithConsoleLogging (Command)**. Executes the supplied command and redirects all output and logging to the console.

- **RunWithConsoleLoggingAndHidden (Command)**. Executes the supplied command and redirects all output and logging to the console, but ensures that the console is hidden.

349

- **FindExeAndRunWithLogging (File, Parameters)**. Uses the FindFile function to find the file. If the file is found, the function executes it using RunWithConsoleLogging, optionally with the supplied parameters.

- **FindExeAndRun (File, Parameters)**. Uses the FindFile function to find the specified file. If the file is found, the function executes it using RunWithHeartbeat, optionally with the supplied parameters.

- **RunCommand (Command, WindowStyle, WaitOnReturn)**. Executes the supplied command. If WaitOnReturn is set to true, the command is executed, and the function waits until the command has finished. If it is omitted or set to false, the command is executed, and the function finishes immediately. WindowStyle is optional and indicates the appearance of the programs window. Possible values are:

0	Hides the window and activates another window.
1	Activates and displays a window. If the window is minimized or maximized, the system restores it to its original size and position. An application should specify this flag when displaying the window for the first time.
2	Activates the window and displays it as a minimized window.
3	Activates the window and displays it as a maximized window.
4	Displays a window in its most recent size and position. The active window remains active.
5	Activates the window and displays it in its current size and position.
6	Minimizes the specified window and activates the next top-level window in the Z order.
7	Displays the window as a minimized window. The active window remains active.
8	Displays the window in its current state. The active window remains active.
9	Activates and displays the window. If the window is minimized or maximized, the system restores it to its original size and position. An application should specify this flag when restoring a minimized window.
10	Sets the show-state based on the state of the program that started the application.

- **ComputerName**. Returns the current computer name. This value typically changes during the deployment.

- **FindFile (FileName, FoundPath)**. Tries to find the specified file based on the FileName at some default locations used during deployments. If found, the path is stored in the FoundPath variable.

- **FindMappedDrive (ServerUNC)**. Returns the drive letter of the specified UNC path if it has already been mapped. It will not map the path if it hasn't been mapped yet.

- **ValidateConnection (ServerUNC)**. Validates that the supplied UNC path can be reached with the current credentials and maps the path to a local drive letter if it isn't already mapped. It returns Success (0) if a connection to the server can be established successfully; otherwise, it returns Failure (1). To get the drive letter of the mapped UNC path, use FindMappedDrive after this function has been called successfully.

> **Real World Note:** If there is already a connection to the server using a different share, the function also returns Success(0). Because a connection to the server could be established successfully, however, it does not map an additional drive. If that's required, you have to use ValidateConnectionEx, which allows you to override that default behavior. Please see ValidateConnectionEx for more details.

- **ValidateConnectionEx (ServerUNC, ForceConnection)**. Validates that the supplied UNC path can be reached with the current credentials and maps the path to a local drive letter if it isn't already mapped. If several mapped drives to the same server are required, ForceConnection needs to be set to true; otherwise, it just ensures that a connection to the server itself is possible, but does not map an additional drive letter if there is already an existing connection to the same server. The function returns Success (0) if a connection to the server can be successfully established. It return Failure (1) if not. To get the drive letter of the mapped UNC path, use FindMappedDrive after this function has been called successfully.

- **ValidateNetworkConnectivity**. Verifies that the current computer is able to communicate over the network and forces all network adapters to get a valid IP address if none is available yet. It returns Success (1) if there is at least one network adapter with a valid IP address with which it can communicate; otherwise, it returns Failure (1).

> **Note:** If there is only a wireless adapter with a working connection, the function returns Failure (1), as well, because a deployment over wireless isn't supported. But this might not be the required behavior for custom scripts.

- **MapNetworkDrive (UNCPath, Username, Password)**. Maps the supplied UNC path using the supplied credentials to the next available drive letter if it is not already mapped. It returns the drive letter if it can be mapped successfully; however, if there is an error connecting to the supplied UNC path, it returns the error description and also logs this information as an error. It is preferable to use FindMappedDrive if the UNC path has already been connected.

- **MapNetworkDriveEx (UNCPath, Username, Password, LogType)**. Maps the supplied UNC path using the supplied credentials to the next available drive letter if it is not already mapped. It returns the drive letter if it can be mapped successfully; however, if there is an error connecting to the supplied UNC path, it returns the error description. In addition to MapNetworkDrive, it allows you to specify how it's being logged if a UNC path couldn't be mapped. If using MapNetworkDrive, it logs this as an error. However, this behavior can be overwritten by specifying a different LogType (please see CreateEntry for a list of available LogTypes) if the failure isn't critical and should only raise an information warning.

- **VerifyPathExists (Path)**. Verifies that the supplied path exists and creates all folders of the path if they don't exist. It returns true if the path exists or could be created successfully and returns false if not.

- **VerifyPathExists (Path, AdjustSD)**. Verifies that the supplied path exists and creates all folders of the path if they don't exist. It returns true if the path exists or could be created successfully and returns false if not. This function is called by VerifyPathExists with AdjustSD set to false. If AdjustSD is set to true, it sets specific permissions on the folders if they are created. Inheritance is blocked, and only users from the local Administrators group and the local system will have access to the files and folders.

- **GetAllFixedDrives (ReturnOnlyBootable)**. Returns a list of all fixed drives. ReturnOnlyBootable isn't evaluated and can be set to false.

- **CreateXMLDOMObjectEx (FileName)**. Returns an MXSML2.DOMDocument object, which is basically the core object for any XML-related operation within the MDT scripting environment. If FileName is supplied, the specified XML file is read and returned. The file must exist at the current location, or a full path must be supplied. Use LoadConfigFileEx if you need MDT to search for the file first. If there are any parse errors, they are logged. If you need to ensure that the specified file doesn't contain any parse errors, use CreateXMLDOMObjetSafe instead.

- **CreateXMLDOMObject**. Calls CreateXMLDOMObjectEx to return an empty MSXML2.DOMDocument object.

- **CreateXMLDOMObjectSafe (FileName)**. Calls CreateXMLDOMObjectEx to return the specified XML file as a MSXML2.DOMDocument object. However, the function will fail if there are any parse errors while reading the specified XML document.

- **LoadConfigFileEx (FileName, MustSucceed)**. Has the same functionality as CreateXMLDOMObjectEx with the addition that it searches through all default locations as explained in FindFile to search for the supplied file. When MustSucceed is set to true, the function fails if there is a parse error while reading the XML document.

- **LoadConfigFile (FileName)**. Uses LoadConfigFileEx to find and load the specified XML file but logs any parse errors only.

- **LoadConfigFileSafe (FileName)**. Uses LoadConfigFileEx to find and load the specified XML file and fails if there are any parse errors while reading the XML document.

- **BDDUtility**. Returns an instance of the Microsoft.BDD.Utility COM object. This is a library within the MDT scripting environment that offers some additional functionality that is rather complicated to do using VBScript. Using this object, you can get the following information:

  - **Supports64Bit**. Specifies whether the processor resources on the current computer support Windows 64-bit operating systems. This information also exposes the global Supports64Bit property within the MDT scripting environment after the Gather step has been executed.

  - **SupportsNX**. Specifies whether the processor resources on the current computer support the No Execute (NX) technology. The NX technology is used in processors to segregate areas of memory for use by either storage of processor instructions or for storage of data. This information is exposed as the global SupportsNX property within the MDT scripting environment after the Gather step has been executed.

  - **SupportsVT**. Specifies whether the processor resources on the current computer support the Virtualization (VT) feature. VT is used to support current virtualized environments, such as Hyper-V. This information is exposed as the global SupportsVT property within the MDT scripting environment after the Gather step has been executed.

  - **Is64Bit**. Specifies whether the processor resources on the current computer are based on a 64Bit architecture, even if the Operation system is running in 32 Bit. This information is exposed as well as the global SupportsX64 property within the MDT scripting environment after the Gather step has been executed.

  - **IsHypervisorRunning**. Specifies whether the target computer is running a hypervisor.

Real World Note: This property isn't 100 percent accurate when it comes to virtual machines. This property should return true only if a hypervisor is running and false if not. However, on virtual machines, this property always return true, even if a virtual machine doesn't have the hypervisor running.

  - **IsUEFI**. Specifies whether the current computer is currently running with Unified Extensible Firmware Interface (UEFI). This information is exposed as the global IsUEFI property within the MDT scripting environment after the Gather step has been executed.

Real World Note: It is possible that the computer may support UEFI, but is running in a compatibility mode that emulates the older BIOS firmware interface. In that situation, this value evaluates to false, even though the computers supports UEFI.

  - **IsAdmin**. Specifies whether the current user is being executed with administrative / elevated permission.

- o **HiddenPartitionsToDrives**. Returns an array of all local partitions, including hidden ones such as the Recovery or Boot partition on systems with Bitlocker.

- o **KeepAlive**. A function that can be called to ensure that the current computer does not go to sleep while running the task sequence steps.

- **SetTaskSequenceProperties (TaskSequenceID)**. Ensures that some common task sequence properties like Name, Version, and ImageFile are set for the supplied TaskSequenceID. The TaskSequenceID must be a valid LTI TaskSequence ID.

- **IsSupportedPlatform (Platform)**. Specifies whether the supplied platform is a supported platform. A list of supported platforms and how they are identified can be found in the ZTISupportedPlatforms.xml file.

- **SetTagForDrive (DriveLetter, TagVariable)**. Stores the information on how to identify the drive specified by the DriveLetter in the specified TagVariable. This is helpful in situations in which the drive letter might change, due to a reboot, for example. The function GetDriveFromTag can then be used again to find out the currently assigned drive letter based on the TagVariable.

- **GetDriveFromTag (TagVariable)**. Returns the drive letter of a drive based on the information stored in the TagVariable. It is used in combination with the SetTagForDrive letter to identify and reference a specific drive even if the drive letter changes during the process, due to a reboot, for example.

- **ClearRelativeDriveLetters**. Marks the current value for OSDTargetDriveCache as dirty, which forces a reevaluation of the appropriate Target Drive when GetOSTargetDriveLetterEx is called. This might be necessary on some disk- or partition-related activity.

- **ForceRelativeDriveReCalc**. Marks, like ClearRelativeDriveLetters, the TargetPartitionIdentifier as dirty. This forces a reevaluation of the appropriate target drive and partition when GetOSTargetDriveLetterEx is called. This might be necessary if a new disk, such as a VHD, has been added or removed.

- **GetOSTargetDriveLetterEx (Required)**. Returns the drive letter for the drive where the operating system will be or is installed. If Required is set to true, it logs an error if no appropriate drive letter is found.

- **GetOSTargetDriveLetter**. Returns the drive letter for the drive where the operating system will be or is installed. It calls GetOSTargetDriveLetterEx with Required set to true, so it logs an error if no appropriate drive letter is found.

- **DeterminePartition**. A deprecated function. It always returns false.

- **ReCalculateDestinationDiskAndPartition (Required)**. Calls GetOSTargetDriveLetterEx to get the target drive for the operating system. It does the evaluation on which partition the OS is or will be installed. It doesn't return a value, but set's the DestinationDisk and DestinationPartition properties.

- **SelectSingleNodeStringEx (XMLNode, XPath, Error)**. Returns the text of a XML node specified by the XPath expression within the supplied XML node. If Error is set to true, a warning is logged if the node isn't found. If set to false, nothing is logged.

- **SelectSingleNodeString (XMLDocumentNode, XPath)**. Returns the text of a XML node specified by the XPath expression within the supplied XML node. It calls SelectSingleNodeStringEx with the option of raising a warning if the node can't be found.

- **SelectNodesSafeEx (XMLNode, XPath, Error)**. Returns a list of all nodes based on the supplied XPath expression. If Error is set to true, a warning is logged if no node is found.

- **SelectNodesSafe (XMLNode, XPath)**. Returns a list of all nodes based on the supplied XPath expression. It calls SelectNodesSafeEx with the option of raising a warning if no node is found.

- **FindSysprepAnswerFile**. Tries to find the Sysprep.inf file. If the file is found, it returns Success (0), and the path to the file can be found in the property OSDAnswerFilePathSysprep. If the file isn't found, Failure (1) is returned.

- **FindUnattendAnswerFile**. Tries to find the Unattend.txt or Unattend.xml file depending on the target operating system. If the file is found, it returns Success (0), and the path to the file is stored in the property OSDAnswerFilePath. If the file isn't found, Failure (1) is returned.

- **IsHighEndSKUEx (SKU)**. Determines whether the supplied SKU supports some higher-end features like Bitlocker or multiple language packs.

- **IsHighEndSKU**. Determines whether the current SKU of the OS supports some higher-end featuers like Bitlocker or Multiple Language Packs. It uses the IsHighEndSKUEx function with the value of the property OSSKU for evaluation.

- **InternetFileDownload (URL, Destination)**. Downloads a file from the specified URL and saves it at the specified destination.

In addition to the preceding functions, the Environment class contains a couple helpful read-only properties that you can use in custom scripting:

- **BootDevice**. Returns the device from which the machine has booted.

- **LogPath**. Returns the path to which all current log files are being written.

- **StatePath**. Returns the path to which the user state can be stored or is stored.

- **ScriptName**. Returns the name of the script currently being executed, excluding the path or file extension.

- **ScriptDir**. Returns the path to the script that is currently being executed.

String Handling

The Strings class can be used for some specific string-handling functions when referencing ZTIUtility.vbs. It's globally available using the oStrings object and offers the following functions:

- **isNullOrEmpty (Value).** Returns true if the supplied value is either Null or an empty string, and returns false if not.

- **AddToList (List, Item, Delimiter).** Adds a new item to a delimited list of items. For example, AddToList ("One,Two,Three", "Four", ",") will return "One,Two,Three,Four".

- **HexWidth (Value, length).** Returns the supplied value as a hex value of the specified length. For example, HexWidth (2748, 8) returns 00000ABC.

- **HexWidthByte (Value, Length).** Returns the first byte of the supplied value as a hex value of the specified length. For example, HexWidthByte (A, 8) returns 00000041.

- **IsWhiteSpace (Char).** Returns true if the supplied character can be interpreted as white space, which includes a real space, a tab, a vertical tab, a line feed, a form feed, or a carriage return.

- **TrimAllWS (String).** Removes all white spaces from the supplied string. For example. TrimAllWS ("Contributing is everything …") returns Contributingiseverything….

- **RightAlign (String, Length).** Returns a string of the given length, with the supplied string aligned to the right. If the length is less than the total length of the supplied string, only a substring counted from the right is returned.

- **LeftAlign (String, Length).** Returns a string of the given length of the supplied string. If the length is less than the total length of the supplied string, only a substring counted from the left is returned. If it's longer, spaces are appended to the supplied string.

- **ForceAsString (Value).** Returns the supplied value as a string. If the supplied value can't be interpreted as a string, an empty string is returned. Arrays are converted into a space-delimited list of items.

- **ForceAsArray (Value, Delimiter).** Returns the supplied value as an array. If the supplied value is a string of delimited items (like from AddToList or ForceAsString), it splits this string at each delimiter into array items.

- **GenerateRandomGUID.** Returns a new GUID. This is very helpful if you need a unique value.

- **base64Encode (Value).** Returns the supplied value as a Base64-encoded string. That's how the values of all MDT properties are stored, for example, in the Variables.dat to survive a reboot.

- **base64Decode (Value).** Returns the original (decoded) value of the supplied Base64-encoded string.

File Handling

The FileHandling class, which is globally available using the object oFileHandling, offers the following functions. By default, all functions write their activity to the current log file.

- **RemoveFolder (Path).** Removes the folder specified by the path. It also removes all files and subfolders and calls RemoveFolderEx with the option to log each action.

- **RemoveFolderEx (Path, Logging).** Removes the folder specified by the path. It also removes all files and subfolders. If Logging is set to true, all actions are logged. If it is set to false, nothing is logged.

- **DeleteFile (FilePath).** Deletes the file, specified by FilePath, and calls DeleteFileEx with the option to log the action. It returns 0 on success or the error code on failure.

- **DeleteFileEx (FilePath, Logging).** Deletes the file specified by FilePath. If Logging is set to true, the action including any occurring error is logged. If it is set to false, nothing is logged. It returns 0 on success or the error code on failure.

- **MoveFile (FilePath, DestinationPath).** Moves the specified file to the specified new DestinationPath and calls MoveFileEx with the option to log the action. It returns 0 on success or the error code on failure.

- **MoveFileEx (FilePath, DestinationPath, Logging).** Moves the file specified by FilePath to the location specified by DestinationPath. If Logging is set to true, the action including any occurring error is logged. If it is set to false, nothing is logged. It returns 0 on success or the error code on failure.

- **CopyFile (FilePath, DestinationPath, Overwrite).** Copies the file specified by FilePath to the specified DestinationPath. If the file exists already at the DestinationPath, Overwrite needs to be set to true; otherwise, the file won't be copied over the existing one. It calls CopyFileEx with the option to log the action And returns 0 on success or the error code on failure.

- **CopyFileEx (FilePath, DestinationPath, Overwrite, Logging).** Copies the file specified by FilePath to the specified DestinationPath. If the file exists already at the DestinationPath, Overwrite needs to be set to true; otherwise, the file won't be copied over the existing one. If Logging is set to true, the action including any occurring error is logged. If it is set to false, nothing is logged. It returns 0 on success or the error code on failure.

- **CopyFolder (FolderPath, DestinationPath, Overwrite).** Copies the folder specified by FolderPath to the specified DestinationPath. If the folder or any subfolder or file exists already at the DestinationPath, Overwrite needs to be set to true; otherwise, the files or folders won't be copied over the existing ones. It calls CopyFolderEx with the option to log the action and returns 0 on success or the error code on failure.

- **CopyFolderEx (FolderPath, DestinationPath, Overwrite, Logging).** Copies the folder specified by FolderPath to the specified DestinationPath. If the folder or any subfolder or file exists already at the DestinationPath, Overwrite needs to be set to true; otherwise, the files or folders won't be copied over the existing ones. If Logging is set to true, the action including any occurring error is logged. If it is set to false, nothing is logged. It returns 0 on success or the error code on failure.

- **MoveFolder (FolderPath, DestinationPath)**. Moves the specified folder to the specified DestinationPath. Use MoveFolder (FolderPath, DestinationPath, false) to disable logging.

- **MoveFolderEx (FolderPath, DestinationPath, Logging)**. Moves the folder specified by FolderPath to the specified DestinationPath. If Logging is set to true, the action including any occurring error is logged. If it is set to false, nothing is logged. It returns 0 on success or the error code on failure.

- **NormalizePath (Path)**. Returns the complete path of the supplied path. This function ensures that a path always has the same format. If, for example, you specify only a file name, the complete path including the drive is returned.

- **GetTempFile**. Returns the path to a temporary file at the current temporary folder that can be used for further actions.

- **GetTempFileEx (Extension)**. Returns the path to a temporary file with the specified extension at the current temporary folder that can be used for further actions.

Real World Note: You need to be aware that neither GetTempFile nor GetTempFileEx actually creates the temporary file. They just return a unique name including a path that can be used to create a file for temporary usage. This could be created, for example, using the CreateTextFile method from the FileSystemObject class, which is available within the MDT scripting environment using the oFSO object.

- **GetTempFolder**. Returns the path to the current temporary folder.

- **GetWindowsFolder**. Returns the path to the current Windows folder. It should be identical to value of the environment variable %WinDir%.

- **CheckFileVersion (FileName, MinVersion)**. Returns true if the specified file has at least the specified version or greater. Returns false if the version is lower or if the file can't be found.

Appendix C

MDT Monitoring Events

When enabling the MDT Monitoring option, MDT sends monitoring events to the MDT Monitoring web service. These events are identified by their EventID. The following list contains all default MDT monitoring events with their corresponding EventIDs for troubleshooting or evaluation purposes.

5625 - Image applied successfully

41000 - Processing phase

41001 - Step/Script processing completed

41002 - Error/Failure happened

41003 - Heartbeat event

41004 - Beginning User State capture

41005 - Successfully finished User State capture

41006 - Error during User State capture

41007 - Error during User State restore

41008 - Successfully finished User State restore

41009 - Heartbeat event

41010 - USMT error and warning report

41013 - Error opening SQL connection

41014 - Deployment failed

41015 - Deployment completed successfully

41016 - Deployment started

41017 - Initiating task sequence-requested reboot

41018 - Applying Windows PE

41019 - Windows PE applied successfully

41020 - Applying image using setup.exe

41021 - Setup completed successfully

41022 - Setup failed applying image

41023 - Applying image using ImageX

41026 - Performing unattended Installation

41027 - Unattended install completed successfully

41028 - Unattended install failed

41031 - Installing application

41032 - Error installing application

41033 - Application installed successfully

41034 - Application returned an unexpected return code

41035 - Beginning backup of drive

41036 - Error creating an image of drive

41037 - Successfully created image of drive

41038 - Unable to establish database connection

41039 - Unable to execute database query

41044 - ValidationError - Attempting to deploy a client OS to a machine running a server OS

41045 - ValidationError - Attempting to deploy a server OS to a machine running a client OS

41046 - ValidationError - Machine is not authorized for upgrade

41047 - ValidationError - Amount of memory is insufficient

41048 - ValidationError - Processing speed is insufficient

41049 - ValidationError - Insufficient space available

41051 - ZTIDomainJoin has attempted to join to domain too many times.

Appendix D

Add Logging to Your Applications – NLog for Beginners

One of the most important aspects of your applications and scripts (beside their actual purpose) is the ability to log information about the currently running actions. For daily usage, it might be useful just to verify whether everything is working as expected, or to have some kind of reporting based on this. But as soon as a problem arises, this information is of huge importance for troubleshooting the current issue. So, you can't log too much, only too little.

As described in Chapter 9, MDT has some very useful and powerful logging capabilities built-in. These capabilities allow you to define different logging levels in the scripts and some granularity on the output when the script is executed. However, these capabilities are only available for scripts.

In Chapter 11, you learned how to build your own custom web service, and we also supply several sample projects in managed code (VB.Net and C#) with the downloads for this book. In case of a web service that runs at a central, but most often remote, location and might be used by hundreds or thousands of different computers in a huge variety of situations, it's even more important to have a powerful logging engine available and log appropriate information while writing the code.

In the preparation of this book, we evaluated several different options and products and finally ended up choosing NLog. It is not only very easy to implement and use, but NLog also is similar to MDT in how it handles its logging. However, there are several other options available, like the .NET Framework's built-in tracing provider, the Microsoft Enterprise Library, Log4Net, and so forth, that all have specific advantages and depending on your needs, might be the better solution.

Implementing NLog

Using additional tools like NLog became a lot easier in the recent years, as they are now mostly available via NuGet. NuGet is the package manager of Visual Studio, which allows you to easily integrate additional tools into your solutions and projects. It does not only take care about downloading the necessary files, it also ensures that all dependencies of that tool are properly resolved and have the appropriate version. It also applies changes to your project, such as to the web.config file, that are necessary for some initial setups.

To implement NLog in any of your projects, you have to do the following:

1. Using any version of **Visual Studio 2013**, open the solution.

2. On the **Tools** menu, select **NuGet Package Manager / Manage NuGet Packages for Solution**.

3. In the **NuGet Package Manager** window, in the left pane, select **Online / All**, and then search for **NLog**.

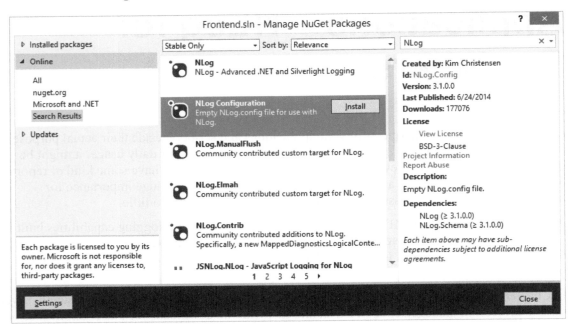

The NuGet Package Manager listing NLog packages.

4. Select the **NLog Configuration** package, and click **Install**.

Real World Note: You typically would have to add the NLog, NLog Schema and NLog Configuration packages to your solution/project. Because the NLog Configuration package depends on the NLog and NLog Schema packages, it's enough just to install the NLog Configuration package and let the NuGet Package Manager handle the dependencies and install them, as well.

---

5. In the **Select Projects** dialog box, select your solution and click **OK**.

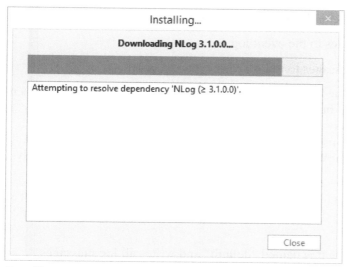

Installing NLog to your project.

NLog Configuration

After NLog has been added to a project using the NLog Configuration package, an additional file is available in the root of the project called NLog.config. This file contains the configuration for what to log and to where.

It's also possible to configure NLog directly in your code; however, as the code is pretty static compared to a configuration file, it just limits the flexibility and is primarily used to enforce certain settings. We recommend doing as much of the configuration within the configuration file as possible.

Components

NLog has three main components that can be configured:

- Targets

- Rules

- Layouts and layout renderers

Targets

Targets are used to display, store, or pass log messages to another destination. There are two kinds of targets,tThose that receive and handle the messages and those that buffer or route the messages to another target. The latter targets are called *wrapper targets*. NLog supports many different targets out of the box, and additional targets can easily be created. The most common targets are

- **File.** Writes log messages to one or more files

- **Database.** Writes log messages to the database using an ADO.Net provider

- **Mail.** Sends log messages by email using the SMTP protocol

- **EventLog.** Writes log messages to the event log

- **AspNetTrace.** Writes log messages to the ASP.NET trace

The most common wrapper target is the AsyncWrapper, which is also used in some samples in this book as it provides asynchronous, buffered execution of target writes. This is especially helpful on targets that can cause a delay in execution or only allow a single message to be processed at any given time. With the use of the AsyncWrapper, the execution of your code continues immediately while the AsyncWrapper takes care that all log messages are properly stored.

There can be several targets defined in the NLog configuration file, for example, to write all log messages to a local log file but also send an email for critical errors or use different files for different levels of detail.

The following snippet shows a target that is named "default" and writes all log messages forwarded to this target to a file:

```
<targets async="true">
    <target name="default"
      xsi:type="File"
      fileName="${basedir}/logs/Default_current.log"
    />
</targets>
```

Rules

Rules define what is actually being logged and to which target these log messages are being sent. Rules are processed starting with the first rule in the list. When a rule matches, log messages are directed to the target(s) in that rule. By default, one log message can be handled by several rules and so also be forwarded to several targets. However, if a rule is marked as final, rules below it are not processed. Each rule can be configured using the following information:

- **name.** Source/logger name. This typically includes a wildcard character *.

- **minlevel.** Minimal log level for this rule to match.

- **maxlevel.** Maximum log level for this rule to match.

- **level.** Single log level for this rule to match.

- **levels.** Comma-separated list of log levels for this rule to match.

- **writeTo.** Comma-separated list of targets that should be written to when this rule matches.

- **final.** Makes a rule final. No further rules are processed after any final rule matches.

The following snippet shows a rule that forwards all log messages with a minimal log level of "Info" to the target named "default":

```
<rules>

  <logger name="*" minlevel="Info" writeTo="default" />

</rules>
```

Layouts and Layout Renderers

One of NLog's strongest assets is the capability to use layouts. In their simplest form, layouts are texts with embedded tags delimited by ${ and }. The tags are called *layout renderers* and can be used to insert pieces of contextual information into the text.

Layouts can be used in many places. For example, they can control the format of the information sent to a file, but also control the file names themselves. There is a huge number of built-in layout renderers available. The most common ones used in the book samples are

- **${callsite}**. The call site (class name, method name and source information)
- **${date}**. The current date and time
- **${level}**. The log level
- **${message}**. The formatted log message

You can find a full list of layout renderers in the NLog documentation. Again, it is available at http://nlog-project.org/documentation.

The following snippet shows how layouts and layout renderers are used to format the log message and also to define the name of the log file:

```
<targets async="true">
  <target name="default"
    xsi:type="File"
    fileName="${basedir}/logs/Default_${shortdate}.log"
    layout="${longdate} ${callsite} ${level}: ${message}"
  />
</targets>
```

Log Levels

NLog uses six different log levels:

- Fatal
- Error
- Warning

- Information

- Debug

- Trace

As you can see, they map roughly to the log levels that are used within MDT (Error, Warning, Information, and Debug), just giving two more levels for granularity. "Fatal" is by definition worse than a "simple" error and is something that could require immediate action. Fatal messages are typically also forwarded via email due to the urgency of the content.

The Trace level writes the most detailed information, even more than the Debug level.

More detailed log levels typically include the less detailed log levels. So if Information level logging is configured for a given target, it also writes the Warning, Error, and Fatal messages. However, that behavior can easily be changed in the rule(s).

The Default Configuration File

The default configuration file that is available after adding NLog to a project as described earlier doesn't log anything at all out of the box. However, it contains a sample rule and a sample target that are commented out. If uncommented, they write all log messages to a file in a subfolder called logs within the root of the (web) application.

```xml
NLog.config  ☐ ✕
<?xml version="1.0" encoding="utf-8" ?>
<nlog xmlns="http://www.nlog-project.org/schemas/NLog.xsd"
      xmlns:xsi="http://www.w3.org/2001/XMLSchema-instance">

  <!--
  See https://github.com/nlog/nlog/wiki/Configuration-file
  for information on customizing logging rules and outputs.
   -->
  <targets>
    <!-- add your targets here -->

    <target xsi:type="File" name="f" fileName="${basedir}/logs/${shortdate}.log"
            layout="${longdate} ${uppercase:${level}} ${message}" />

  </targets>

  <rules>
    <!-- add your logging rules here -->

    <logger name="*" minlevel="Trace" writeTo="f" />

  </rules>
</nlog>
```

The default NLog configuration file with uncommented sample rule and target.

It's a good start for any project, but we recommend a few changes be applied to this configuration file.

Enable AutoLoad

By default, the configuration is read and processed only once at the beginning, when your application starts. Although this is fine if you have a fixed set of rules and targets that are used all the time, it's also a bit limiting if you want to adjust the logging behavior on the fly.

A typical scenario could be that by default only warnings, errors, and fatal errors are being written to a log file to keep the log files small and readable. However, to troubleshoot a certain error, it might be necessary to enable additional logging for Debug or even Trace level log messages, as well. And as that can create a large amount of data within a short timeframe, you might want to disable this again after the cause of the error has been found and fixed.

Now, because the configuration is processed only once on startup, it would be required to restart the application or application pool, which might have unwanted negative side effects. For this reason, NLog can be configured to monitor the configuration file and reload it on any configuration change. To enable this option, you can add the autoReload attribute. Please also see the sample configuration file at the end of this section.

```
<nlog autoReload="true">

   ...

</nlog>
```

Enable Asynchronous Processing

By default, all log messages are handled synchronously. So the code execution has to wait every time a log message has to be written to the target(s). Because that typically happens quickly and NLog also allows you to easily configure what to log, there usually isn't any noticeable impact on the execution.

However, if for any reason a huge number of log messages have to be written or the specified target has a longer response time than expected, it might negatively affect your application. For this reason, targets are typically wrapped in the NLog asynchronous target wrapper. This handles the log messages asynchronously and ensures that all log messages are forwarded to their appropriate target(s), while letting your code continue.

This is actually so typical that it can be configured with a simple attribute async as shown in the following snippet. Please also see the sample configuration file at the end of this section.

```
<nlog autoReload="true">

  <targets async="true">

    <!-- all targets in this section will be asynchronous -->

  </targets>

</nlog>
```

Sample Configuration

In the following snippet, you find a sample configuration file, which also is used in the sample projects supplied with this book. It covers the typical logging requirements for projects as described in this book. It defines four different rules, with three of them commented out. Each covers a different logging detail level. The first two use the same target, so only one of them should be used at a time to avoid duplicated log messages.

The targets in this sample only keep the log messages of the current day in the log file. Older log files are copied to a subfolder called Archive, which the logs from the last seven days. After seven days, they are deleted. This ensures that the drive isn't filled by continuously growing log files. The size limit of each file is set to 5 MB. If more information has to be logged, an additional file with an incrementing number is created. This keeps the log files at a usable size.

```xml
<?xml version="1.0" encoding="utf-8" ?>
<nlog xmlns=http://www.nlog-project.org/schemas/NLog.xsd
      xmlns:xsi=http://www.w3.org/2001/XMLSchema-instance
      autoReload="true">

 <!--
 See http://nlog-project.org/wiki/Configuration_file
 for information on customizing logging rules and outputs.
  -->

 <targets async="true">
   <target name="default"
     xsi:type="File"
     fileName="${basedir}/logs/Default_current.log"
     layout="${longdate} ${callsite} ${uppercase:${level}}:
       ${message} ${exception:format=Message,StackTrace}"
     archiveFileName=
       "${basedir}/logs/Archives/Default.${shortdate}.{#}.log"
     archiveAboveSize="5242880"
     archiveEvery="Day"
     archiveNumbering = "Rolling"
     maxArchiveFiles="7"
   />

   <target name="debug"
     xsi:type="File"
     fileName="${basedir}/logs/Debug_current.log"
     layout="${longdate} ${callsite} ${uppercase:${level}}:
       ${message} ${exception:format=Message,StackTrace}"
     archiveFileName=
       "${basedir}/logs/Archives/Debug.${shortdate}.{#}.log"
     archiveAboveSize="5242880"
     archiveEvery="Day"
```

368

```
            archiveNumbering = "Rolling"
            maxArchiveFiles="7"
        />

        <target name="trace"
          xsi:type="File"
          fileName="${basedir}/logs/Trace_current.log"
          layout="${longdate} ${callsite} ${uppercase:${level}}:
            ${message} ${exception:format=Message,StackTrace}
            ${stacktrace}"
          archiveFileName=
            "${basedir}/logs/Archives/Trace.${shortdate}.{#}.log"
          archiveAboveSize="5242880"
          archiveEvery="Day"
          archiveNumbering = "Rolling"
          maxArchiveFiles="7"
        />

    </targets>

    <rules>
      <!-- Uncomment logging rules as required-->
      <!-- Error and Fatal Error messages only
      <logger name="*" minlevel="Error" writeTo="default" />
      -->
      <logger name="*" minlevel="Info" writeTo="default" />
      <!-- Be aware Debug and Trace will be pretty extensive -->
      <!-- <logger name="*" minlevel="Debug" writeTo="debug" /> -->
      <!-- <logger name="*" minlevel="Trace" writeTo="trace" /> -->
    </rules>

</nlog>
```

Using NLog

So far, you have learned how to add NLog to your existing project and how to configure the output of the log messages. Now you learn how to generate these log messages within your code.

We highly recommend that you add the logging while you are writing the code, the logic. Log everything that might be interesting when something goes wrong. Make sure you add all the information to the log message that is necessary. Always remember that these log messages might be the only information you have available to troubleshoot an error. So, in general, you can't really log too much, only too little.

Creating the Logger Object

We recommend creating a private static object within each class that you want to have enabled for logging. Using the same name within each class ensures that you have a nice standardized way of creating log messages.

So at the top of every class, just add the following snippet:

```
private static NLog.Logger logger =
  NLog.LogManager.GetCurrentClassLogger();
```

Generating Log Messages

Using the logger object as described in the preceding section, you can now easily create log messages in your code. The logger object has an appropriate method that matches the name of each of the log levels. The following snippet shows the syntax for how to create the almost same messages as used previously in Chapter 9:

```
logger.Info("Stealing with Pride is great! ");

logger.Warning("But be careful");

logger.Error("In case of an error");

logger.Fatal("Or even more important on fatal errors");

logger.Debug("You need some details.");

logger.Trace("And sometimes even more details.");
```

As you can see, it's pretty similar to what you used previously in scripting.

One advantage, compared to the logging in scripting, comes when you want to include additional information in the log message. Although that could end up in some pretty long and complex string concatenations in VBScript, NLog can take this information as additional arguments.

```
Logger.Info("Processing event {0} ...", monitorEvent.uniqueID );
```

Another advantage is that NLog has built-in support for properly logging information about exceptions, as well. When an exception happens, you typically know only that something more or less unexpected happened in the code you have called. For proper troubleshooting, additional information about the exception, such as the stack trace, would be required.You could add this additional information to the log message itself, as shown before, but it's not really flexible. On the other hand, if you include only the exception message itself and then later decide that it would be good to have, for example, the stack trace or the inner exception message, as well, you would have to manually update every occurrence within your project with this. Now, NLog can handle this for you, as for every previously mentioned method, there will be an appropriate exception-related method that takes the exception as an argument.

Here is a snippet showing how NLog is typically used to log an exception:

```
try
{
    // some code which may throw
}
catch (Exception exc)
{
  logger.ErrorException("Exception while parsing event.", exc);
}
```

Using any of these methods, all exception-related information will be available when processing the log message itself.

So to write this information to a file, for example, the following layout could be used:

```
layout="${longdate} ${message} ${exception:format=tostring}"/>
```

This will format the log message to have a long date-time string, the message, and the exception formatted as a string. You could easily add the stack trace, as well, or any other information that might be useful for your project.

Index

Beyond the Book – Meet the Experts

If you liked their book, you will love to hear them in person.

Live Presentations

Johan and Maik frequently speak at Microsoft conferences around the world, such as Microsoft Management Summit (MMS). You also find additional information on their blogs:

- Maik Koster: http://maikkoster.com
- Johan Arwidmark: www.deploymentresearch.com

Video Training

For video-based training, see the following site:

- www.deploymentartist.com

Live Instructor-led Classes

Johan presents scheduled instructor-led classes in the US and Europe. For current dates and locations, see the following site:

- www.deploymentartist.com

Twitter

Johan and Maik also tweet on the following aliases:
Johan Arwidmark: @jarwidmark
Maik Koster: @maik_koster